OXFORD MEDICAL PUBLICATIONS

An introduction to psychopathology

An introduction to psychopathology

Fourth edition

Derek Russell Davis

Emeritus Professor of Mental Health
University of Bristol

Oxford   New York   Tokyo

OXFORD UNIVERSITY PRESS

1984

Oxford University Press, Walton Street, Oxford OX2 6DP

London Glasgow New York Toronto
Delhi Bombay Calcutta Madras Karachi
Kuala Lumpur Singapore Hong Kong Tokyo
Nairobi Dar es Salaam Cape Town
Melbourne Auckland

and associates in
Beirut Berlin Ibadan Mexico City Nicosia

Oxford is a trade mark of Oxford University Press

First edition 1957
Fourth edition 1984

British Library Cataloguing in Publication Data

Davis, Derek Russell
An introduction to psychopathology.—4th ed.
—(Oxford medical publications)
1. Psychotherapy
I. Title
616.89'14   RC480.5
153MO 0 19 261467 3
         0 19 261488 6 (pbk.)

Library of Congress Cataloging in Publication Data

Davis, Derek Russell.
An introduction to psychopathology.
(Oxford medical publications)
Bibliography: p.
Includes index.
1. Psychology, Pathological. I. Title. II. Series.
RC454.D29 1984   616.89   84–918
ISBN 0–19–261467–3
ISBN 0–19–261488–6 (pbk.)

Set by Cotswold Typesetting, Gloucester
Printed in Great Britain by Wm. Clowes Ltd., Beccles, Suffolk.

Preface to the fourth edition

In the decade or so since the third edition appeared, interest has grown steadily in the psychological methods of treating mental disorders. Psychotherapy available then to only the relatively few is now much more readily available within the National Health Service. Outside the NHS a diversity of agencies, with staff of varying levels of training, experience, and skill, offer psychotherapy or counselling. There are many schools, each with its peculiarities of theory and approach. The disorders for which treatment is sought are not mysterious. Penetrating accounts of their origins and natures have been given by novelists, playwrights, and poets. But the urgent need now is for further development of explanations in the terms of a modern psychopathology. This new edition gives an up-to-date picture of what is known. I hope that it will help students and practitioners in the mental-health professions to understand better how disorders at all ages come about.

I have thoroughly revised the text of the third edition, leaving out some material and adding new. I have greatly reduced the number of references to the specialist literature. My intention in the Notes and References attached to each chapter is modest. It is to give those who want to read more widely something with which to start when they visit the library.

Bristol   D. R. D.

June 1983

Contents

1. Explanation in psychopathology

Psychopathology, a branch of science, is that part of psychology that seeks to explain disorders of mental activity and behaviour in terms of psychological processes. Of particular interest are disorders of perceiving, thinking, and remembering. Disorder in these functions may be called a psychosis if it interferes seriously with a person's capacity to appraise sensitively and critically the world around him and his position in it. He may then be unable to sustain co-operative relationships with others or cope with the ordinary demands of living.

The causes of a disorder fall into one or more of four classes: external agents affecting the brain directly, e.g. alcohol, drugs or violence producing injury; diseases of another organ, e.g. liver or kidney, which affect the brain; degenerative or other diseases of the brain itself; and events and circumstances outside the person which compose his experience. When the causes lie in the first three classes, the disorder may be called an organic psychosis; when in the last class, either a functional psychosis or, if it is circumscribed and the appraisal of the world is unimpaired, a neurosis. By mental illness is usually meant a functional psychosis.

Psychopathology relates disorders to causes in the last class. Neurology, on the other hand, relates disorders to the site, extent and character of faults in the structure or function of the central nervous system. Psychiatry, a branch of medicine, applies knowledge from several branches of science, e.g. pharmacology and endocrinology as well as psychopathology, in the care and treatment of patients suffering from disorders of mind or behaviour. Psychotherapy, a method of treatment, applies psychopathological knowledge in the relief of suffering or the modification of attitudes or behaviour. Psychoanalysis, which depended originally on the method of free association and Freud's theory of the unconscious, is a specialized form of psychotherapy.

THE DISEASE MODEL

The model on which neurology largely depends reduces a disorder to what is identified as its essential element. This lies typically in a fault in the structure or function of a tissue or organ. Because it has led to great successes in treatment, this 'disease' or 'medical' model has dominated medicine. Diabetes mellitus, for instance, is attributed to a fault in a particular group of cells in the pancreas and failure in the secretion of insulin; pernicious anaemia, to atrophy of the gastric mucosa and failure in the production of a substance required in the absorption from food of vitamin B_{12}. The model raises the question : What causes the fault? This may be due either to an inherited constitutional weakness or to an external agent, such as infection, toxin or trauma. Treatment is designed to correct the fault or replace what is missing. Thus diabetes is treated by administering insulin, which replaces that not secreted by the pancreas, pernicious anaemia, by administering 'intrinsic factor' or vitamin B_{12}.

The successes of the disease model have sustained hopes that it would prove applicable to mental disorders too.[1] In some cases of psychosis there is evidence of disease of the brain, due, for instance, to trauma, intoxication, neoplasm, cerebro-vascular disease or cortical atrophy. These are organic psychoses. In many cases of 'dysphasia', i.e. disorder of speech, in adults there is evidence of damage more or less localized in the cerebral cortex. But in other cases of psychosis or of disorder of speech in young children or backwardness of reading in schoolchildren, disease of the brain is no more than a supposition for which there is little or no evidence. To call such cases organic psychosis or dysphasia or dyslexia is to insist on an explanation derived from the disease model.

There is a long tradition of attempts to explain mental disorders as due to faults in metabolism. A century ago Emil Kraepelin, working in the first psychology laboratory in Leipzig, pointed to the resemblances between the symptoms of mental illness and the effects in healthy subjects of drugs such as caffeine and alcohol in large doses. Since states akin to the psychoses can be so induced, he argued, psychoses occurring naturally have a similar cause, although the exact nature of the toxic agent has not yet been discovered. It has not necessarily been taken into the body from outside and may well be the product of a metabolic dysfunction.

Disorders induced by drugs

Such drugs as caffeine, amphetamine and alcohol may produce excitement, elation, distractibility, and acceleration in the stream of mental activity. These effects are similar to those seen in mania or the acute onset of schizophrenia. Other drugs, e.g. reserpine, reduce and retard mental activity to produce a state akin to depression. Catalepsy may be produced by bulbocapnine. Those who have taken such drugs as cocaine, cannabis indica, mescaline, lysergic acid diethylamide (LSD) or psilocybin may experience a variety of strange phenomena, including auditory and visual hallucinations. They may also report ideas of reference, and show some clouding of consciousness or a sort of perplexed alertness. Patients taking such drugs as methyldopa for the treatment of hypertension may, unusually, develop a psychosis with similar characteristics; the hallucinations they experience may be vivid and fearful.

Phenylketonuria

Expectations that mental disorders would be found to be due to metabolic dysfunctions were greatly encouraged when in 1934 Følling discovered in certain cases of severe mental handicap an error of metabolism of phenylalanine which results in the excretion of phenylpyruvic acid in the urine. Mental development becomes severely retarded if the infant remains untreated, but proceeds more or less normally if the fault is detected within the first few weeks and the patient is put on a diet low in phenylalanine. The dysfunction has been shown to be due to a recessive gene, and occurs when the patient is homozygous for the gene. It is uncommon, and accounts for 0.5–1 per cent of cases of severe mental handicap. A few similar errors have been discovered, but altogether they do not account for more than a very small proportion of such cases.

Hopes have been sustained that metabolic dysfunctions will be demonstrated in cases of functional psychosis. Certain individuals, it is supposed, are predisposed to psychosis by reason of a metabolic weakness, which they have inherited, and which becomes manifest when they are subject to stress. The abnormal products which then result produce the psychotic symptoms. Were it not for the weakness, they would adapt successfully to the stress. There are promising leads towards the definition of the dysfunction, but many claims have been made and abandoned. Adherence to a disease model has also been encouraged by the efficacy shown in the treatment of the functional psychoses by the psychotropic drugs, which first came into general use in 1954–5.

However, the usefulness of the disease model in the explanation of the functional psychoses is open to question. The disorders induced by drugs, it may be argued, are more like the toxic-confusional states, which are regarded as organic psychoses, than the functional psychoses, such as schizophrenia, mania or depression. Recovery tends to be rapid when the taking of the drug is stopped. Nor is there compelling evidence that any of the psychotropic drugs exerts a direct influence on the essential processes in any of the psychoses, although they may modify some of the symptoms.

The inheritance of mental disorder

Adherents to the disease model have attached great importance to the evidence that the functional psychoses are inherited through a pathogenic gene or genes to which the metabolic dysfunction, whatever it may prove to be, can be attributed. The evidence is controversial. To show that a disorder runs in families is not sufficient, for there are other mechanisms of inheritance. Money, for instance, and hence life-style, may be inherited, as may an interest and proficiency in music. Pathogenic attitudes, which are socially transmitted, run in families as strongly as do pathogenic genes. Before any conclusion can be reached, the pattern of occurrence in families has to be proved to conform to—or rather not to depart from—that to be expected from a specific hypothesis. Proof of this kind is not easy. The hypotheses tested so far have probably been too simple.

That a disorder is due to a dominant gene is a testable hypothesis. Two expectations follow. One or other parent of the patient has been similarly affected. If one parent is affected, and the other not, the proportion of the children affected is one-half, or, if both parents are affected, three-quarters. These expectations are derived from Mendel's laws.

The occurrence of *Huntington's chorea*, an uncommon progressive disorder due to a degeneration of the cerebral cortex and mid-brain beginning typically in the middle thirties, fits this pattern fairly well. In the few cases reported in which neither parent has been affected, information has been incomplete, one parent for instance having died young, or the identity of the father being uncertain. The proportion of the children affected has been found to be about one in three. The reason why it falls short of the one in two expected is probably that a relatively high proportion of those inheriting the gene die, before or after birth, before the diagnosis has been made. The incidence of certain other forms of degeneration of the brain, e.g. Alzheimer-type dementia with an onset in middle age, in the families of an affected person has been found to be higher than that in the general population, although not showing any distinctive pattern.

Recessive inheritance

The pattern to be expected when a disorder is due to a single recessive gene is not distinctive, the occurrence in families transmitting the gene being sporadic although more frequent than in the general population. One test lies in the incidence in the children of two affected parents, who are presumed to be homozygous, although such unions are uncommon. When the test has been applied to schizophrenia, the proportion of affected children has been found to be about one-quarter, far short of the 100 per cent to be expected, the distribution between marriages of those that are affected being irregular. Another test lies in the proportion who are affected among the brothers and sisters of the affected. The proportion expected is one in four. Of the brothers and sisters of patients suffering from schizophrenia about 10 per cent have been found to be affected when schizophrenia has been defined rather broadly. A similar hypothesis tested in this way in respect of a certain type of congenital deafness, on the other hand, gets support from the findings.

Twin research

Another method of testing whether a disorder is inherited was suggested in the last century by Francis Galton, who pointed out that if the disorder is inherited, the incidence in the relatives of the affected will be the greater, the closer the blood relationship. That this is so is necessary to a genetical hypothesis, but does not decide in favour of it against an environmental hypothesis, for the closer the blood relationship, the more do the relatives also share the same traditions and experiences.

It has been argued that the effects of environment have been excluded when the concordance rates of identical, or monozygotic (MZ), twins and fraternal, or dizygotic (DZ), twins are compared. The environments are equally alike, it has been claimed, whether a pair is MZ or DZ. The concordance rate, i.e. the proportion of cases in which, when one member of a pair is affected, the other is similarly affected, would be expected to be high for MZ pairs. Because of the differences in their genetical constitution, DZ pairs should show a lower concordance rate than that for MZ pairs, and a rate similar to that for sibs born separately.

These expectations have been borne out in studies of several classes of disorder, amongst them, schizophrenia.[2] However, the significance of the higher concordance rate found in MZ than in DZ pairs is uncertain. An environmental explanation has not been excluded, as has been supposed, because there is evidence that environments are more alike for MZ than DZ pairs. A higher rate in MZ pairs has also been found in such disorders as pulmonary tuberculosis and the common infectious diseases of children, in which the environmental factors are of more practical importance than the genetical ones. The concordance rate in MZ twins is higher in schizophrenia that in other forms of mental illness, and this might mean that genetical factors play a more important part in the aetiology of schizophrenia. This argument too is open to objection.

Comparisons have also been made of concordance rates in MZ pairs between those brought up together and those separated in early childhood and brought up apart. The size of the reduction in the rate in separated pairs gives an indication of the effects of the different environments they have met. However, difficulty in finding suitable cases has put severe limits on the conclusions to be drawn from research of this kind. There has probably been some preferential reporting of the cases or schizophrenia in which a pair shows concordance despite early separation. Also, separation of an MZ pair during childhood occurs in special circumstances only, and to compare the rate in the small minority who have been separated with the general run who have not is unsound. The study of the differences in the experiences of the affected and unaffected members of separated pairs may throw light on the environmental causes of a disorder such as schizophrenia.

Fostered and adopted children

More satisfactory evidence that schizophrenia is inherited genetically has come from studies of persons separated from their biological families early in life and subsequently fostered or adopted. Case-finding and sampling have presented problems, which have not been fully overcome. In particular, it is uncertain how far the results have been biased by 'selective placement', i.e. the tendency to place the children of parents of higher social status in the better homes.

Two research designs have been followed. In the investigation of Heston and Denney,[3] for instance, children separated within 3 days of birth were divided into two groups: those whose mothers were suffering from schizophrenia, and those whose mothers had no history of psychiatric disorder. All of the five adopted who subsequently developed schizophrenia were in the former group, as were all of the four patients with intelligence quotients (IQs) below 70, and in this group there were more felons and more who had been discharged from the army on psychiatric grounds.

In the 'NIMH adoptees' study there were two groups of adoptees who had been removed from their biological parents within the first month of life. The experimental group was made up of patients suffering from schizophrenia, the control group, of persons with no history of admission to a mental hospital. The prevalence in the experimental group of 'psychopathology' in the biological families was found to be much higher than in the control group. There was no difference between the groups in the prevalence in the adoptive families. These and other investigations allow two tentative conclusions to be reached. The prevalence of schizophrenia in those adopted in infancy is raised when a member of the biological family has suffered from schizophrenia. It is not raised by being brought up in a family of which a member not related by blood suffers from schizophrenia, i.e. the shared environment does not influence the pattern of occurrence among adoptees.

Studies of fostered and adopted children do not specify what form the genetical factors take, any more than do those of twins. The results published so far, although they contain some inconsistencies, have given some encouragement to those who put the emphasis on the genetical factors in aetiology, but warrant no more than tentative conclusions. Among the inconsistencies are the closer correlations shown in some respects by half-siblings than full siblings.[4]

Birth order

As evidence that genetical factors play a part in aetiology are cited the findings of research on twins, as evidence that environmental factors play a part, the findings that there is a birth-order effect. It is well known that such abnormalities in young children as pyloric stenosis, patent ductus arteriosus and congenital dislocation of the hip are relatively common in the first-born. The causes are then looked for among factors more likely to affect first-born than later-born children. First-born are neither more nor less favoured genetically than later-born.

Testing whether there is a birth-order effect is easy when families can reasonably be assumed to be complete. The question is put: does the distribution of the members of a representative sample of patients suffering from a particular disorder depart significantly from that expected from the 'null' hypothesis that those from each size of family are evenly distributed between each birth position; of those from families of three, for instance, one-third are expected in each position. When families are incomplete, comparison is made of the distributions in samples of those with and without the disorder. The proportions of each birth order in the general population of new-born children give no more that a rough indication of what is to be expected, and change from year to year as families tend to become smaller. About 40 per cent of the new-born in England are first children.

The reasons for a birth-order effect are not simple or obvious. An excess of last-born children among patients coming from large families—an effect reported in male homosexuality, for instance—might merely reflect a greater frequency of the disorder in the children of older mothers.[5] For this there might be an explanation in terms of chromosome abnormalities, as has proved to be so in the case of Down's syndrome. Another explanation might lie in the closer relationship that last-born children have with their mothers, and another, in the greater frequency with which the last-born suffer parental loss during childhood. This last explanation was invoked to account for the over-representation of last-born in a sample of alcoholics; the numbers of first- and last-born were the same when comparisons were restricted to the patients brought up by both parents.

Social-class differences have also to be taken into account. For instance, studies of large samples have shown that the mean IQs of children late in birth order are lower than the mean IQs of those early in birth order. This effect can be attributed to the disproportionate number of large families, and hence of children late in birth order, who belong to the lower social classes. The first-born in the lower social classes are several times more likely than fourth or later born to be subjected to tonsillectomy and circumcision. In the professional and salaried classes, the first-born are less likely to be subjected to these operations. The later born children of large families tend to have an inferior health record, probably because they are more liable to suffer from infections.

First-born children occupy a favourable position in some respects, e.g. in the inheritance of land when there is primogeniture. Galton pointed out long ago, although on inadequate data, that among the eminent there are a disproportionate number of 'only' children and first and last in order of birth. Correlations between birth order and personality traits have been reported, although the overall picture is confusing.[6]

Sex ratio

Many disorders of mental development during childhood are commoner in boys than girls. On the other hand, admission rates to mental illness hospitals and units are higher for females than for males. No evidence has been found of any sex-linkage in the genetical inheritance of disorders of mental development (except certain chromosome abnormalities) or of mental illness. Explanations of the differences in the numbers of male and female patients seen in clinical practice have been sought, therefore, in differences in social roles, in the conflicts and stresses to which members of each sex are subjected at different times in their lives and in the ways in which they react to them. The relative frequency of a disorder in males and females may conveniently be expressed as the 'sex ratio', which is the number of males in a sample divided by the number of females. The sex ratios of some physical defects are given here as illustrations: congenital dislocation of the hip, 0.13; anencephaly, 0.5; spina bifida, 0.7; Down's syndrome, 1.0; harelip, 1.8; talipes equinovarus, 2.0; pyloric stenosis, 5.0.

THE ADAPTATION MODEL

Psychopathology offers a model complementing, or alternative to, the disease model. This is the 'adaptation' model. Instead of reducing a disorder to the underlying processes in tissues or organs, psychopathology broadens the range of observations to cover the circumstances, context or systems to which the disorder is related, and supposes that the disorder represents the person's attempt to adapt to a change in circumstances.

Medicine took an important step forward in the last century when it came to regard the degeneration of lung tissue, for instance, in tuberculosis, not as due to a constitutional weakness, but as a reaction to invasion by tubercle bacilli in an attempt to limit their spread. Similarly a boil is seen nowadays, not as due to degeneration, but as active adaptation to, and defence against, invasion by micro-organisms. The change in view has important consequences. The cold, pale skin of the patient in surgical shock, for instance, until a decade or so ago likely to be regarded by first-aiders as due to a failure in the peripheral circulation to be corrected by warming the patient up, is now seen as adaptive, blood having been diverted from the periphery in order to sustain vital functions. Treatment, as a general rule, is designed to support the adaptive processes, e.g. by the transfusion of blood.

Depression when explained by reference to a disease model is attributed to a specific metabolic dysfunction in brain tissue (perhaps to do with dopamine), although this has not yet been defined with any certainty. Anti-depressant drugs, intended to correct the dysfunction, are prescribed as forerunners of a treatment as rational and specific for depression as insulin treatment is for diabetes. On the other hand, depression may be explained as reflecting, amongst other things, the gradual extinction of responses that have failed to remove external threats. It is then adaptive in that it not only protects the organism from excessive stimulation, but also allows new, potentially effective modes of response to emerge.[7] These two views have very different implications for treatment.

Homeostasis

If they are adaptive, disorders should conform to the principle of homeostasis. An early version of this principle was stated in 1887 by Fredericq thus: 'The living body is an agency of such sort that each disturbing influence induces by itself the calling forth of compensatory activity to neutralise or repair the disturbance'. The 'pleasure-pain' principle enunciated by Freud in 1920 is similar, although expressed in different terms. W. B. Cannon,[8] who introduced the term homeostasis, expressed the principle in these terms: 'The organism reacts to a disturbance in such a way that the relevant internal conditions tend to be restored'. Yet the assumption of the principle in psychopathology raises serious problems because much disordered behaviour appears to be maladaptive.

Freud[9] made the point in these terms: 'It is not strictly correct to speak of a supremacy of the pleasure principle over the course of psychic processes. If such existed, then the vast majority of our psychic processes would necessarily be accompanied by pleasure or would conduce to it, while the most ordinary experience emphatically contradicts any such conclusion.' A prominent feature of mental illness is that actions tend to be repeated despite the pain they cause the patient. This has been called 'the neurotic paradox'. Moreover, behaviour tends to be inappropriate, inefficient and disorganized, often repetitive or persistent, sometimes vacillating or incomplete. These characteristics constitute the essential problems of psychopathology.

Freud decided at one time to assume that there are two distinct classes of behaviour, one governed by the constructive instinct *Eros* and the other by the destructive instinct *Thanatos*, but this formulation, although it has occasionally been revived, has largely been abandoned. Others have written of derangement, disruption or breakdown of the functions of the brain as a result, Pavlov argued, of the 'overstrain' of excitatory and inhibitory processes, the symptoms of mental illness then being accidental products.

Modern psychopathologists assume that actions, no matter how inappropriate they appear to be, reflect adaptive patterns acquired through learning that are confronted in the particular situation by new demands. Many examples can be given of behaviour adaptive in most circumstances that prove maladaptive in a particular situation. Headlong flight, generally an adaptive reaction to danger, proved disastrous for the Gadarene swine because of the precipice. The migration of lemmings brings them to new supplies of food, but to disaster when they reach the fjords. The tendency of insects to fly towards light is disastrous if the light happens to be incandescent. A fall in ambient temperature tends to produce in children and adults a reduction in bodily activity and the adoption of a posture that conserves heat. These reactions, adaptive in some circumstances, may be fatal for a person out in a storm on a mountainside, when his best chance of survival lies in maintaining a high level of activity and hence of heat production. Again, if the response evoked by a sudden alarm is hasty and excessive in the circumstances, it may cause panic by adding to the cause for the alarm. These examples show the variety of the reasons why in particular situations behaviour may be maladaptive.

Reaction and interaction

In all but the last example, the behaviour is regarded as reactive only. This is usually too simple a view because, leaving out of account the effect of the behaviour on the situation, it defines but one part of the relationship between organism and environment. A person who reacts to a change in the ambient temperature by switching on or off an electric fire, shutting or opening a window or donning or doffing clothing not only keeps steady his own internal state constant (homeostasis), but also regulates, as a thermostat, his environment.[10] The reactions change the situation, and this effect is then the cause of a further reaction. Hostility on the part of one person may be both an effect and a cause of the behaviour of another. Psychopathology has thus come to regard a person's behaviour as a component of interaction rather than as reaction, an item in a sequence of exchanges.

Psychologists broke away from the tradition in laboratories of studying responses to a single, usually impersonal, event when the problems arising during the Second World War turned their attention to the skills required of operators by machines. Human operator and machine came to be regarded as 'intermittent correction servo-mechanisms'.[11] Deviation in the display of the machine evokes a corrective response, a change in the display and a further response. Each response—'the motor output'—produces two kinds of feedback: internal, due to kinaesthetic and other stimuli from the operator himself, and external, from the changes produced in the machine or other components of the system. Responses tend to maintain or restore the steady state that has been prescribed by instructions, e.g. when flying an aeroplane, to keep on a steady course. The feedback is then negative. It is positive if they increase the deviation in the display, i.e. if the disequilibrium increases.

After the war the study of feedback processes, then called 'cybernetics', was extended, notably by Bateson,[12] from interactions of human and machine to interactions of two or more persons. Also, there was a change in term from cybernetics to 'systems theory'. Each person is seen as a component of a system, i.e. an organization of two or more persons interacting with one another and regulating one another's behaviour.[13] A husband and wife form such a system, which is open in that it is also a component of other systems, such as a nuclear and extended family. They are components, too, of the larger system of the community. They are a couple in that their relationship with each other is stronger than, and more or less independent of, the relationships either has with others.

As a system, a couple or family tends to react to external events homeostatically, i.e. in such a way as to preserve the relationships to one another of the persons composing the system. The rules implicitly accepted by a husband and wife as governing their behaviour towards one another, for instance, tend to be respected. A system evolves adaptively through the processes of learning, but if learning is held up by reason of its dynamic conservatism, the tensions within it increase. Homeostasis may fail when the system is challenged by an event of special force or significance. The feedback within relationships then becomes positive. If it is not reversed, and escalates, the system decompensates, coming then to a crisis or turning-point.

A period of instability or disequilibrium follows while those composing the system explore the implications and consequences of the challenge to their assumptions and expectations about one another, or the rules they have accepted, and attempt to find a basis on which to restore their relationships. Exploration is followed by reorganization, the relationships being stabilized on terms more or less different from before, or by the breakup of the system, those composing it then separating. The disorder of behaviour during the period of instability may amount to mental illness. Sometimes the pattern of relationships after reorganization is so restrictive, that one or more become so disabled as to be regarded as mentally ill.

Lovers' quarrels follow this course. They start when something happens which obliges the lovers to review their relationship. Expression may then be given to anger, recrimination or vituperation; there may be confession and explanation. There is no return to the status quo, and they work out new terms that can serve as a basis for reconciliation; these are more or less constructive. Or they separate.

The stress-strain analogy, to which resort has often been made in psychopathology, should be avoided. The term 'stress' tends to be used misleadingly instead of 'strain' to describe the effects of excessive demands on the organism. However, the effects constituting strain in materials cease as soon as the stress ceases, whereas the changes in behaviour occurring at times of crisis are seldom reversed; expectations for instance, are changed. The organism is 'reprogrammed' and responds differently thereafter.

Components of responses

Any response to an event or change in circumstances has three components: behaviour, which may or may not serve as feedback, bodily activity, and mental activity. When the room temperature rises a person switches off the heater, opens a window or doffs clothing. Sweating increases, as does circulation through the skin as a result of the dilation of blood vessels, and hence cooling; respiration becomes rapid and shallow. The person feels hot and uncomfortable, and entertains fantasies about ice and cooling drinks.

Old controversies about the relations of mind and body can be avoided. Mentalistic explanations that give mental activity as the cause of behaviour or bodily activity are unsatisfactory; e.g. he opened the window, or started sweating, because he felt hot, or he ran away, or his heart started thumping, because he was afraid. Nor is it helpful to suppose (as did the 'James–Lange' theory) that mental activity, such as emotion, results from the perception of the running away, or preparing to do so, and the awareness of the thumping heart or dry mouth. Mental activity has several aspects: heightened feeling, i.e. emotion, such as fear or anger, perception of events outside the person and their interpretation, anticipation of what may happen next, rehearsal of possible responses to it, and awareness of bodily activity.[14]

There may be some reciprocity between the components. Sweating and increase in skin circulation proving effective, he did not feel uncomfortable; or, on the other hand, not turning off the heater, he started to sweat and felt uncomfortable. Running away proving ineffective in removing the danger, he felt afraid, his heart thumped, his mouth became dry, he trembled, etc. To the psychopathologist, behaviour, mental activity, and bodily activity are all components of a response of varying pattern to a change in the environment.

The relations between the components tend to be complex. A sudden stimulus evokes an uncomfortable excitement as well as an increase in pulse rate and blood pressure. The excitement subsides as soon as the stimulus is recognized as harmless, but a mild discomfort continues while the bodily effects last. Flushing of the face, a component of a response to an insult or to an embarrassing remark, as well as to a rise in ambient temperature, also gives a message, which forms part of the feedback to the person making the remark, its significance, whether for instance it is a flush of anger or a blush of shame, being indicated by the other changes, such as in facial expression, gesture or posture, with which it is associated.

Emotion, i.e. heightened feeling, is experienced when behaviour has failed or appears to be failing to restore the relevant internal conditions—fear when flight is hindered, for instance, or anger when one cannot strike, hunger when one cannot eat, or love when one cannot make love. The bodily processes of which a person is aware are distinctive. With fear are associated discomfort in the chest, dryness of the mouth, trembling, sinking feelings, and bodily weakness, with anger feelings of fullness and strength. The character of the emotion is also derived from the significance of the events that are anticipated and the responses to them that are rehearsed. With fear the events are seen as threatening, and the responses rehearsed are those of escape or rescue. With anger too the events are threatening, but the responses are of attack and destruction.

Emotional expression, which is a form of communication and conveys messages, may undergo change in mental illness. A depressed patient, for instance, may report an inability to cry or otherwise express feelings. Tearfulness is one of the ways in which a person may appeal to others for help, support or consolation.[15] One of the reasons why it is lacking in depression may be that by going unheeded by the patient's spouse or other family members, i.e. being unrewarded or unreinforced, it has become reduced through 'habituation'.[16] Other messages conveying grief, sorrow or remorse, may suffer a similar fate, and then be replaced by other less conventional messages.

The symptoms of illness may be held to represent messages of an unconventional kind when expression in more conventional ways has been blocked. One of the aims of psychotherapy is then to encourage expression in messages of a more easily recognized form, which others can understand and respond to. Communication is restored in this way, first between patient and therapist, and then between patient and others.

The next chapter reviews the several models on which psychopathology depends. These are simplified representations of the complex processes producing mental disorder and show what the consequences are when none of the responses within an organism's repertoire achieves homeostasis within the organism itself or the system to which it belongs. Some of the models have been developed in the course of experiments in the laboratory, others as a result of more or less systematic observation of the effects of naturally occurring events. Some are derived from studies of humans, others of infra-humans. A model may be used in clinical work as a scheme into which to fit the findings in the history-taking, mental examination, and treatment of patients.

NOTES AND REFERENCES

1. The place of medical models in psychiatry is discussed by Wing, J. K. (1978). *Reasoning about madness*. Oxford University Press.
2. The part played by physical inheritance in the aetiology of the functional psychoses is reviewed by Kringlen, E. (1967). *Heredity and environment in the functional psychoses*. Wm Heinemann Medical Books, London; Shields, J. (1978). Genetics. In *Schizophrenia: towards a new synthesis* (ed. J. K. Wing) Academic Press, London; Gottesman, I. I., and Shields, J. (1982). *Schizophrenia; the epigenetic puzzle*. Cambridge University Press, Cambridge.
3. Heston, L. L. and Denney, D. (1968). Interactions between early life experiences and biological factors in schizophrenia. In: *The transmission of schizophrenia* (ed. D. Rosenthal and S. S. Kety). Pergamon, London.
4. The criticisms made of the NIMH Adoptees Study are summarized by Lidz, T. and Blatt, S. (1982). Critique of the Danish–American studies of the biological and adoptive relatives of adoptees who become schizophrenic. *Am. J. Psychiat.* **140**, 426–35.
5. Hare, E. H. and Moran, P. A. P. (1979). Raised parental age in psychiatric patients: evidence for the constitutional hypothesis. *Br. J. Psychiat.* **134**, 169–77.
6. The birth-order effects found in the National Survey of a 1946 cohort are reported in Douglas, J. W. B. (1964). *The home and the school*. McGibbon & Kee, London. Douglas, J. W. B., Ross, J. M. and Simpson, H. R. (1968). *All our futures*. Peter Davies, London.
7. Davis, D. R. (1970). Depression as adaptation to crisis. *Br. J. Med. Psychol.* **43**, 109–16.
8. Cannon, W. B. (1932). *The wisdom of the body*. Kegan Paul, London.
9. Freud, S. (1978). *Beyond the pleasure principle* (standard edn) Vol. 18, pp. 1–64. Hogarth Press, London.

10. When the person referred to might be of either gender, I have written for the sake of brevity 'he' or 'his' instead of 'he or she' or 'his or her'.
11. Craik, K. (1948). Theory of the human operator in control systems. *Br. J. Psychol.* **38**, 55–61, 142–8. This paper gave impetus to the new movement in psychology.
12. Bateson, G. (1973). *Steps to an ecology of mind.* Granada, St. Albans, Herts.
13. The role of communication in regulating behaviour in systems is discussed by Watzlawick, P., Beavin, J. H. and Jackson, D. D. (1968). *Pragmatics of human communication.* Faber & Faber, London.
14. The relations to one another of the components of the experience of emotion are discussed in the classic textbook: James, W. (1981). *The principles of psychology.* In *The works of William James* (ed. F. H. Burkhardt, F. Bowers and I. K. Skrupskelis. Harvard University Press, London.
15. Hill, J. D. N. (1968). Depression: disease, reaction or posture. *Am. J. Psychiat.* **125**, 445–57.
16. These points are taken up again in the discussion of ethological models in CHAPTER 2.

2 Laboratory and other models

Pavlov's experimental neurosis

That laboratory experiments on infra-human behaviour can elucidate mental disorders occurring in humans was claimed by Pavlov in 1914 when an experiment in which he was testing the capacity of dogs to differentiate shapes had had an unexpected outcome.[1] A dog was fed after the exhibition of a circle and not fed after the exhibition of an ellipse. When the salivary response to the circle had become consistent, the shape of the ellipse was made to approach gradually that of the circle. When the ellipse had become almost circular, the dog began to struggle, howl, tear at its restraining harness and show other unusual behaviour both in and out of the laboratory. Contrary to its usual custom it barked violently on being taken out of the laboratory. It lost the previous pattern of response even when the ellipse was restored to a shape which previously it had differentiated. 'In short', Pavlov concluded, 'it presented all the symptoms of acute neurosis.'

The disorder produced in the original experiment was characterized by an extreme general motor excitation, aggressive and destructive tendencies, and the loss of the pattern of response to conditioned stimuli. In other experiments a general motor inhibition was produced, including 'hypnotic' paralysis of the skeletal musculature, particularly of those muscles most active in a positive response; these features are similar to those of hysterical paralysis in humans. Many other symptoms have been produced: tics, tremors, irregular sexual activities, disturbances in respiration and cardio-vascular functions, apathy, dullness, immobility, and negativism. Some of the disorders lasted over several years. Similar disorders have been produced in sheep, cats, pigs, rats, doves, chimpanzees, and human children.

The form of disorder, Pavlov supposed, depends on the type of nervous system or 'temperament' inherited by the animal, although there are inevitably cases in which the nervous system is 'unsteady' or 'fragile' as a result of misfortune in life, such as traumatic lesions, infections, intoxications, and severe shock. He put the emphasis on the effects of castration and other disturbances in the endocrine system in making the animal more susceptible to breakdown, but showed also that the type of temperament is partly determined by experiences early in life. Thus puppies brought up in their kennels, when compared with litter-mates given greater freedom, display marked 'passive-defensive' reactions and other characteristics of the 'melancholic' temperament.

Because the new patterns of behaviour are inefficient and inconsistent, and the disorders appear suddenly, Pavlov supposed that the demands made by difficult tasks on the central nervous system cause a breakdown in its functioning. Thus he spoke of the 'collision' between excitatory and inhibitory processes in the central nervous system and of the more or less permanent disturbance of the balance between them and of 'overstrain' of excitatory or inhibitory processes as causes of the disorders of behaviour. He did not recognize that, in the face of a problem proving to be insoluble, violence, and variability are potentially adaptive. Nor did he define the external conditions in which the disorders arise.

Others have tried to identify the essential factors. Two seem to be important: the monotonous repetition of conditioned stimuli followed by trivial reinforcements in trials extending over 2 or 3 weeks, and the restraint imposed on the animal by the harness and frame, i.e. frustration and confinement. It has also been pointed out that the situation contains all the ingredients of the 'double bind'.[2] The subject is involved in it, and cannot withdraw from it. He is taught to respond compliantly to it. To respond, first made necessary, is then made impossible because the message is paradoxical and undecidable.

Goat kids have been shown to be more liable to develop the experimental neurosis induced by Pavlov's method when they have been separated from their mothers for a short period immediately after birth.[3] They show other deficiences as well. Their development, both physically and in behaviour, tends to be retarded. Conditioning takes place less easily and produces more disturbance. Exploratory behaviour is reduced, and they tend to show freezing and immobility. They do not show a normal attachment to their mothers. They do not thrive, and many die early. The females who do survive to maturity are incompetent as mothers, and the development of their offspring lags. When there is a normal attachment, the mother serves as 'a conditioned security signal' and reduces the vulnerability of the young to excessive stimulation. Her function is protective in this respect. When so protected, the young do not develop disorders.

These tentative definitions of the circumstances in which experimental neurosis arises have reduced the importance given by Pavlov to temperament or inherent properties of the nervous system as a factor. The inadequacy of Pavlov's theory was perhaps the main reason why interest in research on experimental neurosis declined after reaching its zenith in the late nineteen-thirties. Another reason was that the technical problems proved too complicated when the combinations of symptoms constituting experimental neurosis were considered together. Research after the Second World War concentrated therefore on the acquisition of single symptoms through the processes of learning, e.g. the learning and persistence of avoidance responses.

Audiogenic seizures

Many other forms of disorder have been produced in laboratory animals. Rats trained to jump from a platform to one of two patterns, behind one of which is food, develop disorders when one pattern is removed to give them no choice, and when they are forced to jump by having an air-blast turned on them. Stimulated in this way, many develop seizures. These become less frequent when they acquire a habit of response, which may be a 'position-stereotype'.[4] Seizures have also been produced by ringing a bell close to the rats' cages, i.e. by intense stimulation from which there is no escape. These 'audiogenic' seizures, which resemble human epileptic fits, consist of violent activity, beginning with wild jumping and circling round the cage, during which the animals collide with any object in their path. They grunt and squeal and show tonic and clonic contractions. This excited phase is followed by a 'plastic' phase of inactivity, during which the animals are insensitive to stimulation and can be taken into the hand, laid on the back, and the limbs stretched and moulded.

Certain drugs, e.g. atropine, reduce the frequency of seizures. Others, e.g. nicotine, make the animals more susceptible, as do some dietary deficiencies. There are also genetic factors. Thus when reactors have been crossbred with non-reactors, the pattern of the occurrence of susceptibility in the progeny suggests that susceptibility is due to a single dominant gene.

Work on audiogenic seizures attracted attention in the late nineteen-forties because it brought together psychological, pharmacological, nutritional, and genetic studies, but has not been followed up because the psychological mechanisms have remained obscure.

Instrumental avoidance responses and neurosis

If an electric shock is applied through a grid to his foot, a dog lifts it off the grid. If the shock is preceded by a buzzer, he learns to respond to the buzzer by lifting his foot before the shock is given. This response is an example of an instrumental avoidance response, which is evoked by a 'danger signal', in this case the buzzer.

The learning of an instrumental avoidance response tends to be rapid, a small number of repetitions of a painful stimulus being sufficient. 'The burnt child fears the fire' in the homely model. The response once learnt is made every time the danger signal appears even if it is not followed by the painful stimulus. The making of it precludes further experience of the situation in which it was acquired, and it becomes 'fixated'; it does not undergo extinction although its other effects may be maladaptive, as they were in Masserman's experiments.

Masserman's experiments[5]

Cats put individually into a cage at one end of which was a food-box were trained to take food in response to a stimulus, which was usually a light-flash in combination with a bell. When the habit had been established, an air-blast was made to impinge on the cat's neck just as he was about to take food. One experience of the air-blast was usually sufficient to cause a more or less permanent disturbance of behaviour both inside and outside the cage. A few cats tolerated the air-blast without becoming disturbed. Many cats resisted any attempt to make them re-enter the cage.

If forced into the cage, they tried to escape and showed erection of hair, dilation of pupils, sweating, disturbance of pulse and respiration, restlessness, and various forms of aggressiveness. These symptoms increased if they were pushed, by moving a partition, into the vicinity of the food-box, and increased further as soon as the feeding signal was given.

Many cats were fidgety, distractible, and excitable outside the cage. In a few cases preening and licking were increased as also was the courting of attention from the experimenter. Some cats became solitary but aggressive, others passive and timid. A few avoided food completely, even outside the cage, to the extent of lying beside a plate of food without eating, despite a long period of starvation. A few showed compulsive behaviour inside the cage. One cat hid his head in the food-box without touching the food. Another, trained to operate the feeding signal, continued to do so without going to the food-box. Others developed rituals, such as the making of a circuit of the cage before stalking towards the food-box.

A dog's responses to the buzzer can be abolished by administering a shock immediately he lifts the foot, but not then through the grid. This procedure is effective because a dog restrained in a harness cannot find a new method of avoidance, the choices open to him in the laboratory setting being severely restricted. A similar procedure was not effective in counteracting the cats' avoidance of the food-box and cage. Nor was the avoidance tendency overcome by the resulting increase in hunger.

Masserman found three methods of overcoming the avoidance tendency. He gave some cats a partial control over the situation by training them to operate the feeding signal before exposing them to the air-blast. These cats showed a weaker avoidance tendency and continued to operate the switch as they had been trained to do. They then made tentative approaches to the food-box, and after a while began to take food from it, despite the air-blast. The second method depended on social imitation, the avoidance tendency being weakened when a cat is accompanied into the cage by a cat with normal feeding habits. The third method forced a solution. He put cats back into the cage and, by moving a partition, forced them towards the food-box. When this was combined with severe hunger and highly attractive food—salmon seasoned with cat-nip—they suddenly started to feed again, despite the air-blast, to which they gradually became accustomed, i.e. habituated.

Masserman's experiments, although they were unsystematic and did not test specific hypotheses, are of interest because of the variety of the disorders produced and their resemblances to such human disorders as claustrophobia, obsessional rituals, and anorexia nervosa. They illustrate certain points about 'neurotic' disorders and their treatment.

The immediate effect of the avoidance response is satisfactory in that it relieves the anticipation of danger aroused by the feeding signal or the cage. The maladaptive effect of preventing feeding, which is delayed, does not deter the making of the response. This accords with the principle of the 'gradient of reinforcement', which states that the more closely the effect follows upon the response, the more is the tendency to make the response reinforced. That is, behaviour that relieves anxiety immediately is not deterred by its later consequences. A tendency to take alcohol, reinforced by its immediate effect, is not weakened by the hangover and the other consequences. The patient who suffers from claustrophobia or agoraphobia gains immediate relief from anxiety by staying out of the situation that arouses anxiety; the disadvantages of staying out are less immediate. Again, the patient who compulsively washes his hands because doing so relieves anxiety is not deterred by the later soreness.

In humans, delayed effects do exert some influence on the mode of resolution of conflicts when they are brought into the present in the form of images; these are predominantly but not solely verbal symbols. Images of the hangover, police prosecution, cirrhosis of the liver, disgrace and penury, for instance, may deter one from taking a drink, or images of cancer of the lung, from lighting a cigarette, but they do not have any great force. Deterrence by reminding a person of the consequences tends to have little effect. Behaviour is more likely to change if conditions are established in which a person can learn new ways of gaining relief from anxiety—through social imitation, for instance. Giving the person greater control over the situation means giving opportunities to acquire new habits.

Staying away from the food-box the cats do not suffer the fears that going towards it would arouse. This is an example of what Freud regarded as the essence of a neurosis: the renunciation of a function that gives rise to anxiety. Staying away is defensive, does not change the situation from which the anxiety arises, and prevents the learning of other responses which might make for a more satisfactory adaptation. For these reasons neuroses tend to persist.

A person who comes into the laboratory after a cat has acquired an avoidance tendency might observe the making of the avoidance response or the disturbance produced when the response is prevented, but would not be able to see for himself what the dangers are that are being avoided. Once the response has been learnt, the device administering the air-blast can be dismantled, and the dangers are then obscure. If he wanted to discover the reason for the avoidance tendency, he would have to enquire as best he could into the circumstances in which it had been acquired. Similar difficulties are faced by a psychiatrist who wants to discover the reason for the phobic avoidance of a situation or the phobic refusal to eat.

The effects of frustration

The response elicited by a danger signal is adaptive in that it avoids the danger. But if the conditions change, it may fail to remove the danger and is then frustrated. This is an emergency, and behaviour undergoes characteristic changes. The amount of activity increases. Responses become more forceful, more extensive, and more rapid. The minimum intensity of stimulus necessary to evoke a response is reduced. A simulus of given intensity evokes a response more often. A stimulus has to be less specific to evoke a response. Responses related to other drives or interests are suppressed.

The processes through which these changes come about were said by Cannon[6] to be of biological value in enabling the emergency to be met more effectively, since they are 'energising and directly serviceable in making the organism more effective in the violent display of energy which fear or rage or pain may involve'. Yet in some circumstances the effects of the changes may be maladaptive.

Whether they are adaptive or maladaptive depends on the particular situation. A violent display of energy may be effective in some emergencies, but many of the emergencies met by humans are dealt with more effectively by the exercise of skill, i.e. by responses that are restrained, carefully graded, timed, and co-ordinated. Forceful responses because they are less accurate may make the situation worse and start a vicious circle. An example is the panic attack when a sidden alarm leads to hasty and excessive measures which add to the cause for the alarm. Or, as the adage says, 'dangers breed fears, and fears more dangers bring'.

Vicious-circle effects like these have been studied in experiments in which highly motivated human subjects have been put to a difficult task requiring skill.[7] The skill of a subject who fails to master the task tends to deteriorate progressively because his responses become less restrained and less accurate as the danger of failure appears to him to be more imminent. The vicious circle can be reversed by reducing the level of difficulty to the point at which he can readily succeed. The level can then be raised gradually, all the time making sure that he does not fail again. This is, conditions are created in which he can learn in easy stages, without threat to his control over the situation. A vicious circle is more likely to develop when a subject sets a standard of accuracy he cannot easily achieve, i.e. wants an excessive degree of control over the situation.

Vicious-circle effects are also observed in interactions between one person and another. Fearing that the other is unfriendly a person adopts an unfriendly attitude, which evokes a rebuff and adds to his fear, the feedback being positive.

Progression and regression

If it fails to remove a danger, a response may be superseded through 'progression' to a new, more effective and usually more elaborate mode of response. The superseded response may reappear subsequently. This, which is called regression, has been demonstrated along these lines. Subjects are given opportunity to learn habit A, which is partially effective in the avoidance of, say, an electric shock. They are then given opportunity to learn habit B, which is more effective. Habit B is then made ineffective. There may then be progression to habit C or regression to habit A. This amounts to trying again a solution to a problem found to be successful on a previous occasion. Whether regression does occur as a result of frustration depends on the circumstances in which a habit was superseded. It is more likely to reappear if progression took place when drive strength was high, less likely if it was gradually modified through experience over a protracted period of time. The term regression is sometimes applied to childish behaviour, such as a display of helplessness, observed in an adult as a result of frustration when it is thought to represent reversion to a habit superseded during childhood.

Aggression

The responses made in an emergency may become so little restrained and so crude as to be violent and threaten damage to laboratory equipment. Yet then they are usually too poorly co-ordinated and too vacillating to be effective. They may be described as aggressive if they are intended in some degree to be destructive. There is a typical sequence of changes in the behaviour observed when subjects faced by an insoluble problem recognize that they are failing in spite of all their efforts. Responses become less restrained, then more destructive. The emotion associated with them is more anger than anxiety. They are accompanied by verbal criticism or abuse, which is at first specific, then generalized. The aggression, in words or behaviour, is at first projected, i.e. directed against objects or persons, then introjected, i.e. directed against the self, e.g. in the form of self-reproach or self-disapproval. Efforts to solve the problem fall off. Aggression occurs when more constructive responses have failed to remove a threat, but is only one of the classes of behaviour which then emerge.

Disorganization

Much of the behaviour which results from frustration is clumsy, vacillating, and poorly sustained. A similar disorganization is shown by the mental activity resulting from frustration, and characterizes the emotion called anxiety. Although it is sometimes attributed to breakdown in the functioning of the nervous system, disorganization is adaptive in that it represents reversion to 'trial-and error' behaviour. New modes of response then emerge, one of which may prove successful. But the randomness of trial-and-error behaviour may mean that it is an inefficient way to solve a problem.

Experimental extinction

If it is repeatedly evoked and does not achieve the removal of a threat, i.e. reinforcement is withheld, a response becomes, with each repetition, more delayed, slower in execution and weaker, until finally no response at all is evoked. It is said then to have undergone experimental extinction. Repeated stimulation reduces responsiveness in this way, the psychological process being known as 'habituation'. The decline in responsiveness may become 'generalized' and affect a wider range of stimuli and/or a wider range of responses.

Examples of extinction in human subjects are easily found. A person blinks if an object is waved in front of his eyes, and this response wanes with each repetition. An unaccustomed noise evokes a startled response on the first occasion, and is hardly responded to at all after several repetitions. A generalized decline in responsiveness has been observed in experiments when there has been intensive stimulation without reinforcement. Responsiveness tends to recover with the passage of time or may be restored by a change in the stimulus situation, but recovery tends to be incomplete, for extinction is easier on a second or later occasion; recovery is then slower.

The ease with which a response undergoes extinction depends on the conditions in which the response was acquired. The conditions of learning favouring resistance to extinction are intermittent rather than continuous reinforcement, spaced rather than massed trials, varying rather than consistent setting, and high level of drive. Responses learned under these conditions, which obtain for much of the learning outside the laboratory, undergo extinction only when they are repeatedly evoked in massed trials without reinforcement, i.e. as a result of intensive stimulation. Responsiveness tends then to recover rapidly.

Depression

Depression in patients tends to be characterized by a more or less generalized reduction in responsiveness. This has usually been preceded by a period of overactivity and disorganization, during which anger has been expressed, but is associated with self-reproach. These points are compatible with the view that the reduction in responsiveness of depression is due to intensive stimulation without reinforcement. But whereas in the laboratory responsiveness recovers rapidly, recovery from depression may be protracted, although this is not always so. Depression is depression, it has been said, and not fear or distress or sulking, because it lasts for a long time. A possible reason lies in the persistence of the danger signals. Not responding adequately the patient does nothing to change the situation threatening him. The result is a deadlock.

Anxiety and depression

The emotion resulting from frustration is typically anxiety, which is given its special character by the indefiniteness of the dangers anticipated and the changeableness, incoherence, and disorganization of the responses rehearsed in fantasy. These may include destructive impulses; anxiety is then mixed with anger. An anxious person, who is in suspense, waiting for information to clarify the situation, is watchful and alert, often excessively alert and over-reacting to a wide range of stimuli. The anxious feel helpless in the face of dangers which, although felt to be imminent, cannot be identified or communicated. There is always an element of not knowing what to do.

Hope and despair alternate in anxiety, whereas depression, when this term is used to refer to emotion, is characterized by a more pronounced and persistent hopelessness and dejection, with which are associated self-reproach and feelings of unworthiness and inadequacy. The difficulties faced, although ill-defined, appear general, formidable, and unlikely to be overcome. However, depression and anxiety tend to occur together. Thus any change in circumstances not immediately compensated tends to evoke both a sense of loss of what has been and apprehension about what will be—usually regarded as components of depression and anxiety respectively.

The bodily symptoms associated with anxiety and depression are rather similar. They include tightness or uneasiness in the chest, tending to move up into the throat, sinking feelings in the epigastrium, and light feelings in the head, which may be described as dizziness. The patient is typically pale, less often flushed. Sweating is increased. The pulse is rapid, the heart overacting. There is intolerance of effort, mild exertion producing an undue increase in pulse, respiration, and sweating. Tiring is rapid. The posture is tense, tendon reflexes typically, brisk. Sexual interest is in abeyance. The function of every organ in the body is affected in some degree.

Phobias and separation anxiety

In contrast to anxiety, the dangers associated with fear are definite, immediate and external, and the responses rehearsed are relatively coherent and well organized. The term 'phobia' is used when emotion has a more or less specific reference to a situation or object although the emotion may appear to be out of proportion to the dangers. Phobias for spiders and snakes are relatively common. The cats in Masserman's experiments can be said to have shown a phobic response to the cage. Agoraphobia is a morbid response to public places.

The agoraphobic patient does not feel anxious while he succeeds in avoiding whatever dangers are contained in them. Emotion is aroused when, avoidance responses being frustrated, the dangers appear imminent. The patient then feels unable to cope with whatever demands public places make. These demands might represent threats to his conception of himself or to the assumptions he makes about the world.

Akin to agoraphobia is separation anxiety, which arises when a person faces dangers while being denied, as a result of separation, the reassurance and support of a parent or other significant person. Existentialist theory equates anxiety with the threat of being alone or of being nothing; without the reassurance of another person the sense of self is threatened.

Psychosomatic disease

Such interventions as confinement, restraint, and frustration have been shown experimentally to produce changes also in the functions of such organs as the stomach, colon, skin, and heart.[8] This raises the question: do they play a part in causing the organic diseases for which medical treatment is sought? There has long been epidemiological evidence that they do, e.g. the increase reported in the First World War in the incidence of gastric ulcer in soldiers who had recently been in action in the trenches, and the rise in the number of deaths recorded as due to gastric and duodenal ulcer during the period of heavy air raids during the Second World War. When stocks go down in New York, it was once remarked, diabetes goes up. The survivors of fires and floods, prisoners of war and the bereaved, amongst others, have been shown to have high rates of mortality and morbidity.

The term 'psychosomatic' was coined in the nineteen-thirties to be applied to those organic, or somatic, diseases in which psychological factors are thought to play a part, e.g. heart disease, cancer, disease of the gastro-intestinal tract, urticaria, bronchial asthma, ulcerative colitis, and rheumatoid arthritis.[9] So many diseases have now to be included in such a list as to discourage any inclination to distinguish psychosomatic diseases from those which are not. However, the term persists as a reminder that any analysis of either the effects of a change in circumstances or the causes of a somatic or mental disorder should take into account the interrelationships of the behavioural, mental, and somatic components of the organism's response.

Sensory deprivation

Disorders resembling clinical disorders have also been produced experimentally under conditions of 'sensory deprivation'. In experiments intended originally to elucidate problems then thought likely to be met in space travel, volunteers were put into a darkened and sound-proofed room on their own. Sensory stimulation was further reduced by immobilizing them. Other investigators preferred a method in which subjects were suspended in water, appropriate arrangements being made for the delivery of oxygen for breathing. Research along these lines was carried out in America and elsewhere during the nineteen-fifties.[10] It fell into disrepute because of the untoward effects on a few subjects.

In these conditions many subjects sleep fitfully without distress. Some experience after a time an increasing tension and agitation amounting in a few cases to panic. A few become obsessed with more or less delusional ideas. A few experience hallucinations. These effects develop gradually within a day or two. Recovery tends to be rapid when normal conditions are restored. In what degree the effects are caused by reduction in sensory input, and in what degree by social isolation from other persons or by immobilization and confinement has proved difficult to decide.

Ethological models

Ethology, which grew out of zoology, used to mean the interpretation of character by the study of gesture, but has widened its scope to bring together questions about the immediate causes, function, development, and evolution of, especially, the social behaviour of animals.[11] Its tradition is to observe social interaction under more or less natural conditions. It has provided several models for psychopathology, notably models for the formation of the attachment of one member of a family to another (to be discussed in CHAPTER 4). The growing interest in ethology in the nineteen-fifties gave impetus to the change over from reaction to interaction models.

Ethology has also drawn attention to the various types of response that occur at times of conflict. In a skirmish with another at the boundary of its territory, for instance, an animal may show alternation from attack to flight. Responses are then incomplete and abbreviated to preparatory or intention movements, which reflect the tendencies in conflict. An attack may be redirected to another, even innocuous, object. The substitute responses tend then to be of low intensity, incomplete, eccentric, and imperfectly oriented. The form they take depends upon definable factors in the situation and can be understood by reference to priorities in responding, although they may appear irrelevant or out of context.

A stickleback begins to dig in the sand, for instance, in circumstances in which he might be expected to attack another male. Digging, although out of context because it is not a component of aggression, belongs to patterns of behaviour serving courtship and nest-building. Yawning, lighting a cigarette, chewing gum, handling keys or hankerchief, scratching behind the ear and the several counterparts of preening that occur at times of embarassment or frustration have been given as examples of substitute responses in humans. More controversial examples are the masturbation of adults and children when they are anxious, the rocking, tapping and twirling of children, and compensatory overeating.

When two people meet, they exchange messages, verbal or non-verbal, which indicate status and intention through stance, posture, gesture, emotional expression, and other signs. The stance of the angry, for instance, indicates their assumption of superior status and threatens violence, whereas with fear goes a display indicating inferior status, prostration, and abasement. Those we call depressed convey through posture and emotional expression their subjection and dependence. Their symptoms are messages communicating their distress; tearfulness, for instance, may be an appeal for help. There tends to be a paucity of messages because they have gone unrewarded by those to whom they have been addressed.

The relationships studied by ethologists have been diverse, amongst them, those between rivals, male and female, parent and offspring, and litter-mates. Some of these relationships are lasting, others transitory. The participants in some do the same things, in others different but complementary things. In psychopathology there are other types of relationship to be considered as well, that between sibs, employer and employee, colleagues, etc.

OTHER MODELS

A model from community disasters

Three phases may be recognized in the changes in behaviour observed in the experiments discussed above, although few experiments have been continued into the third phase. In the first phase previous patterns of behaviour are disrupted; there may be transient attempts to restore the status quo. The second phase is one of instability, with more or less sustained attempts to establish new patterns, e.g. as a result of trial-and-error learning. In the third phase there is reorganization and the recovery of stability. In Masserman's experiments the three phases might be described as fright, flight, and return. In experiments on the effects of frustration, there is disorganization of previous patterns, then attempts through regression and aggression to regain control, and the gradual emergence of new patterns.

This three-phase scheme provides a framework into which to fit observations made on human behaviour after community disasters caused by such things as floods, high winds, earthquakes, fires, mining disasters, transport accidents, and landslides. By a disaster is meant an event causing immediate disruption of the normal life of an individual or a community, with or without a threat to life or actual loss of life. Many detailed accounts of disasters have now been published.[1 2]

First phase

Those outside the disaster area, but with ties to the persons and places struck, may show a 'counter-disaster syndrome', characterized by vigorous activity directed towards rescue, first aid or the making of a contribution of some kind. A few of those immediately affected may stay cool and collected, but most behave as if stunned and appear bewildered, aimless, and apathetic, with a restricted field of awareness. They tend to be passive, compliant, suggestible, and retarded. Some show a child-like dependence on those offering help. Families tend to keep together and to find separation hard to bear. A few show confusion or manifestly inappropriate behaviour. Very few lose control and cry, scream or rush about. During this phase survivors tell their stories of the loss of relatives or friends without emotion and as if disinterested spectators. Recall is selective and may be blurred for some details.

Second phase

After a few days they begin to show more emotion—fear, anger, anxiety, and despondency. They feel the need to be with others. They tell their stories over and over again, usually with identical detail and emphasis. At night they dream about the disaster, reliving their experiences with more emotion and rehearsing the steps they might have taken to keep control over what was happening. The play of children shows a similar preoccupation.

Memories at first freely recalled become modified, assimilated, and less available as defences become established. The preoccupation and distress give way gradually to various defensive concerns. These may be for the welfare of family and community. There may follow a euphoric identification with the community and an enthusiastic participation in repair and rehabilitation. Explanations of the disaster are sought. Guilt may be expressed over the community's previous mode of life, in the form of superstitious rumours or statements that people had lived too well and had deserved punishment. There may be angry criticism of the way in which the disaster came about and had been dealt with. Scapegoats are readily found, perhaps in local political leaders or officials.

Third phase

Recovery is gradual. Homes are rebuilt or replaced, and a normal mode of life is resumed. There is often a surprising resilience. Some move away. Although some are able to talk freely about their experiences, recall is more often restricted to a few, stereotyped details, while some experiences are assimilated and lose their identity. There is often for a while a heightened interest and more participation in the affairs of the community, and individuals form closer relationships with neighbours and others.

Bereavement

One of the most influential models for psychopathology is that based on the effects of bereavement,[13] by which is meant loss or dispossession, typically because of death. This 'cessation of interaction with an emotionally relevant person', as it has been called, is followed by a phase in which the bereaved detach themselves from the person lost. Recovery occurs with the 'redistribution of interactional patterns' and the making of new attachments. Roles in family or community change, and the bereaved as they recover assume new responsibilities and meet new demands. These processes go on gradually and may be brought to a satisfactory conclusion in a few weeks or months. When they go awry, the patient may remain ill for months or years.

Lorenz's[14] description of the behaviour of geese who have lost a partner testifies to the view that the course after bereavement in humans is similar to that in other species. 'The first response consists in the anxious attempt to find him or her again. It loses all courage and flees even from the youngest and weakest geese . . . and sinks to the lowest step in the ranking order . . . the goose can become extremely shy, reluctant to approach human beings and to come to the feeding place . . . the bird also develops a tendency to panic. Geese, having lost their partners, took up again their long-neglected connections with parents and siblings.' The effect on mammals of the loss of a partner has been summed up thus: 'One chimpanzee is no chimpanzee at all.'

The effects of bereavement fit into a three-phase scheme. Bowlby[15] called the three phase of mourning: 'yearning' (formerly 'protest'), 'despair or disorganization' and 'detachment' (formerly 'denial'). The third phase he has also called 'reorganization'.

First phase

The loss is sometimes followed immediately by intense, but short-lived attempts to prevent or restore the loss. Sometimes there is a denial of the loss, or a person may faint. For a few hours or days, typically perhaps for 2 weeks, the bereaved appear dazed and feel numb, empty and unreal. Emotional responses are blunted, and there is a sharp reduction in responsiveness in other respects too.

Second phase

The bereaved experience waves of grief and distress, intense feelings alternating with apathy and dejection. They are preoccupied with the loss and the circumstances in which it occurred. They pine and cry for the lost person, and search for him. At times they reproach themselves, at times blame others, for what was done or not done. Interest is withdrawn from other matters. Concentration is impaired, and they are inefficient at work. They sleep poorly, appetite is poor, and they lose weight. Although distress is usually admitted openly, it is seldom that help is sought outside the family. This phase lasts typically for about 6 weeks. Four out of five of the bereaved are said to show considerable improvement within 10 weeks.

Third phase

The bereaved make a gradual recovery as they acquire new habits and make new attachments. The defences shown in the second phase crumble and are abandoned. Memories of the loss, which may be haunting in the second phase, gradually fade, although a few details may be preserved for a long time. They return to a normal mode of life, although the style may be different from before, and achieve social and economic independence. Some widows remarry; rather more widowers do so. Some of the widowed find sexual partners or companions outside marriage. A few return to live with parents.

Some attach themselves more closely again to a sister or brother. Relationships with children tend to become closer. Some find a satisfactory new role as grandparent. Some start a course of study or a new job or career.

Common defences

During the second phase a degree of relief is obtained through a variety of more or less transient defences. Here are some examples. *Business*. The bereaved person carries on his ordinary work with greater energy or for longer hours and looks for new things to do in order to keep busy. The advice given most often by relatives to the bereaved is to keep busy. *Consolation* is sought in various ways, sometimes through unwise or promiscuous liaisons. *Denial*. Anything to do with the person lost is put out of mind. *Searching*. The lost one is looked for as if still alive. *Fantasy restoration*. The permanence or reality of the loss is denied, and fantasies of an early return are indulged in. Images of the lost person may be vivid and mistaken usually briefly for reality. In general, the perceptual set increases alertness to reminders of the lost one. *Mummification*. Possessions are kept ready for an early return. *Reminiscence*. There is preoccupation with the recall of experiences shared with the lost one. *Displacement*. An excessive or inappropriate grief is displayed over some other loss of little relevance. *Intellectualization*. The loss is spoken of in rational terms, but without appropriate emotion. *Idealization*, or at the extreme *enshrinement*. The lost one is represented as if free from all faults. *Identification*. The roles and causes held dear by the lost one are taken up. *Somatization*. Bodily symptoms are developed like those from which the lost one suffered. *Retaliation*. Angry criticisms are made of anyone connected with the loss for what they did or did not do, even to the extent of starting legal proceedings.

Sometimes the second phase is prolonged for a year or more—'prolonged grief'—with persistence of one or more of the defences listed above. Sometimes grief is delayed, not being shown for weeks, months or even a year or more and then beginning suddenly, perhaps on an anniversary. In a few cases the distress is severe enough to amount to illness or to require medical intervention. Out of it a psychosis may develop, with delusions and hallucinations, which represent in an extreme form some of the defences, or with marked changes in mood towards depression or excitement, even elation and business.

A distinction can be made between a sense of loss which is felt to be external, as in normal grief, of which pining is the characteristic feature, and depression, which carries with it a feeling of diminution or depreciation of the self, i.e. a lowering of self-regard or of unworthiness or wickedness. Also, the feelings of the depressed towards the person lost tend to be an ambivalent mixture of love and hate. Suicide occurs occasionally, death then being sought in order either to get relief from intolerable distress or to achieve reunion with the person lost.

Effects on health and mortality

Organic illness sometimes follows closely upon a bereavement. Ulcerative colitis, asthma, peptic ulcer, rheumatoid arthristis, and eczema, amongst others, have been reported to be unduly common, but the evidence is inconclusive.

There is sound evidence of an increase in mortality. Rates are higher for all ages for the widowed than for the married. Diseases of the cardiovascular system show the greatest increases. Part of the increase for widowers is due to suicide, but not for widows. The mortality rate of widowers over 55 years old has been shown to be raised for 6 months after the loss of their wives by about 40 per cent over that of married men of the same age; about 5 per cent of widowers of this age die within 6 months. The rate then falls back to that of married men. The rise in the rate for widows is much smaller and is mainly in the second year after bereavement. The rate of the close relatives has been found to be raised for at least a year, the rise being greatest when the death has been sudden and unexpected. After a community disaster the rate of those affected has also been found to be raised for a year. The probable reason for the raised rates is that there is a 'desolation' effect. There are several processes by which such an effect might be produced.

Judging from the patients referred to psychiatric clinics, severe reactions after bereavement are commoner in women than in men. Severe reactions in married women tend to follow the loss of a husband or child, especially a young child. The death of a child is an exacting test of a marriage. The person lost is occasionally a brother or sister or parent, more often mother than father. In single women, severe reactions follow the loss of one of these, in men, the loss of a wife, young child or parent, also more often mother than father. However, samples from psychiatric clinics cannot be accepted as representative of the general population.

The results of follow-up studies of the bereaved show that severe and prolonged reactions tend to occur when the loss has been sudden, unexpected, or unprepared for. Such reactions appear to be commoner when the relationship with the person lost has been discordant, when the bereaved person has been unduly dependent on the person lost, when the person lost has disappeared, and there is uncertainty whether he is dead, or when the death has occurred under distressing circumstances, e.g. through suicide, or through the supposed negligence or misconduct of the bereaved person or others.

They occur also when grief has not been expressed normally, e.g. when a woman mourns privately a lover she has not acknowledged. They are commoner among younger than older widows, and among widows with dependent children, and especially when young widows perceive the people around them as unsympathetic or antagonistic or are unable for other reasons to express their feelings.[16] Not doing so holds up the exploration in the second phase of the implications and consequences of the loss. There appears to be some truth in the popular belief that to talk about the loss—'to give sorrow words'[17]—helps toward recovery.

Anniversary reactions

The level of anxiety tends to rise on anniversaries of bereavements or other events of special significance. Defences are given up temporarily or more lastingly as aspects of the experiences are recalled and reviewed. On the anniversary of her husband's death or occasionally of her wedding day or other special day, a widow suffers a recurrence of her grief and associated symptoms, and takes stock of her position, and this may be an occasion to talk again about him. A significant excess of suicides has been found to occur within a month of the anniversary of a father's death. In a more complex way a woman may develop an illness at the age at which her mother died. 'Age coincidences' have been shown to be unduly common.[18]

Major surgery

Much has been learnt about the conditions in which disorders occur from the follow-up of those who have suffered community or personal disasters; these have been retrospective studies. Prospective studies are occasionally practicable. Patients have been interviewed, for instance, before they undergo major surgery in order to learn something about the individual differences in the effects on them, and how untoward reactions can be prevented by preoperative preparation.[19]

Patients have been divided into those with low, moderate, and high anticipatory fear. 'High fear' is relatively frequent when the operation is to be on the perineum or lower abdomen. 'Low-fear' patients remain unperturbed before the operation, without disturbance of sleep or signs of emotional tension. They do not seek information about the operation, and are apt to adopt a joking or facetious attitude, with denial of potential difficulties and dangers.

'Moderate-fear' patients show signs of emotional tension intermittently, and suffer from some disturbance of sleep. They express some forebodings, but are able to suppress disquietening thoughts. They ask for information about what they will experience, and find reassurance in the skill and goodwill of the staff. High-fear patients show signs of sustained emotional tension. they are restless and unable to concentrate during the day, and suffer from insomnia at night. They tend to adopt attitudes of passivity, resignation or fatalism, although they may entertain fantasies of mutilation or annihilation. They turn repeatedly for reassurance to the staff, on whom they show a child-like dependence.

After the operation low-fear patients seem surprised when they experience pain and regard it as unnecessary and due to the ineptness of the staff. A few show angry resentment or refuse to co-operate. Moderate-fear patients tend to be model patients, with relatively little emotional disturbance throughout the recovery period. High-fear patients continue to display a relatively high level of fear and to be childishly dependent and propitiating, with frequent expressions of gratitude and admiration.

Untoward reactions are less frequent if during the pre-operative period low-fear patients have been told of the dangers, discomforts, and deprivations they will experience, how they will be helped and how they can help themselves. Moderate-fear patients are helped by objective statements which are as comprehensive as possible. The excessive reactions of high-fear patients are partly due to misinformation and misinterpretation, which can be corrected, but they tend to misunderstand objective explanations, and are helped by emphasizing the grounds for optimism and by accepting their dependence.

Adaptations to other forms of stress have been studied, amongst them, the stress of examinations.[20] The coping strategies shown by students tend to be suited well to the immediate challenge, less well to their professional development. The techniques they use depend on how much information they have gained about what the examination entails. Those experiencing the most discomfort beforehand are the students ill-equipped with the necessary knowledge and skills.

Disorders induced in political prisoners

Drugs have been administered to political prisoners in order to induce abnormal mental states, which allow confessions to be extracted. These are often extravagant and resemble the self-accusations which form a prominent symptom of some depressive illnesses, much that is recalled being wholly or partly false and being derived not from real experiences but from fantasies.

Similar material may be recalled by neurotic, guilt-ridden individuals when they are brought under the influence of narcotic drugs. Whether drugs are essential to the extraction of confessions from prisoners is doubtful. More likely, the confessions are the result of prolonged psychological stresses which induce despair, resignation, and hopelessness to a degree to amount to a temporary psychosis. The literary accounts of the methods applied to political prisoners emphasize the degrading conditions, repeated interrogation, loss of sleep, frustration, solitary confinement, which deprives the prisoner of reassuring social contacts, deterioration of physical health, and cold, pain and hunger.[21] Thought-reform procedures have been used which challenge the prisoner's beliefs and then offer a new belief system. This tends to be accepted because it restores security, orientation, and identity. The three phases have been called: confrontation, reordering, and renewal.[22]

The tradition of extracting confessions goes back to the persecution in the middle ages of those accused of witchcraft. The accused who did not confess that they had bound themselves to the devil were liable to be burned or hanged. Those acknowledging their offences could plead that while being under the influence of the devil they had been victim rather than servant. This rallied succour from others, but also confirmed their belief that one part of their personality and been possessed by the devil. The disowning of a part of the self and the feeling of being under the control of an external power occur as symptoms of mental illness.

On one occasion in Northern Ireland a method was used, which was derived from experiments on the effects of sensory deprivation, in order to prepare detainees for interrogation in depth.[23] The detainees were made to stand in a controlled position against a wall, which has the effect of reducing proprioceptive cues to body image. Sleep was made difficult, and diet was restricted. An opaque hood was put over the head. A continuous noise— electronic mush—masked extraneous sounds. The effects were a high level of anxiety and psychological disorientation. Depersonalization, disorder of body image, and hallucinations were produced in some cases. Since the method was applied over a period of hours only, recovery, it may be supposed, was rapid. How often, and in what degree, there were more persistent effects is disputed.

Several descriptions have been given of the psychoses induced in prisoners of war.[24] They show an increase of activity for a while after capture, with restless excitement and exploratory activity, which, purposeful to start with, becomes more and more dispersed and random. Activity then subsides, and they become relatively inactive, except for isolated, repetitive, and stereotyped acts. Mortality rates tend to be high among those who suffer from severe stresses during imprisonment, especially from diseases of the cardio-vascular system, but also from cancer, gastro-intestinal disease, tuberculosis, accident, and suicide. The lasting effects of imprisonment in concentration camps have also been studied in detail.[25]

Models from biographies and literature

The models available to psychopathology have been increased by studies of the distinguished and of the characters depicted in novels and plays. P. J. Möbius, for instance, one of the pioneers at the end of the last century, wrote well-researched interpretations, which he called 'pathographies', of the disorders shown by J. J. Rousseau, Goethe, Schopenhauer, and Nietzsche. Karl Jaspers, in his classic *General Psychopathology*, set great store by pathography because 'we may see what can never be observed for the average institutional inmate, and what will add depth to our knowledge'.[26] He wrote about Nietzsche, Strindberg, Van Gogh, Hölderlin, and Swedenborg. Freud wrote about not only artists and writers, e.g. Leonardo da Vinci and Dostoevsky, but also such fictive characters as Lady Macbeth and Rebecca West.[27]

Freud found a model in the legend of Oedipus Rex in Sophocles' play. Thus he referred to 'being in love with one parent and hating the other'—(the 'Oedipus complex')—as being 'among the essential constituents of the stock of psychical impulses' formed in childhood and as important in determining the symptoms of later neurosis.[28] However, his formula, which is based, as is usual in psychoanalysis, on the child's feelings towards his parents, gives a one-sided account of the complex interactions in a family. For him, the son is the transgressor whereas in the Greek plays the father, feeling threatened because he has been told by the oracle that he will perish at the hands of his son, instructs the mother to destroy him at birth; instead she abandons him. The father later starts the quarrel which ends in his death. In the story of Hamlet in Shakespeare's play, which psychoanalysts have regarded as similar to that of Oedipus, the stepfather, not the son, is the aggressor, who reacts to the threats in his stepson's behaviour. Here an interaction model serves better than the reaction model on which Freud depended.

The Electra complex, the counterpart in girls of the Oedipus complex, is derived from the story of Electra, who in the plays of ancient Greece, e.g. Aeschylus' *The Oresteia*, while still grieving for her father, Agamemnon, encourages her brother, Orestes, to kill her mother, Clytemnestra, and Clytemnestra's paramour in retribution for their murder of Agamemnon. Versions of this story have been used by modern playwrights, notably T. S. Eliot, Jean Giradoux, Eugene O'Neill, and J. P. Sartre.

Hamlet and *The Oresteia* are two of the many plays which are studies of madness. Amongst others are Shakespeare's *King Lear* and Ibsen's *Ghosts*. Among literary accounts of madness are Dostoevksy's *The Brothers Karamazov*, Strindberg's *Inferno*, Thomas Mann's *Death in Venice*, and Virginia Woolf's *Mrs. Dalloway*.

Hamlet is notable in that it offers several explanations of Hamlet's madness. Several characters in the play attribute it to a life event, such as his father's death, his mother's remarriage or Ophelia's rejection of him. Hamlet and his friend Horatio interpret it as 'an antic disposition' put on in order to hide from others the strong feelings aroused in him by the revelations of the ghost of his murdered father. But he also warns his mother not to suppose him to be mad in order to defend herself by denying the truth in his accusations. 'Repent what's past', he urges her.[29] The audience are in a better position than any of the characters to understand his madness because, being told much more about its circumstances and connections, they can see it in its full context.

King Lear shows how madness can arise out of a crisis in a father's relationships with his daughters. His unrealistic expectations being disappointed, he becomes estranged from them. The turmoil of the storm on the heath is then a metaphor for his anger and disorganization, the hovel for his degradation and despair. He makes a short-lived recovery when he is able to restore his relationship with Cordelia on new terms.

Ghosts is one of the several plays by Ibsen which show how behaviour is constrained by the ghosts of the past, and how a crisis in a system of relationships gives an opportunity to review what has happened and then to break free, as in *A Doll's House* and *The Lady from the Sea*; Oswald in *Ghosts* and Rebecca West in *Rosmersholm* fail to do so.

The Brothers Karamazov is one of several novels of its time in which is discussed the relationship between a character—Ivan—and a visitor, who is his double and an embodiment of one side of him, of his 'thoughts and feelings, but only the most vile and stupid'. In *Death in Venice* Thomas Mann describes how Aschenbach's sense of his own corruption, which has its roots in his relationship with his father, is translated into delusional ideas about the plague affecting the city.

Inferno and *Mrs. Dalloway* are rich sources of descriptions of disorders of perception. *Inferno* is an account of Strindberg's mental illness, which started after the breakdown of his second marriage, and in which he experienced hallucinations and became preoccupied by delusions. *Mrs. Dalloway*, which gives a version of an illness she had suffered 10 years earlier, was described by Virginia Woolf as 'a study of insanity and suicide, the world seen by the sane and insane side by side'. The accounts writers and artists give of their experiences make an important contribution to knowledge of the phenomena of mental illness especially. Although they have disadvantages, they have the great advantage that they are given unprompted by an investigator's questioning.

NOTES AND REFERENCES

1. Pavlov, I. P. (1941). *Lectures on conditioned reflexes, 2: conditioned reflexes and psychiatry.* Lawrence, London.
2. Double-bind messages are discussed again in CHAPTER 5.
3. Liddell, H. S. (1960). Experimental neurosis in animals. In *Stress and psychiatric disorder* (ed. J. M. Tanner). Blackwell, Oxford.
4. The various forms of disorder produced in frustrating situations are discussed with special reference to the fixation of responses by Maier, N.R.F. (1956). Frustration theory; restatement and extension. *Psychol. Rev.* **63**, 370–9.
5. Masserman, J. H. (1964). *Behaviour and neurosis.* University of Chicago Press.
6. Cannon, W. B. (1929). Bodily changes in pain, hunger, fear and rage (2nd edn). Appleton & Co., New York.
7. In the writer's experiments pilots were put to a task similar to flying an aeroplane on instruments, e.g. Davis, D. R. (1946). The disorganisation of behaviour in fatigue. *J. Neurol. Neurosurg. Psychiat.* **9**, 23–9.
8. Hill, O. W. (ed.) (1976). *Modern trends in psychosomatic medicine.* Butterworths, London.
9. The objective of psychosomatic medicine has been defined as 'to study in their interrelation the psychological and physiological aspects of all normal and abnormal bodily functions and thus to integrate somatic therapy and psychotherapy.'
10. Solomon, P., Kubzansky, P. E., Leiderman, P. H., Mendelson, J. H., Trumbull, R. and Wexler, D. (eds) (1961). *Sensory deprivation.* Harvard University Press, Cambridge, Mass.

11. Hinde, R. A. (1982). *Ethology*. Fontana, London.
12. Accounts of the behaviour of the survivors from many kinds of disaster are reviewed by Bennet, G. (1983). *Beyond endurance*. Secker & Warburg, London. See also Beach, H. D. (1967). *Management of human behaviour in disaster*. Department of National Health and Welfare, Ottawa.
13. Parkes, C. M. (1972). *Bereavement: studies of grief in adult life*. Tavistock Publications, London.
14. Lorenz, K. (1967). *On aggression*. Methuen, London.
15. Bowlby, J. *Attachment and loss*, Vols 1 (1969), 2 (1973), and 3 (1980). Hogarth Press and Institute of Psychoanalysis, London. The three volumes give an extended review of the research issues. Of particular relevance to bereavement is Vol. 3 with the subtitle: 'Loss sadness and depression'.
16. Maddison, D. and Walker, W. L. (1967). Factors affecting the outcome of conjugal bereavement. *Br. J. Psychiat.* **113**, 1057–67.
17. The passage in Shakespeare's *Macbeth* (1V.3.209–10) continues: 'The grief that does not speak whispers the o'er-fraught heart and bids it break.'
18. Hilgard, J. R. and Newman, M. F. (1959). Anniversaries in mental illness. *Psychiatry* **22**, 113–21.
19. Janis, I. L. (1974). *Psychological stress*. Academic Press, London.
20. Mechanic, D. (1962). *Students under stress: a study in the social psychology of adaptation*. Free Press, New York.
21. Koestler, A. (1947). *Darkness at noon*. Penguin Books, Harmondsworth.
22. Lifton, R. J. (1961). *Thought reform and the psychology of totalism*. Penguin Books, Harmondsworth.
23. (Compton) Report of the enquiry into allegations against the security forces of physical brutality in Northern Ireland arising out of events on 9 August 1971. HMSO (1971), Cmnd 4823, London.
24. Hinkle, L. E. and Wolff, H. G. (1955). Communist interrogation and indoctrination of 'enemies of the state'. *Archs Neurol. Psychiat.* **76**, 115–74.
25. Eitinger, L. and Strøm, A. (1973). *Mortality and morbidity after excessive stress: a follow-up investigation of Norwegian concentration camp survivors*. Humanities Press, New York.
26. Jaspers, K. (1963). *General psychopathology* (trans. J. Hoenig and M. W. Hamilton) Manchester University Press, Manchester.
27. Freud, S. (1955). *Some character-types met with in psychoanalytic work* (Standard edn) Vol. 14. Hogarth Press, London.
28. Freud, S. (1958). *The interpretation of dreams*. (Standard edn) Vols 4 and 5. Hogarth Press, London.
29. A person may defend himself by supposing the other to be mad or, as Hamlet puts it (III.4.145–6): 'Lay not that flattering unction to your soul, that not your trespass but my madness speaks.'

3 Disorders of mental processes

Much that can be written about disorders of mental processes depends on the reports of patients who inspect their own mental processes in response to questions about what they are experiencing or have experienced. Inferences may also be made from what they are observed to do or say. The reports can be recorded, but not the mental processes themselves. By abstracting from the reports and inferences, which are assembled more or less systematically, general descriptions of the phenomena of mental illness can be formulated. These are usually arrived at without any assumptions about the origins, causes, consequences or significance of the phenomena. Attempts can then be made to define the conditions in the brain or the environment in which certain phenomena or certain disorders occur.[1]

One form in which the question may be put is: given certain conditions, what are the disorders which typically occur? This question may be asked about the disorders occurring in patients who have sustained diffuse, i.e. not localized, damage to the brain. This may be the result either of the concussion caused by mechanical injury due to accident or of acute or chronic intoxication by alcohol or drugs. The latter cases are complicated more often than the former by previously existing disorders of personality.

DIFFUSE BRAIN DAMAGE

Recovery takes place in four stages. The first stage is one of confusion, of which poverty, slowness and, especially, incoherence of mental activity are the main features. The patient may be aroused momentarily by intense stimulation, but does not respond otherwise, and shows little or no spontaneous activity. What he does do is slow and aimless. If he vocalizes, it is to groan or shout meaninglessly.

The second stage is one of delirium, the typical features being fearfulness, agitation, and vivid, usually visual imagery. Consciousness is clouded and the patient responds erratically to external stimulation, his attention not being sustained. When he does respond coherently, he tends to imitate what the examiner says or does. What little he says spontaneously tends to be so disturbed as to seem meaningless or to consist in the repetition of common phrases. His speech is slurred, and his limb movements are slow and unsteady.

For the most part the patient lies dreaming. Mental activity is largely autonomous, but in some degree affected by external stimuli, which dimly and incompletely perceived are clothed with meaning and are often terrifying. Quietness and weakness of lighting favour autonomous activity. Brighter lighting by giving better definition to the external environment results in greater control over the imagery, but this control fatigues rapidly. Crudely perceived stimuli, such as shadows, are invested with meaning and may be mistaken for threatening persons or animals. Several factors account for mistakes of this kind: the high, although variable, level of arousal, the lowering of vigilance, the impairment of perception, and the reduced and deficient testing of reality.

There may also be some enhancement of imagery by random activity of nervous tissue as a result of intoxication. Sensations are then blurred, to produce 'white noise', for instance, which is then elaborated. The patient may then see visual patterns like lace curtains, usually coloured. When there is also peripheral neuritis, meaning may be attached to skin sensations such as numbness, pins and needles or itching, and a patient may be seen to brush off his skin what he seems to take to be lice, cockroaches, threads etc., uttering curses as he does so. There may be a similar basis in the phosphenes due to optic neuritis for some of the vivid visual experiences of patients in delirium tremens, such as the pink rats, spiders, and dragons of the popular stories; these do occur occasionally although more ordinary images are commoner.

The delirious do not clearly distinguish between what is imagined and what is perceived. They do not at the time disown what they imagine even when it is grotesque. In contrast, schizophrenic patients tend to disown their hallucinations, regarding them as intrusions. After recovery, patients may still be uncertain whether some of their experiences in delirium were imaginery or real, telling of them, sometimes as if they had happened, and sometimes as if they had been strange dreams.

The amnesic syndrome

Characteristic of the third stage of recovery is the amnesic syndrome.[2] This has sometimes been called the Korsakow syndrome because the salient symptoms are like those described by Korsakow in 1890 as accompanying the peripheral neuritis due, typically, to intoxication by alcohol.[3] These include 'weakness of the psychic functions', showing itself in sleeplessness, rapid fatiguing, irritability, apprehensiveness, and preoccupation with fearful imagery. However, the essential components of the amnesic syndrome are: disorientation in place, situation, and time, and disorder of memory for recent events especially. Other symptoms are commonly associated, e.g. reminiscence and confabulation. New material is learnt with difficulty, and perception is disordered. The patient shows little spontaneity. Mood is one of indifference, although occasionally one of euphoria. Sexual interest is in abeyance.

Disorientation

Patients do not know where they are, how they got there, or what kind of situation they are in. They have been unconscious, but they have not yet found out what has happened or, if they have found out, have forgotten. When questioned, they try to orientate themselves from casual or incomplete perceptions, which they accept uncritically. They make absurd mistakes, and are little put out when corrected.

They do not know what time of day it is. They do not usually give the date correctly, making mistakes even in the year. Sometimes they do not know what season it is. Typically they give their birthday and year of birth correctly, less often their age. What is said about year of birth, age, and present year is often contradictory. When this is pointed out, the patient may attempt a facile reconciliation.

Disorder of memory

One way in which the disorder of memory is shown is difficulty in finding the way about. Patients have to be shown over and over again where the ward lavatory is, and lose their way when retracing their steps to their beds. They leave articles on one side and forget where they have put them. Incapacity in the learning of new visuo-spatial relationships comes more often to notice than unreliability in other respects, perhaps because it is less easily covered up.

Patients give a poor account of what has happened to them in the immediate past, and do not remember, for instance, the meals they have had, visits that day from relatives or friends or meetings or interviews with the doctor. They do not retain information. Mental tests do not reveal any deterioration in well-established habits or skills or any loss of knowledge. On the other hand, new material is not recalled correctly even after several presentations, as may be shown in the learning of a series of digits or in the 'paired associates' test. Mistakes are repeated, despite correction, the patient seeming to be unable to 'unlearn'. The span of apprehension of a digit series may be unimpaired. Some of the difficulty in remembering may lie in a poor strategy for 'encoding' what is experienced. Because of a low level of drive or interest it is not put into a context of other experiences.

Patients fail also to recognize persons, places or objects they have seen for the first time after they have become ill. In the recognition of material presented in a test, a patient may respond to it as not identical to or in some way changed from the original. The probable reason for this 'reduplicative' paramnesia lies in the disorder of perception. The field of awareness tends to be restricted, a few details or qualities—'high lights'—being attended to while others are neglected. What is perceived is fragmentary and incomplete, and is filled out by imagery. The patient makes as a result false identifications and interpretations, which are accepted uncritically. The mistakes tend to have a paranoid colouring. For instance, a patient may identify the other patients in the ward as detectives, who are there to watch him because of the crimes he supposes he has committed. Yet patients tend to be appropriate in their dealings with other patients, nurses and doctors, probably because they are ready to fit in with the roles suggested to them by others.

Reminiscence

The amnesic syndrome tends to be associated with the preferential recall of incidents from the remote past. These appear to have been uncovered as a result of the disorder of memory for recent events. However, when tested, recall from childhood is found to be no more accurate or complete, perhaps less so, than that of healthy persons of similar age. When the damage to the brain is progressive, as in cases of dementia due to cerebro-vascular disease or cortical atrophy, and there is a progressive dissolution of memory, the new, complex, and poorly organized memories succumb, it has been said, before the old, simple, and well-organized ones.

The new perishes, the old endures. This law, stated first by Ribot in 1882, was restated by Hughlings Jackson in the more general form that the most complex and highest mental functions are affected more than the simpler, lower, and more automatic functions. A patient who has lost many of his professional skills may yet continue to dress himself, feed himself, and occupy himself in simple ways without apparent change, and retain an appropriate social manner, until late in a progressive disease, and thus hide from the casual observer the degree to which his memory is impaired. However, acceptance of Ribot's law without qualification is likely to lead to overestimation of the degree to which the memory of remote experiences is preserved. The clinical findings are less consistent than the law would lead one to expect; the formula it gives is too simple.

Reality testing

A usual feature of the amnesic syndrome is the lack of self-critique. Patients do not check the correctness of what they say, and persist in contradictory statements or 'entertain incompatible propositions', e.g. about their age, date of birth, and the present date, or about a sequence of events. Nor do they look a second time or search for further information in order to confirm the reality of what they experienced or to corroborate their identifications and interpretations. They do not look to others for corroboration. The reduction in the testing of reality in these ways may reflect their disengagement from what goes on around them.

They may be put out slightly by inability to remember when questioned and then make facile excuses or fill in gaps in memory by confabulating. Asked who is the Prime Minister, a patient replies that he has not read the newspapers recently. Asked what he has done that morning, he may tell of events that have never happened. What he tells may be obviously fabrication. Sometimes the fabrication is a fluent and plausible reconstruction based on one or more key details, and may deceive the unwary, unless note is taken of its changeability. Much of what is fabricated has been suggested to the patient; some is derived from imaginary experiences. Confabulation is thought to occur more often in association with the Korsakow syndrome due to alcohol than during recovery from concussion.

The residual effect

In most cases of concussion recovery is complete in a few days. In the cases of more severe damage to the brain, whether as a result of concussion or other causes, the amnesic syndrome may persist after recovery has advanced as far as it is going to, and this may take months or a year or two. Patients then develop methods of getting over the resulting difficulties, like those developed by the elderly when their memory is impaired. The effects of their incapacity are reduced by restricting walks to familiar territory, not taking on anything which might be taxing, and keeping to an orderly routine. A special effort may be made to memorize important details, or resort is made to *aides-mémoires*. The forgetting of a name or other detail is covered over by a circumlocution or evasion, or a facile excuse is made. Patients seem either to be unaware of or denying their incapacity. In general, they adopt a mode of life which takes account of their disabilities, and these are not apparent while they are able to continue in their routines.

Catastrophic reactions

The disabilities may be revealed when a patient is obliged to move into unfamiliar surroundings, e.g. on admission to hospital. The precariousness of the adjustment may be shown up by an untoward event, which a healthy person would take in his stride. Brain-damaged patients readily become panicky when there is a slight dislocation in a plan. Even a small dose of alcohol may result in a loss of control. Pressed on a task he is unable to master, a patient may become, in various combinations, anxious, agitated, angry, sullen, evasive, restless, and tearful. At the same time his behaviour disorganizes rapidly. A 'catastrophic reaction' like this may take a psychologist by surprise while administering mental tests, when the degree of the patient's disability has not been recognized. The tendency to react in this way may be referred to as emotional lability. Once a catastrophic reaction has been provoked, it may sometimes be very difficult to bring the patient back into the situation. Sometimes the display of emotion ends as suddenly as it starts.

Retrograde amnesia

Whatever the degree of recovery from concussion, the patient is unable to recall any event that happened within a period before the injury. Whether an event preceding the inuury is recalled depends on its relationship in time, its importance to the patient having no influence. The period of 'retrograde amnesia' shrinks with recovery, memories being restored in order of the time of the events; those more remote from the injury return first. In most cases of concussion the period after recovery is of a few moments or seconds. In a few it lasts for more than 30 minutes. No patient recalls the blow causing the concussion. If he does recall a blow, it was not the cause of the concussion, but it may have caused other injury within the skull, such as the rupture of a blood vessel.

The fact that retrograde amnesia is typically for a few seconds suggests that engrams require a brief period, and only a brief period, to become established. Possibly the biophysical processes creating enduring engrams ('long-term traces') take a few seconds to be accomplished. Alternatively, an experience survives in memory, it may be supposed, it it is reinforced by the events following it, which give it a context and a significance. Another explanation is required for the failure before recovery to recall the events covered by the shrinkage of the retrograde amnesia. Discussion of the memory processes should also take into account some observations made on football players while they were in a confused state immediately after being concussed. They were able to recall for a few minutes afterwards the blow itself and other events immediately preceding it, but could not do so subsequently.[4]

Post-traumatic amnesia

The patient is able to recall little other than a few high lights of what happened within the circumscribed period of the 'post-traumatic amnesia'. Memory of a few incidents is restored as recovery continues, but there is no shortening of the period for which memory is defective. This period is longer, perhaps much longer, than that of the impaired consciousness observed by the nurse, for it covers also the period during which the patient responded more or less adequately to events although unable because of the amnesic syndrome to recall them subsequently. The length of the post-traumatic amnesia is a guide to the severity of the brain damage and thus to the severity of the residual defect.[5] As a rough and ready rule, if it is less than 24 hours, recovery is usually complete. If it is more than 3 days, a degree of residual defect is to be expected, but there are cases in which a full recovery is made although it is very lengthy.

HALLUCINOGENIC DRUGS

Support for the disease model of mental illness has been looked for in the resemblances between the effects of drugs and the symptoms of mental illness. Of particular interest are the effects of such hallucinogenic drugs as mescaline and LSD. The imagery they produce, resembling that of the mentally ill in some respects, also resembles that of patients in especially the second stage of recovery after concussion, when no chemical agent has to be taken into consideration. The question may then be put: is the special character of the imagery a direct effect of the drug, or is it a result of the patient's disengagement from the world around him and the suspension of reality testing? This is part of the more general question: How far is the character of imagery in mental illness, while under the influence of hallucinogenic drugs, in dreaming during sleep, in the states immediately before or after sleep or under conditions of sensory deprivation determined by the conditions in which the imagery occurs?

The effects of LSD vary from occasion to occasion and person to person. Some subjects report that the objects they perceive are brightly coloured. Some experience vivid, but colourless, visual imagery. Some have claimed that the drug has been 'mind-expanding' and has given a greater and sharper—'transcendental'—experience of reality, and others, that they have achieved a new way of looking at the world, a greater awareness of ultimate reality, and a greater understanding of the meaning of human relationships. Claims like these have not been borne out in the behaviour of subjects, who have impressed observers as remote, apathetic, and disinterested and as capable of no more than shallow relationships with others.[6]

Tests of perception under controlled conditions have given no support to the claim that under the influence of LSD reality is more clearly or accurately perceived. On the contrary, the imagery of perception is obscured by 'noise', and the testing of reality by repeating observations in different ways is reduced. Some subjects complain that the things around them appear unreal. The things, although familiar, do not have a normal significance for they are perceived as if they have been changed in some way. These feelings wear off slowly as the pharmacological effects decline, but may continue a day or two longer. The impression the subjects then make on others of being detached, irritable, and suspicious is similar to that some mentally-ill patients make.

Some differences between the hallucinations induced by drugs and the hallucinations occurring in mental illness can hardly be attributed to differences in the conditions affecting disengagement or reality testing. The former tend to be more vivid and coherent than the latter. The former tend to be predominantly visual, the latter predominantly auditory. The former tend to be accepted by subjects as being their own thoughts whereas the latter are typically disowned as intrusions from outside. These differences, suggesting that some at least of the essential processes are different, argue against explanations of mental illness in biochemical or metabolic terms.

PHENOMENA OF MENTAL ILLNESS

Perception, imagery and hallucination

What is imagined differs from, and is not usually mistaken for, what is perceived. It is experienced as coming from within the person, and not from the outside. Also, it is less constant, less distinctive, and less vivid. Its content is dependent on the will in a different way. If in doubt a person seeks more information about the outside world, i.e. tests reality, in order to discover whether what is experienced has any origins in reality.

Imagery is sometimes experienced as coming from outside although it has no basis in reality.[7] It is called hallucination if it is mistaken for perception. A variety of somewhat similar phenomena occur. The terms have a certain convenience although the distinctions are arbitrary and depend on sometimes difficult evaluations of what a person says about his experiences in response to questions. Pseudo-hallucination is imagery as vivid and immediate as perception, but not mistaken for it. The imagery of a vision is experienced as if it came from outside although not from ordinary reality as perception does. Illusion is the fanciful elaboration of the perception of something outside, e.g. the faces seen in the flames of a fire; what is imagery and what is perception may not be clearly distinguished. Sensory experience is sometimes described in fanciful terms, e.g. a person suffering from ringing in the ears ('tinnitus') as a result of disease of the ears tells of a noise like escaping steam or the sea flowing over shingle. The words 'like' or 'as if' are crucial and label the descriptions as metaphors. Obsessions are recurring, obtrusive images or thoughts which are accepted as having origins within the person although they cannot be stopped.

Other recurring, obtrusive images are disowned and attributed to an outside agent; these are hallucinations. The uncritical acceptance of such an origin, which may be called a lack of insight, suggests that the person is suffering from a functional psychosis such as schizophrenia. Hallucination in the functional psychoses is more often auditory than visual although it may belong to any of the sensory modes. The patient hears the voice of a persecutor or tempter, for instance. He may also see a threatening figure, or feel that he is being burnt or beaten. Electric currents are being passed through him, or he is being lifted off the bed. Genitals are being interfered with. Semen is smelt. Poison is tasted. All these experiences are mistaken for perceptions. Hallucinations of vision, taste, and smell may also occur at the start of an epileptic seizure.

Young children often fail to distinguish between imagery and perception and suppose that what they imagine is external and perceptible to others, but as they grow older they become more reliable in making the distinction; little is known about how they learn to do so.[8] Adults make mistakes too, especially at a time of high expectation or arousal. A widow mourning her husband sees or hears him for a few moments. In a wood at night dark shadows are seen as a lurking beast. Waking from a frightening dream, a person feels that what he has experienced has happened in reality.

Testing reality

Mistakes like these are corrected when the person recognizes that they conflict with other information or the views of others. Normally experiences are continually reappraised in the light of the further information becoming available, although uncertainty whether, for instance, a dream experience has had a basis in reality may linger for some hours after waking. Further information is sought by testing reality. A person takes another look or, hearing a voice, makes a head movement to test whether the change in the sound's strength and character conforms to the expectations he has of an outside sound. Corroboration is sought in what others say or do.

Imagery may continue to be attributed mistakenly to reality when the testing of reality is impaired. There are several reasons why this happens. After a long period of intense activity and wakefulness, attention is partly withdrawn from the outside world. Sufficient information is available, but it is not then used. This may also happen when a person has been bereaved or become depressed. Also vigilance may be reduced, and with it awareness of the outside world, by a disease, such as concussion, a drug used in treatment or intoxication by alcohol or drugs.

Also, the information available may be reduced. At the extreme is the paucity of the information available to the subjects of experiments on sensory deprivation. A person on his own is denied the corroboration or refutation of reality by others. In a wood at night a person cannot improve the lighting although other ways may be found to get more information, e.g. by exploring the dark shadows with a stick. On the other hand, running away from what is taken to be a beast prevents reappraisal. This is an important example of a way in which a mistake is perpetuated.

This may happen too when what is perceived appears to conform to expectations, whether these are derived from previous experience of similar situations or from delusions. Seeing what he expects to see, a person does not check, and does not correct any mistake. Reality testing is impaired when arousal is high because perception is then selective. Also, there is then shrinkage and disintegration of the perceptual field, with narrowing of the range of cues utilized. Attention is preoccupied by details of particular significance, with some neglect of other details which supply their context. Perceived out of context, they are liable to be misinterpreted. This is a special example of reduction of the information available.

Integrating information

In order to illustrate some of the points, let us consider an ordinary magazine picture. To the left is seen the face of an ugly, angry, distressed old woman. When attention is held by detail, the significance of other details and the meaning of the picture as a whole is missed. When the picture is looked at as a whole, the woman is recognized as a soap-box orator surrounded by an audience, who are seen against a background of familiar buildings. Once the information is integrated to form the concept 'Speakers Corner' or 'Hyde Park', perception is stabilized, and the uncomfortable feelings aroused by the woman's face are relieved. 'Hyde Park' is a hypothesis that provides a general explanation of what is perceived. It is a 'final' one in that it stabilizes perception and leads to contentment.

However little the information available, a tentative hypothesis always emerges, e.g. 'a lurking beast' provides an unstable explanation of the shadows in the wood. Such an initial hypothesis is replaced as soon as more information becomes available. Perception is kaleidoscopic as each hypothesis leads to reorganization of the perceptual field. Initial hypotheses are tentative and are expressed in such terms as 'It looks like . . .' or 'It sounds as if . . .'. The final hypothesis is nearly always expressed as 'It is . . .'.

The perception of the anxious

The perception of the anxious i.e. of those with high arousal, has been shown to differ from that of the non-anxious in several respects.[9] The amount of information required before a final hypothesis is reached is greater, i.e. the anxious want a greater degree of certainty. The number of hypotheses entertained before the final hypothesis is larger; up to this point perception is less stable. One reason for the instability of the perception of the anxious lies in the tendency, referred to above, to be preoccupied by details; these have often a sense of heightened 'personal reference'. This tendency is shown also in their responses to the ink-blots of the Rorschach test. Whereas those of the healthy tend to refer to each ink-blot as a whole, the responses of the anxious tend to refer to details. Some of the responses of the anxious are determined by the shading in the ink-blots which is perceived as clouds or smoke.

Perception in psychosis

Patients suffering from an acute psychosis entertain hypotheses which, being derived largely from fantasies, have little reference to any specific part of the perceptual field. The hypotheses are replaced only slowly as further information is provided, and lack the tentative 'like' or 'as if' quality. They are held to with a rigidity that seems to reflect difficulty in assimilating information, and are deficient as interpretations of the world around them. These patients appear to be perplexed, and to show 'effort after meaning', but what they perceive lacks coherence. Typically, their perceptual world is bleak and impoverished. These effects may be added to by the medication given for the treatment of the psychosis.

The perception of patients with a chronic schizophrenic defect state show the above characteristics to a marked degree. The few hypotheses they report under experimental conditions are of poor quality and refer indefinitely to a small part of the perceptual field. They do not explore the relationship of one part of the field to another. Thus a patient when questioned about what he sees in another magazine picture replies: 'girls and pigeons'. He itemizes without stating the relationship between the items, whereas a healthy person replies, giving a concept: 'Trafalgar Square'—a final hypothesis—or 'girls feeding pigeons'. The amount of information the patients require before reaching a final hypothesis is relatively high, the number of hypotheses before it, relatively few.[10]

The social context of perception

The responses to the Rorschach ink-blots of patients with a chronic schizophrenic defect state tend to refer to small detail or white spaces and to be determined by vague forms; colour predominates over shape. In the earlier work, which was governed by the view that mental disorder is 'intra-psychic', these characteristics of the responses were taken to indicate incoherence and lack of meaning in what the patients perceive. In recent work,[11] responses to the ink-blots have been regarded as messages in the context of interaction with the tester and as representing attempts to share percepts, ideas and feelings with him. They fail as messages when patients have not accepted his frame of reference.

The responses can be examined in order to define what has gone wrong, not only in perception, but also in communication. So examined they may show failure on the part of patients to share a 'focus of attention' with others and to convey a 'sense of closure'. The meaning of response is left blurred, incomplete, inconsistent, or contradictory. Sometimes patients express themselves in negative terms: e.g. 'It doesn't look like a . . .', or in subjunctive terms: e.g. 'Were I sick, I'd say it resembled a . . .', or by asking questions: e.g. 'Is it a . . .'. They tend to interrupt and disrupt exchanges with the tester, e.g. by making irrelevant, tangential or inappropriate remarks, or by using peculiar words, constructions or pronunciations. The disorders in the processes of perception and communication and in the content of what is communicated are related and are difficult to separate.

Impairment in reality testing, lack of information, and selectivity of perception account for some of the features of hallucination in psychosis. Other explanations are required for other features. One such feature is the disowning of images. Another is the organization and interpretation of what is selectively perceived in accordance with dominant ideas which are delusional. A deluded person pays attention to the saltiness of the soup offered him and interprets it as due to the poison put there by people hostile to him. What to one person sounds like a whistling noise, perhaps due to the wind, to which he pays little attention, is heard by another as a voice talking about his wrongdoing. Such phenomena are usually called hallucinations although they might be called illusions since they contain fanciful misidentifications of something external.

Delusion

A delusion is defined as a fixed, idiosyncratic belief, amounting to a conviction, which is unusual in the culture to which the person belongs. An idea shared with other members of a cultural group is not a delusion even if it is erroneous or irrational. Unlike a normal belief, which is subject to amendment or correction, a delusion is held to despite evidence or arguments brought against it. A delusion is said to be 'primary' when it emerges as an entirely new interpretation of an event which the person feels has a special significance for him.

Delusions are usually taken to indicate mental illness, but something akin to them is common in everyday life. A person insists on the correctness of an idea he overvalues, or of an interpretation, denying any significance to evidence appearing to refute it. It is a question of degree. A delusion is preoccupying and exerts a dominant influence on the way in which a person perceives the world around him and his position in it.[12] Also, it gives him a special position. A person usually gets angry when an overvalued idea is contradicted, whereas the emotional response when a delusion is challenged tends to be bland or otherwise inappropriate.

Extravagent ideas are relatively common at times of frustration. A person when frustrated supposes there to be serious deficiencies in the behaviour of others, i.e. he projects the blame on to others. He may feel that things or people are against him. Ideas like these if they persist amount to a delusion of persecution, especially if he believes that there is a conspiracy, i.e. that the action against him is concerted.

Frustration may also lead a person to believe that the fault, more or less specific to the situation, lies in him. This tendency to reproach himself may be quickly reversed by a degree of success. On the other hand, he suffers from delusions of guilt if he comes to suppose that the fault in him is more general, e.g. that he is weak, wicked or damned. Ideas like these reflect a sense of unworthiness or loss of self-esteem. They occur typically in depressive illnesses in association with misery and hopelessness, and make a person liable to hallucinate voices talking about his faults.

A fixed belief of physical illness or, more extreme, that organs are rotting or being destroyed, is a hypochondriac delusion. This reflects preoccupation with bodily sensations and their misinterpretation in accordance with ideas of being of little worth or rotten. A belief, that he has lost his identity, does not exist or is nothing, is a nihilistic delusion. Hypochondriac and nihilistic delusions may occur together; their combination is severely disabling.

A belief that he has an exalted position or power is a delusion of grandeur or omnipotence. Some of those who suffer from paranoid schizophrenia reveal, as well as hallucinations, typically auditory, more or less coherent or 'systematized' delusions of persecution and grandeur, without showing any awareness of how abnormal are the ideas they express. The delusions of others may be contradictory and incoherent.

A delusion although appearing to be maladaptive may persist because it is rewarded by the effects it has on others. Also it explains for patients what would otherwise cause anxiety because it provides the basis for a stable organization of what they perceive. There is often some sense in it although the sense is expressed extravagantly, confusingly or metaphorically. Thus delusions have been called 'unlabelled metaphors'.[13] A girl discloses the belief that she is the Virgin Mary. What perhaps she means is that she feels she is still a virgin although she fears she is pregnant. In this case the delusion with its implications of her essential goodness mitigates the intense anxiety which being seduced and perhaps being pregnant would otherwise have evoked. It partly distorts and partly denies the significance of what has happened. The delusion that he is being poisoned may give a man some relief from the anxiety caused by his erectile impotence. Thus soldiers serving under stressful conditions and aware of some loss of sexual interest may half-believe that 'they' are putting bromide into the soup.

Again, a man who declares that his wife is being persistently unfaithful to him may be understood to mean that she is having sexual intercourse with others on many occasions. He is deluded if he insists unreasonably that this is so. Yet the delusion may serve to explain for him why she no longer responds to him sexually or shows the same love and concern for him. Her behaviour towards him may provide some justification for these beliefs, which are further strengthened if, upset by his accusations and suspiciousness, she turns against him. A husband who is not deluded entertains other explanations of what is happening between his wife and himself; his doubts and uncertainties are reduced when he is reassured. A delusion, because the belief is not negotiable, tends to be confirmed by the reaction it evokes, a delusion of persecution, for instance, by the hostile reaction; moreover, even conciliatory reactions may be perceived as hostile.

Paranoid delusions

Paranoia, which in its derivation from the Greek means no more than mental derangement, has been used as a name for what was once thought to be a distinct class of mental illness, characterized by delusions of persecution and grandeur. Paranoid delusions refer to the fixed beliefs of patients that they are the victims of the malevolence of others. They are more pronounced than 'ideas of reference' that what is happening around them has a special and sinister reference to them. Paranoid delusions and ideas of reference carry the implication that the person has been singled out for the attention of often eminent people or public bodies.

Paranoid delusions share with some other delusions two features of great interest. Firstly, they provide explanations of what is experienced in terms not of processes, whether interpersonal, i.e. what is happening within a relationship, or intra-psychic, i.e. what is happening within the person, but of agents typically from outside and typically persecutors. Both forms of explanation may be heard in everyday conversation. Thus a person whose car is not running well may look for an explanation in such processes as the flow of fuel or its ignition or alternatively feel himself to be the victim of incompetent garage mechanics or car designers or, at the extreme, of vaguely identified enemies.

A mentally ill patient may feel himself to be under the influence of others who intrude into his thoughts. He may identify the intruder, whose voice he hallucinates, as male or female, English or foreign or belonging to a known person. At the extreme, he feels that he is possessed by a malevolent agent or demon who has entered into, invaded or taken control over his physical body. In other cases the entering person is experienced as benign and related to him in some way, as in cases of reincarnation when the entering person is identified as someone who has had a previous existence.

Paranormal psychology typically attributes 'paranormal' phenomena to the activities, usually capricious, of agents. In psychopathology, what the patient experiences as an agent is explained by reference to such a psychological process as 'dissociation' or 'splitting'. This results in the experience of a 'second self', of which the intruder is a special instance.

The second feature of interest in paranoid delusions is that the patient feels that he is being observed by another, or others, who comments on what he is thinking or doing; it may be a running commentary. Sometimes the hallucinated voice has an external reference, being in this respect an illusion, e.g. the patient interprets what is heard by others as a whistling or humming noise as a voice or voices making remarks, occasionally about indifferent matters, but more often about him. The voice is sometimes experienced as coming from within him or being his own audible thoughts on which others are eavesdropping. Because it observes and comments, the voice may be said to serve a 'meta' or second-order function, which is also what the second self does.

Depersonalization

This term is applied to a person's complaint either that he feels himself to be changed, or that the world appears different or unreal because he is different.[14] If the world is seen as if in a dream, or as vague, unreal or, although familiar, as having no significance, the complaint is called derealization. The essence of depersonalization is loss of identity or loss of the sense of the reality of one's self. It is nearly always accompanied by a sense of being divorced from one's body—the 'out-ofbody' experience.

To depersonalize may also mean, in a broader sense, to negate another person by ignoring his feelings or treating him as an object or thing. This was experienced in an extreme form by inmates of the concentration camps of the last war, deliberate measures being taken by the captors to bring about this result. The passive 'ontologically insecure' person, in Laing's phrase,[15] may feel under threat of being depersonalized or of losing his autonomy when he enters into a co-operative relationship with another. A healthy person, in contrast, is a free and responsible agent, according to the existentialist view, who determines his own development and identity by making choices.

Healthy persons who have been going through a period of intense excitement in the face of danger may experience depersonalization and derealization, in the narrower sense, usually when they begin to relax as the danger recedes, e.g. aircrew may have this experience on the way home from a sortie over enemy territory; memory of the period has subsequently a dream-like quality. Depersonalization and derealization may be associated in mental illness with hallucinations and delusions, especially hypochondriac delusions.

Out-of-body experiences

Most people feel that they are located just behind their eyes but on occasions have had the experience of being detached from themselves and separated from their physical bodies. Then they may distinguish the active aware 'I' from the observed 'me'. The 'I' differentiates between 'me' and 'not me', and the 'ego-boundary' between them. They may then see their bodies as if from a different position in space, sometimes from just behind one shoulder. An out-of-body experience like this is usually associated with depersonalization and derealization, but may occur on its own, usually fleetingly, without illness or stress, even when feeling relaxed. Persons who have been near death, e.g. as a result of a heart attack, occasionally report after recovery that they have viewed from outside and with a detached interest the medical procedures undergone by their bodies.[16]

The second self

The disembodied self may be called the outer or second self.[17] This observes and knows the inner or first self, but is little known by him. But the first self may feel under the influence or control of the second self. The second self may take several forms. He may be experienced as a visual 'autoscopic' hallucination. A dreamer often feels himself to be a detached observer of his own behaviour. Explorers, the shipwrecked and single-handed sailors have described feelings, usually at times of intense fatigue, of being accompanied by a shadowy figure.

Writers have used the second self as a literary device for depicting the conflicts within a person as if they were played out by characters who are ostensibly independent, but whose fate is linked in the narrative, the two selves being imbued with different, usually contrasting qualities.[18] A second self, or double, appears especially in the novels of writers of the Romantic movement at the end of the eighteenth century, many of whom took opium. Examples of particular interest are found in the novels of Dostoevsky, who suffered from epilepsy.

Patients with delusions of grandeur sometimes claim a second identity of distinction. In this way they appear to make amends for the inferiority they feel in a particular respect. Thus a person who has grown up in disadvantaged circumstances claims to be an unacknowledged member of the royal family. In cases of reincarnation the entering person is usually someone of great distinction.

More often the second self is experienced as representing the forces of evil who as pursuers or tempters are trying to gain control over the person. These forces are unacceptable aspects of the self which have been split off or dissociated because doing so preserves the person's conception of himself. The disowning of auditory or other images by hallucinating patients reflects, it may be supposed, a similar process. These patients sometimes speak of their struggle against evil or alien forces, which they externalize.

RECOGNITION AND RECALL

An object or person is perceived as belonging to a class, e.g. 'that is a pencil'. It is recognized, i.e. identified, as being a particular person or object, e.g. 'that is my pencil'. Identity is confirmed by testing reality, e.g. by looking for particular features. The full experience of recognition includes more or less specific images defining the context of the previous experience of the object or person, and a feeling of familiarity, 'pastness' and 'personal reference'.

The term 'agnosia' is applied to the disorder when there is no recognition, the necessary sensory data being available but not being integrated in the brain because of brain disease. Agnosia is rare, if it occurs at all. In most of the cases in which the term might be applied, other causes can be found for the lack of recognition, e.g. impairment or distortion of the sensory data because of disease in the sense organs, inattention, disorientation or a general memory defect.

The disorder is called 'restrictive paramnesia' when a more or less definite aspect of a situation arouses feelings of familiarity, pastness, and personal reference, but the memories evoked do not sufficiently define the context of the previous experience. The person remains perplexed until he succeeds in recalling the relevant details. The phenomenon, common in the healthy, occurs typically when an object or person, known well in one context, is seen in unaccustomed surroundings.

The disorder is 'reduplicative paramnesia' when an object or person evokes feelings of familiarity, but without any sense of personal reference or identity and is thought to be in some way changed. The patient remarks typically: 'I have seen something like that before, but not that one'. It occurs in brain-damaged patients, usually in association with other disorders in recall.

A probably related phenomenon, which has been called the 'Capgras syndrome',[19] may occur in mental illness in association with other delusional misidentifications, the patient asserting that a person, typically someone with whom he has had a close relationship, has been replaced by an imposter who is an exact double. Also in mental illness, e.g. in hypomania, a person not previously known to the patient evokes feelings of familiarity and is misidentified, e.g. as a relative or a person suggested by a delusional idea. The misidentification may be insisted on although it is admitted that the person's appearance has been changed.

The essence of the phenomenon of '*déjà vu*' and the similar phenomena '*déjà entendu*' and '*déjà pensé*' is the sense of familiarity evoked by a situation which the person feels he is reliving, a feeling not related to a single aspect but bearing on the situation as a whole. Images which would define the context of the previous experience are conspicuously absent, the person typically remarking: 'I have seen all this before, but I can't think where or when.' With the sense of familiarity goes a harrowing perplexity and a decided displeasure.

The phenomenon has been evoked by electrical stimulation of the temporal lobes of the brain, and may occur as a component of the aura of an epileptic fit with a focus in a temporal lobe. However, many people have experienced the phenomenon when there has been no reason to suppose any cause in brain pathology or epilepsy. Psychological explanations are tentative. The source of the sense of familiarity, it is supposed, lies not in reality but in vívd imaginary experiences—hence the lack of defining images. The situation evokes fantasies of special significance but without reference to any previous experience of reality, the fantasies being disowned because they belong to unacceptable aspects of the self.

Disorders of recall

Remembering depends on the incorporation of experiences into 'schemata' of related experiences.[20] The individual experience loses its identity. What is incorporated depends on what is perceived selectively in a complex field as well as on the attitude prevailing at the time, i.e. on selection, abstraction, and interpretation. Recall consists in the reconstruction of a version of the original experience around one or more key details, this being facilitated by the revival of the attitude. The result is an incomplete caricature, some aspects being exaggerated, others diminished. To suppose that recall depends on the revival of individual memory traces or 'engrams' is too simple a view of how remembering works and gives rise to misleading expectations of what should be recalled.

The literal or 'rote' recall of material, which is the task set by most psychological tests of memory, is exceptional. A few experiences do retain their identity, among them being details 'over-learned' by repetition and rehearsal. This is one reason why a particular experience in a disaster, which is rehearsed over and over again in the 'second phase' may remain more or less intact. A second reason is that it does not become assimilated as all ordinary experiences do because it is not recalled subsequently. When recall is imminent, anxiety is evoked, and the person engages in some other activity which prevents recall. The failure of recall is thus due to defensive avoidance or 'repression'.

Recall of memories so preserved may occur under certain conditions. These include dreaming, hypnosis, narcoanalysis and some phases of psychosis and of the delirium following brain damage. In all these conditions there is some disengagement from the business-in-hand which has prevented recall.

The psychological processes underlying failure to recall are thus of two kinds: the irreversible merging of experiences with other related experiences, and the defensive avoidance of events potentially available to recall. Normal forgetting is due to the obliteration of the memory by later experiences.

THINKING

Word-association tests

One of the earliest methods of studying thinking was the word-association test. In such a test a list of stimulus words is read to the subject, who is instructed to respond with the first word that comes to mind. If the response word has to stand in a particular relation to the stimulus word, the association is said to be controlled. Francis Galton made use of an uncontrolled test in order to study in himself the processes by which one idea leads to another. This was a century or so ago when it was thought that the essence of learning lies in the linking together of ideas through their repeated association, and that complex experiences can be analysed into elements that have become linked in this way. Emil Kraepelin was probably the first to apply a word-association test to patients.

After Freud had drawn attention to the ways in which responses are influenced by conflicts, C. G. Jung prepared a test to be applied as a diagnostic method to patients suffering from schizophrenia. Some of their responses showed one or more of several features. Sometimes they are repetitions or derivations of the stimulus word or 'clang' associations based on the sound and not the meaning of the stimulus. Or there is 'blocking', the response being unduly delayed, or no response being made at all. Responses may be accompanied by laughing, giggling, turning away or other inappropriate behaviour. The association from stimulus to response may be remote; uncommon, strange or apparently senseless responses are then given. In general, these patients give a smaller proportion of common responses and a higher proportion of idiosyncratic responses than healthy subjects.

One reason might be that responses are less affected by the controls implicit in the test situation. Eugen Bleuler,[21] a colleague of Jung at the Burghölzli, near Zürich, describing the patients' responses as incorrect, bizarre, and unpredictable, supposed that the disease 'interrupts, quite haphazardly, associative threads'. When associations which hold mental processes together are lost, groups of ideas are split off—hence the term 'schizophrenia'. Kraepelin had already argued that the basic disturbance is a 'derailment' of associations.

In modern theories, the splitting off of groups of ideas is regarded, not as haphazard, but as determined by the conflicts affecting the patient. Jung attributed the failure to respond quickly and surely to a concealed cluster of ideas and feelings, which he called a complex. A stimulus word associated with a complex evokes anxiety, and the abnormal features of the response reflect the way in which the anxiety is dealt with. Interruption of associations is a normal method of defence against anxiety, as Galton pointed out. The degree to which there is interruption varies from occasion to occasion. A greater number of ideas tend to be affected by interruption more often and to a greater degree in schizophrenia than in other forms of mental illness or in health.

Indications of the degree to which each stimulus word evokes anxiety may be given by changes in respiration rate and volume, heart rate, blood pressure or electrical conductance of the skin, e.g. of the palms. Continuous measurement and recording on a polygraph is relatively easy. This is the method of the 'lie-detector'. Ideas concealed by reason of guilt are indicated by abnormal features in the responses and also by sharp changes on the polygraph. In cases of schizophrenia in which interruption in associations is marked, the polygraphic changes have usually been found to be small or very small, because, it is supposed, interruption succeeds in reducing anxiety.

Sentence-completion tests

Another method of analysing disorders of thinking in mental illness lies in sentence-completion tests. The patient is asked to complete as he thinks fit a sentence of which he is given the first few words, e.g. (i) 'The man fell down because . . .', (ii) 'Fish can live in water because . . .', (iii) 'The present economic position of the country obliges us . . .'. The stimulus words are chosen to test hypotheses about the nature of the thought disorder. The responses are more controlled than they are in word-association tests. Similar tests were used in early attempts to evaluate intelligence, and by Piaget in studies of the thinking of children. Cameron[22] used Piaget's material in tests on patients suffering from schizophrenia.

The completions given by these patients are unlike those given by children. Thought disorder in schizophrenia is not a form of regression therefore. They show the same features as the responses made in word-association tests. They tend to be subjective, i.e. related to inner thoughts and feelings, and to be expressed in private words ('neologisms') or poor approximations to correct words. Some contain a confused mixture of ideas, some related to the stimulus, and some to fantasies. Cameron called the intrusion of ideas derived from fantasies 'the interpenetration of personal themes', and the bringing in of ideas only distantly related to the stimulus as 'overinclusion'; this reflects the inability to preserve conceptual boundaries. Sometimes ideas are strung together as they are in dreams without logical sequence or causal connections or conjunctions ('asyndesis'). Completions then consist of loose clusters of terms in place of integrated concepts. Complex ideas may be expressed in an abbreviated form or by reference to a single attribute ('metonymy').

Clear and well-constructed completions are given when the stimulus words evoke no anxiety. On the other hand, thought disorder affects completions when the stimulus touches on delicate matters or are difficult. Examples (i) and (ii) are relatively difficult and tend to produce disordered completions. In completion of (ii) one patient wrote 'of the character and inability to moisture air'. In completion of (iii) another patient wrote 'taxation', and another 'this humour because the other one was Jesus Christ not Emmanuel the more we admired you'. The first example shows asyndesis, the second, metonymy, and the third, amongst other things, interpenetration of personal themes. Features like these have not been produced experimentally in healthy subjects.

Object-sorting tests

An example of a simple sorting test is the Goldstein-Scheerer Colour-Form test, which asks the subject to sort and then re-sort squares, triangles, and circles of four different colours. In the Vigotsky test the objects are wooden blocks of varying colours, shapes, and heights. Another example is the Weigl wool-sorting test, the subject being asked to sort skeins of wool according to hue, brightness or saturation. In another test, a variety of everyday objects are sorted according to material, size or use.

The subject when he sorts has to abstract a quality or concept, such as colour, form, material or use, and to neglect differences in other qualities. He has to maintain a 'set' and then to change it when the quality determining the sorting changes, e.g. after having put similar shapes together irrespective of their colour he is required to put similar colours together irrespective of their shape.

The capacity to form concepts, long regarded as of crucial importance, is evaluated in all intelligence tests. In the Binet Scale, for instance, questions about the sameness of objects, e.g. 'In what way are wood and coal alike?' are introduced in Year VII. During the First World War Goldstein observed the special difficulty experienced by the brain-damaged in problem-solving tests, and attributed it to their failure to adopt an 'abstract' attitude towards objects and thus to transcend 'concrete' experience. It was soon questioned whether in cases of schizophrenia, then thought to be due to abnormality of the brain, there is an inability to abstract and a tendency to behave 'concretely'.

Some of the earlier investigators did conclude that in schizophrenia behaviour is abnormally 'concrete', but their methods have been severely criticized, and it has been argued instead that the special features of the performance of schizophrenic patients on sorting tests are due to a tendency to be 'overinclusive'. The way they sort objects is often arbitrary or meaningless, or is based on an unusual or eccentric concept or a pun, e.g. when a red rubber and a book 'which is read' are put together. Sometimes objects are put together on the basis of irrelevant similarities or are linked by weaving around them a story, which is often strange or incoherent. Another test often used by clinicians is to ask the patient what a proverb means, e.g. 'It's an ill wind that blows nobody good'. Interest lies in the degree to which the answer is 'abstract' or 'concrete'. A firm judgement is hardly possible. Any conclusion about the ability of schizophrenic patients to abstract and to transcend concrete experience is vitiated by their failure to maintain an appropriate set and to accept, or even to enquire about, what the tester proposes as the rules and conventions of the test.[23]

On intelligence tests there are no distinctive patterns of scores in schizophrenia. It has been claimed, however, that schizophrenic patients tend to score relatively highly on such subtests of the Wechsler Adult Intelligence Scale as 'arithmetic' and 'block design', and relatively poorly on 'picture completion' and 'comprehension'. The former invite factual answers, the latter, the appreciation of social relationships and less 'concrete' answers. Intelligence tests play a part in the diagnosis of mental illness because they provide good opportunities for observing disorders of thinking. The scores a patient obtains may be misleading; for instance, he may fail to give an acceptable, scorable answer to a question although there are good indications from what he says or does that he knows what would be acceptable.

Clinical observations

Disorders of thinking are revealed in the linking of ideas in talking or writing, whether spontaneously or in answer to questions. At the one extreme is 'word salad', when a lot of ideas are jumbled together without any clear connection between them. At the other, there are occasional 'breaks' or 'blocks' in the stream of talk; these may be described by the patient as his thoughts being withdrawn. In between are: incoherence, loosely linked ideas, a sequence of ideas but with inadequate or irregular syntax, intrusion of irrelevant ideas, circumlocution, talking past the point, repetition, reticience, and impoverishment of expression. There may also be disturbance of the tempo, cadence, and rhythm of speech. All these disorders occur in schizophrenia. In mania, or hypomania, there is 'flight of ideas', with rapid, usually comprehensible jumps from one idea to another.

The terms used to describe the disorders of thinking observed clinically in schizophrenia have been governed by the view that the disorders constitute 'soft' neurological signs, i.e. as yet ill-defined signs of an underlying disorder in brain function. In recent years the terms have been revised in order to fit more readily into the view that in schizophrenia the meaning of what is said is kept blurred, tentative, indefinite, incomplete, inconsistent or contradictory in order to reduce the anxiety aroused in relationships with others.

Dysphasia

Disorders of thinking may also arise as a result of a more or less localized lesion in the cerebral cortex, especially in the dominant hemisphere. A distinction can usually be made, although this may be somewhat arbitrary, between 'expressive' (or 'motor') dysphasia and 'receptive' (or 'sensory') dysphasia. In cases of expressive dysphasia the lesion tends to be more anterior, in cases of receptive dysphasia, more posterior.

The patient with expressive dysphasia understands what is said to him, or what he reads. Often he has difficulty in 'word-finding' and cannot retrieve the name of an object even when it is in front of him although he may be able to say what its use is. He has a picture of the words he wants, but can only say what he wants with difficulty. He speaks the wrong words, or words which are mutilated or otherwise garbled, or repeats or echoes what has been said. He makes grammatical errors. The patient with receptive dysphasia can express himself up to a point, but has difficulty in understanding what is said, even to the extent of seeming to be deaf.

Differentiation between the disorders of thinking in functional mental illness and dysphasia due to a lesion in the cortex is usually, but not always, easy. The dysphasic patient gives the impression that he is struggling to express himself in speech or to understand, i.e. that he wants to but cannot. He uses non-verbal messages in attempts to convey what he fails to convey through speech. The presence of other neurological signs may of course clinch the diagnosis. The impression made by schizophrenic patients, on the other hand, is that they can express themselves but do not want to do so clearly. Their non-verbal messages may be as confusing as their verbal ones.

DAY-DREAMING AND DREAMING

Freud became interested at an early stage in the development of psychoanalysis in the interpretation of the 'manifest' content of dreams as experienced in order to discover the 'latent' meaning. Interpretation thus undoes the 'dream work' by which neurotic conflicts are transformed and disguised to form the manifest content. Although there are formidable difficulties to be overcome if reliable conclusions are to be drawn, the interpretation of dreams has made important contributions to the development of psychoanalytic theory. Amongst other things, it has provided evidence of the hostility and sexual wishes felt by children towards their parents (the 'Oedipus complex') and of the 'wish fulfillment' in dreams of desires denied satisfaction in reality. It continues to play a part in psychoanalytic treatment.[24]

Also of interest are the phenomena of day-dreaming and dreaming because of their similarity in some respects to the phenomena of mental illness. The imagery of day-dreaming is predominantly verbal, but verbal imagery is gradually replaced by visual imagery as the person relaxes. The imagery of dreaming is predominantly visual although there is some contribution of imagery related to other sensory modes.

Day-dreaming

Some day-dreaming is retrospective and recapitulates and reviews recent experiences so that they are assimilated and incorporated into 'schemata'.

Some rehearses plans for the immediate future more or less creatively, or represents strivings after solutions for pressing problems, potential solutions being rehearsed and sifted. These are wish-fulfilling. Mostly the solutions lie well within the bounds of possibility. Extravagant solutions, which may be preoccupying at first, are gradually modified or abandoned as impracticable.

In the 'hypogogic' state, which immediately precedes going to sleep, thoughts continue for a while to revolve around the events and problems of the day and the hopes for the morrow, but gradually lose their coherence and orderliness. What are apparently random associations enter into them more and more, and there is a gradual change-over to visual imagery. Thinking seems effortless, and the subject becomes a passive spectator of an erratically moving scene over which he has little control although he recognizes that it has reference to him.

Thinking in the 'hypnopompic' state, which precedes waking, is less effortless and may be accompanied by perplexity as well as a sense of effort to find meaning in dream experiences. Visual imagery gives way gradually to verbal and abstract thinking. Stimuli from the outside world, like the ringing of the alarm clock, are woven into the imagery and misinterpreted for a while. In this state a person may entertain new ideas which he recognizes as having a bearing on the practical problems of his waking life and be able to preserve them.

Already before he is fully awake a person submits what he recalls of his dreams to analysis and interpretation in order to reconcile dream experiences with reality. Mostly he dismisses them as dreams although he may feel uncertain about doing so. The uncomfortable feelings associated with them may persist for some minutes or hours, not being dissipated until he has become fully re-engaged in the real world. Fragments of them, with the affective colouring little diminished, may be recalled several hours later. Occasionally they are misinterpreted as having happened in reality, and the misinterpretation may persist as a delusional idea, although it is more often corrected as a result of the testing of reality.

Dreaming

Reporting in verbal terms on the predominately visual experiences of a dream, a person selects what he regards as significant. He omits much else, and introduces new items, as well as changing the emphasis, distorting, and interpreting. All these changes, wittingly or unwittingly made, compose what Freud called 'secondary elaboration', which is a further transformation and disguise of the latent meaning.

In dreaming, images having little apparent connection with one another are strung together to form a narrative with a loose dramatic form. The theme may have some bearing on the problems with which the dreamer has recently been concerned, and the scenes may be linked by an interest or drive. They may all have a sexual significance, for instance; just as there are 'sexual' dreams, so there are 'hunger' or 'cold' dreams. Or there may be a succession of frightening episodes, the dreamer feeling threatened and pursued, but not knowing by what or whom, and trying to run away, but not being able to; this is an 'anxiety' dream. Sometimes the dreamer feels angry and violent, but awakes before putting aggressive intentions into effect. In some dreams there is little affect except one of mild pleasure, the dreamer feeling no responsibility, no surprise, and no remorse about the events of which he is a passive spectator; moral judgement is suspended.

Psychoanalytic theory

The images of dreams are assumed to be symbols standing for something—an idea, object or person; this is their 'latent meaning'. They may be composite, i.e. derived by 'condensation' from more than one element. The focus of the dream narrative shows 'displacement' from what is significant in the latent meaning to what is acceptable. The result is that the content 'manifest' in the dream is a shortened, impoverished, and trivialized version of the processes in the 'unconscious', their transformation being due to the mechanisms of censorship and repression. To these mechanisms are due the strangeness, looseness, and apparent senselessness of the ideas manifest in dreams, and also the similar qualities of the ideas in the disordered thinking of the mentally ill.

   The essence of psychoanalytic theory is that certain ideas are inaccessible to recall under ordinary conditions because being actively repressed they are 'dynamically unconscious'. Other ideas descriptively unconscious but available to recall are 'preconscious'. Dynamically unconscious ideas become manifest in a disguised form, not only in dreams, but also in free associations, parapraxes and symptoms. By 'parapraxes' are meant actions, such as slips of the tongue and pen, errors, chance actions, accidents, and jokes, which are faulty because of the interference of some unconscious idea. The psychoanalyst interprets what becomes manifest in these ways to expose what he infers to be the latent meaning.

   In his later writing Freud used the terms 'Id' to refer to the unconscious and 'Ego' to refer to the conscious. The Id represents the instincts and the constitutional make-up present at birth. The Ego becomes differentiated from the Id through the influence of the external world, to whose demands it adapts. The 'Superego', manifest in conscience, shame, and guilt, is the agency by which the influence of the parents and others is prolonged; their judgements and prohibitions are internalized by 'introjection' in early childhood. In serving its adaptive function the Ego reconciles the forces of the Id and Superego and the demands of the external world in such a way as to maximize pleasure and minimize 'unpleasure'. The shift in emphasis to the adaptive function of the Ego, with the change in terminology, has made possible some reapprochement between psychoanalysis and psychology.[25]

NOTES AND REFERENCES

1. A useful source for descriptions and definitions of the phenomena of mental disorder is Scharfetter, C. (1980). *General psychopathology*. Cambridge University Press.
2. Whitty, C. W. M. and Zangwill, O. L. (1977). *Amnesia* (2nd edn). Butterworths, London.
3. Victor, M. and Yakolev, P. I. (1955). S. S. Korsakoff's psychic disorder in conjunction with peripheral neuritis. *Neurology (NY)* **5**, 394–406.
4. Yarnell, P. R. and Lynch, S. (1970). Retrograde amnesia immediately after concussion. *Lancet i*, 863–4.
5. Lewin, W., Marshall, T. F. de C. and Roberts, A. H. (1979). Long-term outcome after severe head injury. *Br. Med. J.* **2**, 1533–8.
6. Bennet, G. (1967). LSD—1967. *Br. J. Psychiat.* **114**, 1219–22.
7. A series of papers covering recent work on hallucinations has been edited by R. K. Siegel and L. J. West (1975). *Hallucinations: behaviour, experience and theory*. Wiley, London. Current ideas on the neurophysiology have been summarized by Slade, P. (1976) Hallucinations. *Psychol. Med.* **6**, 7–13.
8. But see Piaget, J. (1960). *The child's conception of the world*. Routledge & Kegan Paul, London.
9. Davis, D. R. and Cullen, J. (1958). Disorganisation of perception in neurosis and psychosis. *Am. J. Psychol.* **71**, 229–37.
10. See also Reich, S. S. and Cutting, J. (1982). Picture perception and abstract thought in schizophrenia. *Psychol. Med.* **12**, 91–6.
11. Wynne, L. C. and Singer, M. T. (1963). Thought disorder and family relations of schizophrencis: a research strategy. *Archs gen. Psychiat.* **9**, 191–8; ibid. Classification of forms of thinking, pp. 199–206.
    Singer, M. T. and Wynne, L. C. (1965). Thought disorder and family relations of schizophrenics. III. Methodology using projective techniques. *Archs gen. Psychiat.* **12**, 187–200; ibid., IV. Results and implications, pp. 201–11.
    Wild, C., Singer, M. T., Rosman, B., Ricci, J. and Lidz, T. (1965). Measuring disordered styles of thinking. *Archs gen. Psychiat.* **13**, 471–6.
12. The characteristics of psychotic delusions are discussed by Taylor, F. K. (1979). *Psychopathology* (revised edn). Quatermaine House, Sunbury-on-Thames.
13. Bateson, G. (1973). *Steps to an ecology of mind*. Granada, St. Albans, Herts.
14. Sedman, G. (1972). An investigation of certain factors concerned in the etiology of depersonalisation. *Acta psychiat. scand.* **48**, 191–219.
15. Laing, R. D. (1960). *The divided self*. Penguin Books, Harmondsworth.
16. Examples of experiences under extreme conditions of being out-of-body and of 'the other person' are given by Bennet, G. (1983). *Beyond endurance*. Secker & Warburg, London.
17. Laing writes of the 'embodied' and 'unembodied' self.
18. Keppler, C. F. (1972). *The literature of the second self*. University of Arizona Press, Tucson, Arizona.
19. Enoch, M. D. and Trethowan, W. H. (1979). *Uncommon psychiatric syndromes* (2nd edn). Wright, Bristol.
20. Modern theory is based on the work of Bartlett, F. C. (1932). *Remembering*. Cambridge University Press, Cambridge.
21. Ideas about the looseness of associations were central to the concept of schizophrenia advanced in 1911 by Bleuler, E. (1950). *Dementia precox or the group of schizophrenias*. International University Press, New York.
    See also Hoenig, J. (1983). The concept of schizophrenia—Kraepelin–Bleuler–Schneider. *Br. J. Psychiat.* **142**, 547–56.

22. Cameron, N. (1939). Schizophrenic thinking in a problem-solving situation. *J. ment. Sci.* **85,** 1012–35.
23. The research use of object-sorting tests is illustrated by Wild, C. (1965). Disturbed styles of thinking. *Archs gen. Psychiat.* **13,** 464–70. See also Wild *et al.*, (1965) op cit., n. 11.
24. A crucial step in the development of psychoanalysis, taken in 1900, was Freud, S. (1958). *The interpretation of dreams* (standard edn) Vols 4 and 5. Hogarth Press, London.
25. Hartmann, H. (1964). *Essays on ego psychology.* Hogarth Press, London.

4 Disorders of mental development

The life cycle

A family regarded as a system is subject to a series of crises, at which it decompensates, goes through a period of instability and reorganizes. One such crisis occurs at the birth of a child. A couple change then their relationship to each other so as to incorporate the child into a system of three. There is a further reorganization when another child is born. The 'nuclear' family of parents and children—a subsystem of an 'extended' family—is part of a social network. It remains stable for several years, but breaks up when the children in their teen years emancipate themselves from their parents and pair off with partners outside the family. The couples so formed start on another cycle.

For each individual there are many turning-points, transitions or crises at which habits and roles change. Old habits are abandoned, and new habits are developed which are appropriate to the new circumstances. Mental illness according to 'crisis theory'[1] arises at crises and reflects failure to achieve through changes in habits and roles a stable reorganization of the system. This theory revives, with a change of emphasis to the psychological, nineteenth-century ideas relating insanity to the great physiological epochs of life: puberty and adolescence, pregnancy, lactation and the puerperium, the climacteric and old age.

Crises are conveniently divided, following Erikson[2] into 'developmental' and 'accidental'. Developmental crises are expected in the normal sequence of the life cycle, e.g. being born, going to school, leaving school, starting a job, pairing, becoming a parent, children leaving home, retiring from work, and being widowed. Examples of accidental crises are the untimely death or the desertion of a member of the family or other loved person, loss of a job, illness, and the unexpected pregnancy of a daughter.

The distinction between a developmental and an accidental crisis is arbitrary and lies mainly in the degree to which the person has been prepared. The loss of a spouse is a developmental crisis if it occurs at a usual point in the life cycle, accidental if it is untimely. Timing and circumstances decide whether a daughter's pregnancy is a developmental or accidental crisis for a woman. Her change of role to that of grandmother is easier if it is developmental. The crises out of which mental illness arises are more often accidental than developmental.

THE BIRTH OF A CHILD

Some circumstances

A typical family consists of a man and a woman, whose sexual relations are largely if not entirely confined to one another, and one or more children of whom the majority are joint offspring. In about half the cases both man and woman go out to work, and in about half only one of them, usually the man, the other looking after the home. About 15 per cent of children are born to a mother without a husband living with her. Of these mothers about 40 per cent live with their parents.[3]

Some two-thirds of new families live within half-an-hour's journey from parents. The ties with the wife's family are usually closer than those with the husband's. There is thus a 'matrilocal' tendency, which tends to be more marked in the working class than in the middle class. Most wives with young children tend to see their mothers once a week or more often, their mothers-in-law rather less often. The wife's mother tends to play an active part in the life of the new family and to provide help when there is illness or other difficulty. She is usually a key member of the 'support system' for a child, and it is she who looks after the children, in partnership with the father, when a woman has to go into hospital for the birth of a child or for other reasons. One in four children are born into a family of four generations, one or more great-grandparents still being alive.

The trend in Britain during the last two or three decades has been for ties with parents and childhood friends to weaken after marriage and consequently for nuclear families to become more isolated, with weakening of the support system for the children. On the other hand, families who have loosened their ties with kin are more ready to develop the new patterns of living required by changing social conditions.

The mean age of the mother at the birth of her first child is 24 years; it is 26 years at the birth of a child of any order of birth. About one-quarter of mothers are under the age of 21 at the birth of the first child, this proportion being higher in Social Class V. About half of those marrying have had a child within 2 years of marriage, about three-quarters within 5 years. The mean number of children per married couple has now fallen below 2. A little more than 10 per cent of marriages remain sterile. One in every 41 children is adopted. About 13 per cent of all maternities are conceived extramaritally; two-thirds of these are legitimized by marriage before the birth of the child. About 60 per cent of all live births to mothers under 20 are born within 8 months of marriage.

About 160 000 pregnancies were notified as terminated under the Abortion Act in England in 1980, while there were about 623 000 live births. A quarter of the women were under 20 years old. More than half were single.

The crisis for the mother

Over 98 per cent of children are now born in hospital, about 10 per cent of deliveries being aided by the application of forceps, and 10 per cent by Caesarean section. The average length of stay in hospital is about 6 days, but stays of 24 or 48 hours are now common. Two-thirds of mothers feed their babies on the breast; about one-quarter are still doing so at 4 months old.

Her attachment to the baby

During the days immediately following the birth, a mother learns rapidly how to respond to the baby, who already at birth has a repertoire of responses including following and fixating on an object with the eyes; this means that there is 'eye contact' of mother and baby. The baby receives and responds to messages from the mother through all the sensory modalities, likewise she from the baby. The interaction is reciprocal, and exchanges between mother and baby, although brief, are reinforced by their effects.

If the baby is removed from her soon after birth, for fostering for instance, a woman pines and shows other signs of bereavement. These effects provide evidence of her attachment or 'affectional bonding' to the baby.[4] They are lessened if the baby is removed immediately after birth before there has been any contact. The evidence suggests that contact immediately after birth is of special importance and that the attachment process is largely completed within 3 or 4 days. Women who have had this early contact tend to be more attentive, when observed 1 month after the birth, look at the baby more often, do more fondling and kissing, and are more inclined to breast-feed. Skin contact and holding seem to be important. Extended contact appears to favour attachment.

There appears to be a 'sensitive period of learning' for the human mother immediately after birth like that in mammals. Studies in mammals have shown that there are profound effects both on mothering and the offspring's health when learning during the sensitive period after birth is prevented by separation for however brief a period. A mother whose baby has been removed from her to go into a special care baby unit may report that she has felt less attached to this baby than to her previous children. On the other hand, success in what she does for the baby strengthens her attachment and relieves her doubts and uncertainties as well as any anxiety arising, for instance, when there are signs of respiratory distress. Habits of attending to the baby are then learnt quickly. Attending to the baby herself, rather than having things done for her by a nurse, seems to be important.

The commonest cause of early separation is removal of the baby to a special care unit. Separation in order to carry out paediatric procedures is less frequent and shorter than it used to be before the importance of early attachment was recognized.

There are still questions to be answered about the effects of analgesic and anaesthetic drugs on the responsiveness of mother and baby to one another during the sensitive period. In what degree is the mother's readiness to attach affected by her active participation in, and keen awareness of, the baby being born? In what degree is her attachment affected when the baby's responsiveness is reduced, either as a result of asphyxia during delivery or of medication? In what degree does the postnatal depression—the 'blues'—felt by mothers a few days after delivery, now regarded by hospital staff as so common as to be almost normal, reflect the lack of fulfilment given by the experience of childbirth as nowadays conducted? And how do the blues affect the patterns of interaction of mother and baby?

Interference with the attachment process during the neonatal period can seriously affect the relationship of mother and child subsequently, and in this are to be found some of the origins of difficulties in rearing the infant. Separation, by delaying for instance putting the baby to the breast, makes it less likely that the mother will breast-feed thereafter.

Non-accidental injury to children

There is evidence also that in a disporportionate number of cases mothers who have maltreated their children, or done them physical injury, have suffered separation from them in the neonatal period because they have been removed to a special care unit or for other reasons. Low birth weight is unduly common in the history of infants who have been injured. Only a very small proportion of the mothers suffering separation maltreat the child subsequently.

The proportion of live-born children who are physically absued is of the order of 6 per 1000. In series of children injured by a parent, the modal age has been found to be 2 months; more than half are less than a year old. The mother has been responsible for the injury more often than the father; in a few cases there has been collusion. Social conditions are usually poor. A high proportion of the fathers have been unemployed. A child injured once is likely to be injured again. When a first child has been injured there is a very high probability that a later child will be injured.

Parents who injure a child have nearly always themselves been deprived of affection as children and to have been depressed. They have had unrealistic expectations of the child and looked to the child for satisfactions they have not been able to get. They have become desparate when the child cries and does not respond to comforting, or unduly put out, because of unrealistic expectations, when the child soils or wets. Physical injury is only one of the ways in which a child may be maltreated. Knowledge of the factors associated with non-accidental injury can be applied successfully in reducing the number of children injured.[5]

Children are the victims of nearly half the murders reported. Mostly the killer is a parent, more often the mother than the father. Infanticide is not restricted to the puerperium as used to be thought to be typical, although most of the victims are under 1 year old; very few are over 7. The mother usually kills herself or attempts to do so. The father if he is the killer usually kills the mother as well. Most of the killers have been severely depressed and psychotic at the time of the killing.

Mental illness associated with childbirth

Pregnancy, a developmental crisis, requires new adaptations of the young couple, the woman's roles especially beginning to change as soon as she becomes aware that she is pregnant. During the first trimester she may suffer from a variety of symptoms, e.g. nausea and vomiting, in which psychological factors probably play some part. The second trimester is relatively untroubled. Depression not amounting to definite illness is common in the third trimester. Definite mental illness may start during the pregnancy, but does so much more commonly during the puerperium. The incidence then is many times higher than that in non-pregnant women of the same age. The peak is in the first week, onset in the latter half being typical. The onset of about half the mental illnesses associated with childbirth is in the first month. The incidence is raised for at least 2 years. There is a raised risk that a woman who has become mentally ill during one puerperium will become ill again after the birth of another child.

Puerperal psychosis used to be attributed to the sepsis, toxicity, and pyrexia that before the days of the antibiotics occurred as a complication of delivery, but it occurs also when there is no physical illness and a normal delivery. Similar illnesses have been reported to occur after a child has been adopted. In some respects the pattern of occurrence is accounted for as well by endocrine as by psychological factors, but endocrine factors have been looked for without positive findings, and psychological factors are now given importance.[6] The blues have popularly been attributed to milk fever or delay in establishing lactation; both this delay and the blues may reflect a high level of anxiety.

There is no association between puerperal psychosis and social class or social mobility. In some series there has been a disproportionate number of the unmarried, whether single, widowed, separated or divorced. Psychosis is relatively common after the birth of a first baby. Several series have contained a disproportionate number of mothers who have married late and are in their middle or late thirties. As a group the patients have had stormier pregnancies and more complications of delivery, and there is an association between puerperal psychosis and Caesarean section. There is no association with multiple births or stillbirth.

Sexual difficulties have been unduly frequent in the patients' marriages. The mother has tended to have been uninvolved with her husband, although dominating him. Weak and passive he has given her poor support. Typically she has been unduly dependent on her mother although there has been discord between them. During the puerperium the conflicts in this relationship have been revived and transferred into her relationship with the baby. Although rejecting her mother as a model she has recognized the similarity of her behaviour towards her baby to that of her mother towards her; she dreads being like her mother. This is an exaggeration of a process that goes on in every mother during the puerperium when she reviews her experience with her mother, usually with reassurance, and recalls other experiences from her childhood, some of them painful.

These conflicts are reflected in the symptoms. Her feelings towards the baby change rapidly, being determined more by fantasies than facts. She may experience homicidal or aggressive impulses towards the baby, or express delusions that the baby has died and that she has been responsible for the death. She tends to neglect the baby, and her attachment is impaired for this reason or because of a period of separation. It is usual nowadays to nurse mother and baby together during a puerperal illness in order to encourage attachment.

The crisis for the father

His wife's pregnancy or the birth of a child may be the occasion of mental illness in the father although there is probably no increased incidence then. However, symptoms affecting the alimentray tract especially—the 'couvade' syndrome[7]—have been found to be unduly common after the first trimester and until the baby is born. Whether identification with the mother is the most important process, as has been said, is uncertain. A psychosis developing at about the time of the birth is typically paranoid, the baby being seen as a rival for the mother's affection. Men who become ill in this way have had close, dependent relationships with their mothers and poor identifications with their fathers, who in many cases have died or left the home early in the patient's childhood, and they have been demanding of or dependent on their wives. In many cases they have shown homosexual tendencies.

The crisis for the baby

The risk in childbirth to the life of the mother is nowadays small, the maternal mortality rate being 12 per 100 000 total births. The perinatal mortality rate for the baby, i.e. for death between the twenty-eighth week of pregnancy and the end of the first week after birth was 13.4 per 1000 total births in 1980. This rate is nearly twice as high in Social Class V (unskilled) as in I and II (professional). About half the babies dying in the perinatal period are of low birth weight.

There are also risks in childbirth of brain damage severe enough to affect development.

Several factors have to be taken into account when the effects on the baby are being considered:

Birth weight. Of all live births about 6.5 per cent are of low birth weight, i.e. below 2.5 kg. A few are of 'very low birth weight', i.e. below 1.5 kg.

Length of gestation. 'Shortened' means less than 38 weeks. 'Light' or 'small' 'for dates' means of low birth weight but gestation over 38 weeks. Estimates of the length of gestation are unreliable when the date of conception is uncertain.

Parity, i.e. order of pregnancy, which may be different from birth order, i.e. rank among sibs born alive. The perinatal mortality rate is higher for the first than for later born.

Plural pregnancies, i.e. twins, triplets etc. About 1 in 80 maternities is a twin pregnancy. There are rather more than twice as many DZ as MZ pairs.

Complications of pregnancy, e.g. threatened abortion, pre-eclampsia, tox-aemia, and antepartum haemorrhage.

Other diseases in the mother, e.g. essential hypertension, heart disease, diabetes, and mental illness.

Foetal pathology. Some complications of pregnancy, e.g. toxaemia, and other diseases in the mother, may be associated with foetal pathology, e.g. alcoholism may result in the 'foetal alcoholic syndrome' of retardation in growth, malformation, and mental retardation. There is a wide variety of other abnormalities arising independently of factors in this list, e.g. from chromosome abnormalities and pathogenic genes, infections such as rubella, and drugs affecting the embryo.

Complications of delivery, e.g. malpresentations such as breech, delivery by forceps, Caesarean section, prolapsed cord, prolonged labour, foetal distress, and asphyxia, which may be graded as slight, moderate or severe.

Abnormal postnatal signs, e.g. delay in establishing respiration, poor sucking reflex, cyanotic or apnoeic attacks, shrill, i.e. 'cerebral', crying, twitching and irritability, jaundice, and neurological syndromes, such as hyperexcitability, apathy, and asymmetries.

Other factors. These include Social Class, ethnic group, legitimacy, the age and physical and mental characteristics of the mother and father, and the level and quality of the support for the parents from their parents or other members of their extended families.

There are many associations between these factors. Lightness for dates, for instance, is associated with low maternal age, primiparity (in older mothers especially), plural pregnancy, short stature and poor nutrition of the mother, Social Class IV or V, and smoking by the mother. Low birth weight with shortened gestation is associated with high parity and complications of pregnancy. Complications of delivery are unduly common when the mother is of short stature, in poor health or of inferior social class. Pre-eclampsia is unduly common when the home is disturbed, as also is prolonged vomiting in the first trimester of the pregnancy.

Cerebral palsy means disorder of motor function due to disease or injury arising at or near birth or during the first 2 years after birth when physical development appears to have been normal during intrauterine life, at least in its gross aspects. The child's intellectual capacity appears to be normal in some cases even when the disorder of motor function is severe. However, motor disorder may affect the growth of intelligence by reducing the child's capacity to explore the world around him. The term 'cerebral palsy' is usually restricted to cases in which the disease is not progressive. Its causes are uncertain.

The prevalence of cerebral palsy lies between 1 and 2.5 per 1000 population between 2 and 15 years of age. The main types are paraplegia, diplegia, quadriplegia, and athetosis. In diplegia, quadriplegia, and athetosis, birth weight tends to have been low relative to the length of gestation, in paraplegia, very low. A history of complications of delivery and abnormal postnatal signs is common in all types. Another perinatal factor is jaundice due to haemolytic disease of the newborn. Among postnatal factors are intracranial infection, thrombosis, embolism, and trauma. The distribution of cases between social classes does not differ from that of the general population. The prevalence has probably been falling during the last two or three decades, perhaps as a result of the better management of childbirth and better care during the neonatal period.

Brain damage at or near birth

Disorders over a wide range, from anti-social behaviour on the one hand to severe mental retardation on the other, as well as clumsiness, over-activity, tics, distractibility, lability of mood, and reading and other educational difficulties, have also been attributed to brain damage sustained at or near birth, even when there are no neurological signs. This view has been given some credibility by the frequency, by comparison with matched controls, with which the history given of such patients includes complications of pregnancy or delivery or abnormal postnatal signs. However, that these findings have been made in retrospective investigations is a reason for caution in accepting them as evidence.

There are other reasons for caution. (1) Many of the disorders attributed to brain damage at or near birth occur also in cases in which there is no reason to suppose that any such damage has been sustained. (2) Children in whose cases there is unequivocal evidence of brain damage in neurological signs and a history of abnormal postnatal signs do not always or even usually show any disorder of mental development subsequently. (3) Follow-up studies of children who have sustained brain injury in accidents have tended to show that psychological factors are more important in determining the course of mental development than is the apparent severity of the injury. (4) The association between the severity of asphyxia at birth and the intelligence quotient in later years has been found to be non-existent or very small when cases with definite neurological signs have been excluded.

The effects on mental development of complications of delivery, on the one hand, and low birth weight, on the other, are difficult to distinguish from one another and from the effects due to intrinsic abnormalities and the effects of poor conditions in the home. Low or very low birth weight is unduly common in the histories of those with severe disorders. About 40 per cent of those of very low birthweight survive beyond the first year. A third of the survivors are normal mentally and physically. Half have some form of defect, such as cerebral palsy, blindness, or Down's syndrome. The remaining one-sixth show disorders of mental development without there being any other recognized defect.

Most of those of low birth weight develop normally and, when those with recognized defects have been excluded, there appears to be no correlation between birth weight and intelligence quotient subsequently. However, such minor disorders as poor reading at 7 years old and poor scores on verbal reasoning tests at 11 years old have been found to be associated with various childbirth factors. Behaviour disorders during the pre-school years, such as over-activity and restlessness, although unduly common in children with a history of low birth weight or complications of delivery, are more closely related to conditions in the home.[8]

Whether complications of delivery or low birth weight are themselves causes of disorders of mental development is uncertain. If they are, there is room for such a concept as 'minimal brain damage'. However, any association between the childbirth factors and disorders of mental development or behaviour disorders may be indirect only. Both the childbirth factors and the two forms of disorder are unduly common when the mother is in poor health or in Social Classes IV or V. If birth weight is low, or if there have been complications of delivery, a baby is likely to spend longer in hospital after the birth or to be removed to a special care unit and as a result to have less close contact with the mother during the sensitive period in which she becomes attached. The developing relationship between mother and baby is also more likely to be interrupted in early childhood by admission to hospital because of, not only bronchitis and pneumonia, but also cataract, inguinal hernia, and convulsions.

The birth of a baby of low birth weight or with any blemish or abnormality or removal to a special care unit has repercussions on the parents' attitudes and behaviour. Guilt is aroused, confidence is impaired, and getting to know the baby is delayed or disturbed. These and other effects are mitigated if the hospital staff are sensitive to them and take steps to counteract them and espcially to encourage the parents to participate in the caring procedures.

The family triangle

The birth of the first baby forces changes in the relationship of the mother and father to each other so as to incorporate the baby into the system. The new family may be portrayed as a triangle, the sides being the ties between mother and father, mother and baby, and father and baby. A firm base in the relationship between mother and father facilitates the caring role of each without rivalry for possession of the baby or rivalry with the baby for the attention or affection of the other. The marriage deteriorates if these rivalries are not resolved, e.g. because the father sees the baby as a threat to him, as Laius saw the new-born Oedipus. Sooner or later one of the parents then leaves the home. The satisfactory resumption of sexual intercourse after the puerperium is reassuring, as is a developing co-operation in providing care for the baby. Nearly all couples have resumed regular sexual intercourse by 12 weeks after the birth although less frequently for a while than before the conception of the baby.

The support system

The mother and father are key components of the system which regulates and gives security to the infant. Typically they are supported themselves by members of the mother's family, especially the maternal grandmother and aunt, and members of the father's family. If it is sound and flexible, the system survives untoward events such as the mother's illness and admission to hospital. Should this happen, the gap may be filled by a coalition of the father and his mother-in-law, with some participation by other members of the family. The contribution made by neighbours tends to be small.

A new family is vulnerable if the system is weak or ineffective, perhaps because they have moved away from the extended family. More often the reason is the estrangement of the mother from her family or the absence of the maternal grandmother through her death. The system is stronger if the new family have been accepted within the community of the neighbourhood.

THE FIRST YEAR

Mothering

An essential condition for the mental health and development of the child is, in the words of Bowlby's famous declaration,[9] 'a warm, intimate and continuous relationship with his mother in which both find satisfaction and enjoyment'. As a corollary, the causes of mental ill health and retardation are to be sought in disturbance or interruption of the mother–child relationship. This thesis lies at the heart of explanations of mental disorder in infancy and childhood although it has to be qualified in some respects.

Bowlby put the emphasis on the specialness of the child's relationship with the biological mother or the substitute who assumes the mothering role. Certainly, she plays a major part in the support system and is likely to achieve a greater expertise in caring for and communicating with the child than others do. However, there are no differences except in degree, it has been argued, in what the father, grandmother, and others do; this is to mother, i.e. their roles are interchangeable.

The mothering person quickly discovers that the infant responds differentially to the messages she conveys through movement, touch, sight, hearing, and smell as she holds, rocks, cuddles, fondles, gazes, and coos. She may impute more meaning into his behaviour than it warrants, reading a great deal, for instance, into his smile at, say, 8 weeks old although it then means little more than that she has produced in him a degree of relaxation. Complex patterns of non-verbal communication are built up during the first weeks and months.[10] Physical contact is of particular importance as also is eye-contact. Thus the infant's eyes engage the mother's while feeding from breast or bottle, and at 2 months old follows hers to look in the same direction as she does. Feeding is the occasion on which there is the most interaction.

Visual perception

By about 5 months old the infant has learnt to distinguish his mother from others on sight. Pattern vision improves at about this time as he learns to co-ordinate his eyes and to achieve binocular fusion of images. As a result his responses to facial expression and gesture become more discriminating. Binocular vision is less firmly acquired, and the infant becomes liable to squint if an eye fails to achieve a sharp image because of a defect, e.g. congenital cataract, that impairs central vision. If the defect is not corrected within, say, the first 2 months the eye is likely to become 'amblyopic', i.e. to lose more or less permanently its capacity even though there is no longer any structural abnormality.

The infant's attachment to the mother

The quality of the relationship of the infant to the mothering person changes in the third-quarter of the first year.[11] Any effects on the infant of removal from one person to another, as in fostering or adoption, in the first 6 months tend to be short-lived. Separation from the mother, e.g. because of admission to hospital if it takes place before 7 months is followed by a relatively benign reaction, which may include a high degree of alertness; this may persist for a while after the infant is reunited with the mother.

Separation if it takes place after 7 months old is more disturbing. The infant tends to cry excessively, clings, seeks to be nursed, and shows a fear of strangers; gradually he becomes withdrawn. Recovery is slower and less certain. The change in the effects suggests that the infant has become more firmly attached to the mothering person. This makes him more attentive to her, especially auditorily, and prepares him to learn to perceive and discriminate sounds, especially speech sounds, in the second-half of the first year. At this age infants seek their mothers and are comforted by them if anything untoward happens—hence the term 'eight-month' anxiety.

Auditory perception

By the beginning of the second half of the first year the infant shows well-developed patterns of non-verbal communication. Auditory messages become more important when he is able at 9 months old to crawl and later to walk away from his mother. She then serves as a base from which he can go out with confidence to explore the world and to which he can return if he is frightened.

At 9 months old the infant listens, vocalizes as a means of communication, babbles tunefully, imitates vocal sounds, and understands such words as 'no-no' and 'bye-bye'. By his first birthday he shows a remarkable capacity to imitate sounds, not only human voices but also inanimate sounds. This imitation and his responses to spoken instructions show that he is learning fast to discriminate sounds and to perceive and understand words. He is on the way to acquiring language through the give-and-take of communication with his mother and others.

Learning in these respects may be delayed or distorted in several ways. Interaction in the early months may be impoverished because of the disability of the mother, or because she has not formed a normal attachment to him. A mother may deliberately reduce physical contact. Some infants—'non-cuddlers'—learn to avoid physical contact. A mother may avoid eye-contact. A few infants do not respond normally to her by reason of intrinsic factors.

Another reason for slowness in learning to perceive auditorily lies in the infant's failure to form a normal attachment to a mothering person in the second-half of the first year because of separation and transfer from one person to another. Developing capacities may then show some regression. If learning does not take place or is interrupted in the second half of the first year, the capacity to understand speech may be more or less permanently impaired.

Of particular interest is what happenes if deafness is not detected and special measures are not instituted to provide auditory stimulation, e.g. if his mother does not speak directly into his ear, or he is not fitted with a hearing aid. His babbling, broadly similar at 6 months old to that of a normal infant, although there are detectable differences much earlier, does not develop further, and if the measures are not taken until late in the second year, he is found to have 'missed the bus' and lost the capacity to learn to understand speech, or to be able to learn very slowly only.[12]

Sensitive periods of learning

The hypothesis that there is a senstive period for learning to perceive auditorily and hence to understand speech rests mainly on the findings in children whose deafness is not detected. It supposes that there is an optimal period during which learning proceeds rapidly; once this period has passed, the capacity to learn wanes. Learning to listen starts at birth, the infant learning to orientate himself towards sounds that have acquired meaning through his experience of them. The second half of the first year is crucial, but the capacity to learn does not greatly decline until well into the second year.

There are several examples of sensitive periods that have been authenticated in studies of animal behaviour: the acquiring of territorial habits by dogs as soon as they become sexually mature; the imprinting of anserine birds on a parent bird immediately after hatching; the learning of songs by chaffinches during their first year; the acquiring of mothering habits by mammals, e.g. sheep, within an hour of giving birth; and the 'primary socialization' of puppies when they are weaned, typically from 3 to 10 weeks or so after birth.

Human examples include the attachment of mother to baby immediately after birth and of infant to mother in the third-quarter of the first year. If sucking responses are not acquired during the first few days after birth, difficulties in feeding persist, and whatever has been learnt is not readily modified subsequently. There is a sensitive period for vision in the first 2 months. Any failure to learn then to form a sharp image on the retina means that binocular fusion of retinal images is not achieved at 6 months old, and the child squints, the vision of one eye being largely suppressed. Habits of control over urination are normally acquired in the second year, but are vulnerable then if there are disturbances in the home; if they regress, relearning is slow. Speech normally becomes fluent and rhythmic in the third, fourth, and fifth years; stammering tends to begin during these years, and is not easily got rid of.

Sensitive periods may be explained in psychological terms by supposing that learning is rapid at certain times because circumstances are favourable and the learning of a new skill has been prepared for by the learning of other skills. There is a normal sequence in the emergence of habits. The acquisition of one habit provides favourable conditions for the learning of another habit. There is a typical age at which each habit is acquired, but there seems to be no reason why it should not be acquired earlier if the conditions are right.

Reading, for instance, typically learnt at 6 years old, is often learnt at 3 years old.

Why does the capacity to learn decline? It may be that learning slows because of inherent properties of the central nervous sytem, but there is no evidence in support of this view. There are probably other reasons. The deaf child may learn to lip-read and to communicate by sign language. These habits reduce his needs to learn to listen. A young child who has turned away from social relationships as a result of disturbing experiences does not learn to speak, and soon ceases to listen to speech. Not being able to communicate through language, he is further handicapped in forming social relationships.

Physical maturing

Physical maturing, i.e. growth and differentiation of the central nervous system or other organic systems, plays some part in the timing of the onset of sensitive periods, but it is too simple a view that the onset is decided by the laying down of the nervous mechanisms, for in many instances the nervous and other apparatus has existed for some time beforehand. The apparatus for pulmonary breathing is in readiness in man for months before it comes into use at birth. Then anoxia or sensory stimulation brings into operation mechanisms already available but held in a state of inhibition. The rapid appearance of sexual responses after the administration of hormones to the sexually immature makes it clear that existing but dormant mechanisms have been activated. Patterns of behaviour may make a fleeting appearance before they normally become established. Smiling, for instance, may be observed during the first day or two after birth, and then not again until the third month. Integrated locomotory movements, not normally established until the end of the first year, may be observed during the first week. Another reason for doubting the importance of physical maturation is that precocious mental development, as in musical or mathematical prodigies, typically occurs without any evidence of abnormal growth in organic systems.

Vulnerable ages

If it is arrested because circumstances are unfavourable, learning tends not to be resumed after the sensitive period has passed. Habits are thus vulnerable while they are being acquired and before they become established, adverse circumstances then leading not only to the arrest of learning but also to regression. For instance, a 2-year-old child may stop talking, begin again to wet his bed, and cling again to his mother, as the result of admission to hospital, moving house, the birth of a sib or other disturbance in the family.

There is an analogy here with what happens when the development of an embryo is affected by a noxious agent, such as a virus, e.g. rubella, a drug, e.g. thalidomide, or irradiation by X-rays. The type of malformation depends upon the age of the embryo, those organs being most affected which are going through a 'period of differentiation'. The character of the malformation allows the damage to be dated. Similarly, knowing which mental functions are most affected, and which preserved, a clinical investigator can arrive at a hypothesis stating the age at which development became disordered and hence what were the relevant circumstances.

Feral children

The concept of sensitive periods revived interest in the results of training 'feral' children who have come under observation after they have been living wild. These cases are few, and the lack of information about their mental development previously has made it difficult to decide what significance should be given to the results. Victor, the wild boy of Aveyron, one of the most famous cases, was captured in 1799 when he was 11 or 12 years old after several years of living wild in the woods.[13] After devoted care by Itard over 5 years he had been transformed from a dull, insensitive, solitary, fearful savage into an almost normal child. He had learnt to be clean, well-behaved, and affectionate, to make himself understood by mime and gesture and to respond to printed symbols, but he did not speak, except for a few words and did not understand speech. This historical curiosity shows up the limitations of methods of teaching and confirms that children who have not acquired language skills at the proper time may not do so subsequently even though they may learn rapidly in other respects.

PRE-SCHOOL YEARS

The growth of intelligence

The position a person holds among his peers in respect of intelligence-test scores tends to remain constant throughout the school years, and this constancy in IQ has been taken to show that intelligence is a permanent characteristic that reflects a person's genetical constitution. Changes in IQ do occur, however, and the constancy is relative. A change of 15 points (about 1 standard deviation) or more is likely to be shown by more than half of any sample of children during the years from 6 to 16, a change of 30 points by 1 in 10.

Constancy increases gradually during early childhood. Developmental quotients (DQs) estimated during the first 2 years do not provide a sound basis of predictions of the rate of mental development subsequently. Thus when a first test is made at 2 years old and a second 2 years later, the correlation coefficient tends to be less than 0.5, whereas for a first test at 10 and a second at 12, the coefficient tends to be above 0.9.

Mental-test scores of children under 2 years old show little correlation with the IQs of their parents. Coefficients, negligible when the children are under 18 months, become significant when they are $3\frac{1}{2}$ years old, being of the order of 0.35. They increase to more than 0.5 at 7 years old. Social-class differences are not found on mental tests at 18 months old, but there are highly significant differences at 3 and 5 years old. At 5 years old the mean IQ of children in Social Classes I and II, as judged by the occupation of their fathers, is about 1 standard deviation above the mean for all children; for those in Social Classes IV and V, it is 0.6 standard deviations below the mean, i.e. a difference of 25 points. The rate of mental development from 2 to 5 years old thus correlates with social class. In assessing these results it should be borne in mind that the coefficients found when tests scores at younger ages are correlated with test scores at older ages might be misleadingly low because the tests measure different abilities at different ages.

The nature–nurture controversy

Those who argue that genetic factors are of major importance in determining the rate of mental development during childhood and hence the IQ refer to the findings of twin research. Thus the correlation coefficient for the IQs of identical (MZ) twin pairs has been found to be 0.95, that for non-identical (DZ) pairs to be 0.65. Being brought up apart for at least 5 years was found to have had strikingly little effect on the coefficient in a sample of MZ twin pairs.[14] How much weight should be given to the findings depends on judgements on the value of the evidence from twin research in deciding the relative importance of genetic and environmental factors. A birth-order effect has been reported, but is probably small.

The evidence from studies of fostered and adopted children has not been conclusive. Even when the children have been fostered in early childhood, the coefficients for correlations of the IQs of the children with those of the foster parents remain insignificant, whereas those with the biological parents tend to be only slightly smaller than those for children living with their biological parents. On the other hand, the IQs of fostered children are consistently higher than would be expected from the IQs or other characteristics of their biological parents. Even when the biological parents are both of low intelligence, the fostered children are found to develop relatively normally.

Those who hold to the view that genetic factors are of major importance dismiss lack of opportunity as a cause of failure to acquire the abilities and skills which make for success on intelligence tests on two grounds. The first is that the material used in such as the Binet Scale is widely available and within the experience of all children. However, it is now known that the conditions in which infants and young children learn are more specific than used to be supposed. Thus much of the learning goes on in the setting of a relationship with a parent or other person. Also the conditions have to be favourable at the proper time.

The second ground lies in the lack of improvement in IQ shown by children who have grown up in poor circumstances when they are moved to more favourable circumstances. The facts are not all on one side. The IQ does tend to rise gradually when circumstances are more favourable for learning although there may be some resistance, as in Victor's case, to certain kinds of learning.

It has traditionally been assumed that the mental development of children whose fathers are in Social Classes IV or V is relatively slow because they have inherited unfavourable combinations of genes from parents who are poorly endowed genetically. This assumption has been weakened by the finding that the social-class distribution of the grandparents of intellectually retarded children does not differ from that of the general population. The parents have moved down in the social scale. Whether this has been due to their poor intelligence or to educational or emotional difficulties is uncertain.

Another explanation of the slower mental development is that the parents provide less intellectual stimulation and fewer opportunities to learn, or alternatively that they provide less adequate care and protection because of the incapacity of the caretakers or the disorganization of the family. In support of this last explanation is the greater frequency with which children from less favoured homes suffer from bronchitis, pneumonia, infective diarrhoea and vomiting, and sustain accidents; for these reasons admission to hospital is more frequent. The explanations do not exclude one another, and there may be something in all of them.

The conditions affecting mental development

The rate and course of mental development have been regarded in recent years, not as reflecting genetic or other intrinsic factors but as determined by external conditions. The urgent task of research has been to define the conditions, the questions asked being about the social context and when and where rather than how or why.[15]

The level of stimulation

The importance given to opportunity and stimulation as factors owes much to the demonstration many years ago that rats, brought up with a free run of a varied environment, show greater learning and problem-solving capacity in maturity, i.e. are more intelligent than rats of the same strain reared in the restricted environment of a cage. The lower the age at which the enriched experience is gained, the greater is the effect. Studies of the mental development of young children have shown positive correlations between measures of mental development and of intellectual stimulation due to the involvement of the parents in play and the provision of toys and books. Thus the IQs of fostered children, although correlating poorly with the IQs of the foster parents, have been found to correlate with measures of the intellectual stimulation of the foster homes.

The social context

The social context has received increasing recognition. Bowlby laid stress on maternal deprivation, by which is meant an insufficiency of interaction between the child and a mothering person. This could come about in various ways, he pointed out: lack of any opportunity to form a lasting attachment to a mother-figure, during the first 3 years especially, separation for a period from the mother-figure, or a change from one mother-figure to another. In support of his thesis he referred, on the one hand to the frequency with which separation from the mother for a period of 6 months or more in the first 5 years occurs in the histories in cases of psychopathic disorder, and on the other hand to the retardation in social and intellectual development shown by children brought up in institutions when compared with those who are fostered.[16]

There are other ways in which a child may be deprived. The interaction between the child and the mothering person may be insufficient although they live continuously together, because of the disability of either or both as a result of previous experience. The effects of deprivation depend upon the age at which it occurs, its completeness and its duration, and are likely to be especially damaging when it starts in the first year and continues into the second and third year. Language, the capacity for abstraction and the capacity for lasting attachments are then the most likely to be affected. How reversible the effects are is open to question.

Lack of protection

Three models can be offered which illustrate other effects of the social context on development. The first is drawn from experiments on the separation for a short period immediately after birth of young mammals from their mothers, who in consequence fail to attach to the young, to be attentive to their needs and to protect them from potential disaster.[17] The behaviour of the young when not so protected becomes disordered, and mental and physical development is retarded. The essence of the theory suggested by the model is that retardation in development is a disorder due to lack of protection from excessive stimulation at a vulnerable time. This theory does not specify the reasons for, or the nature of, the disorders affecting the mental development of young children.

Failure in primary socialization

The second model comes from an investigation into the causes of failure in a school for guide dogs for the blind.[18] Dogs kept alone in kinnels until after they were 14 weeks old, and not removed before then to a foster home where they would have had opportunities to form an attachment to a human master within the sensitive period, did not make such an attachment. Primary socialization being thus (unintentionally) prevented, none of the dogs benefited from instruction in the school when they entered it at about a year old. A high proportion of the dogs removed to a foster home within the sensitive period were successfully trained. Similar difficulties have been reported in the training of gun dogs. The reasons for failure lie as much in erratic social behaviour as in any cognitive defect. The descriptions given of the dogs who failed in the school are very like those given of the children who require special schooling.

Short stature

The third model depends on an analogy with slow physical growth, which like slow mental growth has been assumed to be due to physical inheritance. But the rate of physical growth depends also on nutrition. Children from homes where there is poverty may be shorter by 3–4 inches than children of similar age from homes providing an adequate diet. The steady increase in the mean height of school children over the last few decades has been attributed to, among other things, the general improvement in diet. The effect has been particularly striking among those who have moved from a poor to an affluent country. However, there are also children whose short stature is due not to any poverty or lack of food available but to their eating habits. Although plenty is available, they eat so little and selectively—usually more outside than at mealtimes—that their diet contains too few calories to promote growth. Their habits are to be understood by reference to their relationships within the family. Meals are social occasions at which the conflicts between the child and his parents often come to a head. Growth speeds up when the diet improves as it tends to do after puberty as the young person begin to emancipate himself, i.e. short stature in these cases is remediable.[19]

By analogy, short mental stature may be due to an inadequate intellectual diet or to failure to benefit from the opportunities available because of a narrowness of interest and a restrictiveness and repetitiveness in what is attempted. The difficulties in teaching such a child may appear to be due more to a resistance to learning than to a lack of capacity. If this is so, slow mental growth too is potentially remediable.

Interruption in mental development

At 2 years old a child typically uses 50 or more words, his vocabulary for comprehension being larger still. He is beginning to put words together. He looks at picture books with enjoyment over the objects he recognizes. Handedness has been established. Toilet habits are still precarious, but are being acquired. He is demanding of his mother's attention and quickly becomes anxious if he does not know where she is. All these skills are developing rapidly, but are vulnerable if there is any change in circumstances.

Admission to hospital

One such change is admission to hospital, which in Britain is the experience of one child in five before 5 years old. Several investigations have been made into the effects of admission since attention was drawn to the depression children may then show. Admission may be traumatic, not only because the child is separated from his mother and other family members, but also because he is confined to a cot, prevented from exploring, and subjected to a variety of bewildering procedures. The 2-year-old child has been studied especially because the effects on social behaviour, language, and toilet training are especially marked at this age. Some adverse effects are the general rule in children admitted under 5 years old, and most mothers report some deterioration in behaviour after the child returns home. Especially vulnerable are 'only' children, youngest children, children from extended family households (in which there tends to be multiple mothering), children with recent experiences of separation, and children who have had no previous separation.[20]

Interruption in mental development may also occur as a result of a variety of other experiences. These include illness of the child without admission to hospital, separation from the mother because of her admission or for another reason, the loss of a significant member of the family, e.g. father or grandmother, whether through death, removal or departure for another reason, and the birth of a sib. However, the evidence that events like these are unduly common in the histories of the children showing interruption is equivocal.

The birth of a sib, which is the experience of two out of three first-born children, may be associated with separation from the mother when she goes into hospital for the delivery. This may be upsetting even when the father and grandmother or other family members fill in the gap in the support system. The first child, especially if he has been highly dependent on his mother, is vulnerable when a second child is born, and may show 'sibling rivalry' for the attention of his mother and some regression in habits. The arrival of the new baby is a crisis because it changes his place in the family and the roles he is expected to play. Nearly always he learns quickly to fit into the changed position in the family system, for which he has usually been prepared. Nevertheless, the birth of a sib is occasionally mentioned by parents as having been associated with slowing or arrest of mental development, but then it has been combined with other changes in the family or perhaps illness.[21]

CIRCUMSCRIBED DISORDERS OF DEVELOPMENT[22]

Some disorders of mental development are circumscribed and affect a single function mainly. Handedness is an example.

Handedness

Most people prefer the right hand for all purposes requiring skill or strength. In nearly all races, whether primitive or civilized, the hand preferred by the majority is the right, and this is known to have been so at all times in history, on the evidence of pictures and of the design of implements. Some 5–10 per cent of adults write with the left hand, and in any other skilled task left-handedness is shown by a similar proportion. The proportion is higher in groups of children defined as neurotic, delinquent or educationally subnormal. In special schools, for instance, it is typically about 20 per cent compared with about 7 per cent in ordinary schools.

Handedness develops gradually, right-handedness developing more rapidly and consistently than left-handedness. There are corresponding preferences in the use of the eyes and feet (or rather leg). Differentiation into an active and passive hand starts at about 36 weeks old and is usually well developed by 2 years old.

Left-handedness runs in families, but the pattern of occurrence does not conform to any simple hypothesis of genetic determination. In some cases, the left hand is preferred because of a physical defect or injury to the right hand which reduced its efficiency while habits were being acquired. In some cases, parents or teachers unwittingly or deliberately encourage the use of the left hand, either because they are left-handed themselves or they suppose the child to be naturally left-handed by reason of a family tendency. In other cases, left-handedness develops as a reaction to training and then reflects resistance or negativism.

Language functions tend to be localized in the left cerebral hemisphere, from which originate the motor and sensory nerves serving the right side of the body. This specialization or 'cerebral dominance', which is not accompanied by any discernible difference in structure, is greater in the right-handed than the left-handed. Thus the right-handed seldom suffer from any disorder of language functions as a result of a lesion in the right hemisphere whereas the left-handed are liable to do so from a lesion in either hemisphere. As judged from the effects of lesions, the right and left hemisphere are dominant in the left-handed in about equal proportions of cases whereas the left hemisphere is dominant almost invariably in the right-handed.[23] Dominance is established gradually during the first few years.

Stammering

Stammering describes various forms of speech defect, such as hesitancy, blocks, repetitions of initial consonants and prolongation of sounds. Usually it begins before the child is 9 years old, although occasionally not until puberty. The onset is commonly in the fourth year, while the rhythm of speech is being acquired, or soon after the first attendance at school. The habit once acquired tends to be intractable. Boys are affected more often than girls, the sex ratio being 2:1. Satisfactory evidence of a birth-order effect is lacking. Stammerers have been said to show perfectionist tendencies, but they tend to be somewhat retarded in their school work although some excel. There is probably no association between stammering and left-handedness although it has often been claimed that there is. The parents of stammerers have been said to show perfectionist tendencies themselves, to be domineering and to have reacted to hesitances in the child's speech by reproof or correction.

Bedwetting

About a half of children have acquired control over urination at night by 3 years old. At 5 years old, about 11 per cent still wet their beds. At 8 years old, about $4\frac{1}{2}$ per cent do so occasionally, and another $3\frac{1}{2}$ per cent regularly. Girls tend to be ahead of boys in becoming dry at night. At puberty about 1 per cent still wet their beds, most of them regularly. After 9 years old bedwetting is almost entirely restricted to families of whom the father is in Social Classes III, IV or V. A high proportion of those wetting come from deviant or problem families; in many cases the wetter's relationship with his mother has been interrupted.

An organic cause is found in few cases only. Wetters are divided into those who have never established control and those of 'onset' type who have begun to wet again after a period of months or years of being dry. The histories of the former tend to disclose that training in other respects has been clumsy and inconsistent, and that mental development in other respects has been retarded. The mother may report difficulties in establishing feeding, whether from breast or bottle. The child has been potted, not in accordance with his inclinations, but at the mother's convenience or the dictates of a system; such training induces contrariness. Disturbances in the second half of the second year, such as those resulting from illness, with or without admission to hospital, separation from the mother, the mother going out to work, the birth of a sib, or house-moving tend to have adverse effects on the development of control. Onset wetting tends to follow closely upon one or more of such experiences. It is associated at first with other signs of disturbance but these remit.

Simple delay in speech development

Relatively benign forms of delay in speech development occur without development in other respects being affected. Simple delay may be complicated by faults in articulation. Comprehension of speech is normal, and the child communicates with his mother by gesture and physical contact especially, but does not use speech to a normal degree. Non-verbal communication tends to be well developed. The child tends to have a close relationship with, and to be unduly dependent on, his mother, who is over-protective; his family is typically close-knit. These children, who are more often boys than girls, tend to catch up when they are 5 or 6 years old, but are vulnerable to separation and may show serious disturbance if they are admitted to hospital or occasionally when they start at school. Their learning may be limited by the anxiety which social contacts outside the family provoke. Difficulties in reading, writing, and spelling are unduly common.

Reading difficulties

The causes of failure to acquire correct habits in reading, writing, and spelling, that are commensurate with other abilities are to be found among such factors as irregularity of attendance at school, frequent changes of school, faulty methods of teaching, failure to detect bad habits, and unfavourable attitudes towards reading, such as apathy and resentment. These may arise from lack of encouragement by parents or lack of confidence and self-reliance such as may be found in children who have been over-protected at home or come from disturbed homes. In some cases, the parents have induced negative attitudes by making excessive demands, being coercive and critical or showing excessive anxiety. There is a higher proportion of poor readers among the children of fathers in manual occupations than among those in non-manual occupations. The proportion when the father is in an unskilled occupation is very high. Serious backwardness in reading is much commoner in boys than girls. It has been estimated that some 10 per cent of children need special help.

Whatever the causes may be, a child who has not learnt to read properly by the time he is 9 years old is likely to have developed unfavourable attitudes toward reading as a result of discouragement and frustration at school. His resistance to reading is apparent as soon as materials are put before him.

It has been claimed that among the backward in reading there is a minority whose difficulties are not attributable to such factors as those above. To these cases the term 'specific dyslexia' has been applied. The reading disorder is specific in that the development of reading skills has lagged behind, and sometimes far behind, that of other mental functions. Visual patterns as complex as words, such as numbers and musical notes, are perceived and discriminated normally. There has been no lack of educational opportunity, and no lack of intelligence as assessed by intelligence tests. Boys outnumber girls. Many of the fathers are in occupations which put them in Social Classes 1 or 11.

In support of the view that specific dyslexia is due to a defect, not yet defined, in brain structure or function, it has been asserted that the reading disorder tends to be associated with mirror-writing, mirror-reading, delays and disorders in speech, and clumsiness. The insecurity and anxiety of those affected are held to be consequences of the reading disorder and not related to its causes. The disorder is said to run in families.

Whether there is a special class of backward readers to which the term 'specific dyslexia' can be properly applied is controversial. There is no generally accepted evidence that they can be differentiated from the general run of backward readers in respect of causes, response to various forms of treatment or prognosis. The symptoms such as speech delay and clumsiness, which with backwardness in reading make up the syndrome of specific dyslexia, have not been found in systematic investigations to show any tendency to cluster. The use of medical Greek informs that the investigator has resolved to look at the reading disorder as a medical rather than an educational problem in its origins, although the remedial measure he proposes may be educational. The term 'specific learning difficulties' in reading, writing and/or spelling is to be preferred in these cases.[24]

DISORDERS OF MENTAL DEVELOPMENT

Specific defects

For medical purposes it is useful to make a distinction between specific defects and undifferentiated cases. Examples of specific defects are Down's syndrome, cerebral palsy, kernicterus, phenylketonuria, and cretinism. Among the identified causes are chromosome abnormalities, complications of delivery, maternal iso-immunization because of a Rhesus factor in the blood, and a metabolic abnormality inherited through a recessive gene. Cretinism is an example of an endocrine dysfunction, the cause of which is unknown or uncertain.

Specific defects can be demonstrated in about two-thirds of the severely disabled in mental-handicap hospitals, and in less than one-quarter of the less severely disabled. Down's syndrome is the commonest of the specific defects, accounting for about one-quarter of all the cases in these hospitals. Cases with neurological signs, such as cerebral palsy, and cases with sensory defects are the next most common. Other than these, there are no specific defects accounting for more than one per cent of the cases in hospital. In about 3 per cent, however, the cause lies in a pathogenic gene, such as that causing phenylketonuria, cerebral lipoidosis or epiloia.

The incidence of chromosomal abnormalities, such as those found in the several varieties of Down's syndrome and in Turner's and Klinefelter's syndromes, the last two being due to abnormalities affecting the sex chromosomes, lies between 2 and 6 per 1000 births. Neural-tube defects and congenital heart defects have each an incidence of the same order, as has cerebral palsy. There is no evidence of any chromosomal abnormality or pathogenic gene in these cases.

Undifferentiated cases

These represent, it is supposed, the extreme of the normal biological distribution of intelligence or other related variables. These variables are assumed to be graded and to be determined by the summation of multiple factors, each of which exerts a small effect. How much of the determination is genetic, and how much environmental, is controversial. The evidence is inconclusive. The questions are probably unanswerable.

The number of cases with IQs in the range from -2 to -4 standard deviations from the mean, i.e. between 70 and 40, conforms to that to be expected from the shape of the normal distribution curve, i.e. about $2\frac{1}{2}$ per cent of the whole population. However, there is an excess of cases with IQs below 40, this probably being due to specific defects. Nearly all of the 2–3 per cent of children with IQs between 80 and 55, which is the range found in special schools, have an undifferentiated disorder. Of the 1 per cent with IQs below 55, some have an undifferentiated disorder, and some have specific defects.

Special educational needs

Until the Education (Handicapped Children) Act 1970 became law, children with IQs below 55 were liable to be excluded from schools. Being described as unsuitable for education at school or 'ineducable', they attended training centres provided by the local authority's health committee. The Act transferred training centres to the education committee and in doing so removed the distinction in this respect between training centres and special schools. It has ensured that education is provided for all children, however severe their disorders.

The Education Act 1981, which followed on the Warnock Report, introduced the terms 'learning difficulties' and 'special educational needs' as well as improving procedures and practices in the assessment of children. The proportion of children with special educational needs has been estimated as being about one in five, but this proportion is arbitrary. Most of these remain in ordinary schools. Special schooling is required for 2–3 per cent of children. These include the relatively few who have severe physical, sensory or developmental handicaps, e.g. cerebral palsy, neural-tube defects, defects of sight and hearing, and Down's syndrome and other specific defects, and the many without specific defects who have severe learning difficulties, whether for cognitive or emotional reasons.

The changes in law and terminology reflect the greater recognition of the educational needs of children with disorders of mental development. The IQ loses its central position in the assessment of children, and more weight is put on the analysis of the particular learning difficulties shown by the child.

Much current research is concerned with the conditions affecting learning in early childhood, especially those lying in social relationships, and with the ways in which the obstacles to learning can be overcome. That is, the disorders are seen as remediable or preventable in so far as the necessary conditions for learning can be created, preserved or restored. To optimize the conditions is of special importance when learning is affected by a specific defect, whether this lies in a chromosome abnormality, damage to the brain at birth or subsequently or other structural abnormality.

Cases with specific defects come indiscriminately from good, moderate or poor homes, but a disporportionate number of undifferentiated cases come from families in Social Classes IV or V as judged by the father's occupation and also from families of abnormal composition, families who are functioning poorly or families showing 'social pathology' and being known to social agencies because of their irregular habits, criminal tendencies or alcoholism. Half or more of the undifferentiated cases come from families with four or more children.

In undifferentiated cases most functions tend to be affected in some degree. The child is likely to have been slow in sitting up and walking although once he has begun to walk he has made rapid progress. Handedness has also been developed slowly, and left-handedness is unduly common, as is squinting. Control over urination has been developed late. There is an excess of children of short stature. Simple sensory and perceptual skills have been acquired normally, as have psychomotor skills, but verbal and academic skills are poorly developed. The children tend to show some detachment in social relationships.

In some cases mental development has lagged from birth, in others it has proceeded normally to start with and has then been interrupted, becoming arrested, delayed or distorted. The age at which the interruption occurs, which tends to be at a time of a significant event in the family, can be judged by the passing of the 'milestones' in development. When the interruption occurs late, the child comprehends speech and makes some use of it, but remains illiterate. The social detachment appears to be due in most cases to failure to form an attachment normally during the second half of the first year. In some cases the attachment has been formed, but has been disturbed or broken in the second or third year.

Speech and language are particularly affected, skills in practical tasks less so. More than a third of the children in whom there is delay, as defined, in the development of speech and language show a more or less general, undifferentiated disorder of mental development. In a quarter or more the delay is simple, and the disorder of mental development is circumscribed. Other causes of delay are deafness and structural abnormalities of lips, tongue and palate. A child shows delay if at 18 months old he does not comprehend simple commands or identify common objects when named orally, if at 21 months old he does not use words with meaning, or if at 3 years old he does not link words in sentences. Delay in comprehension is a more serious disorder than delay in expression.

There is at present no agreement about ways in which the undifferentiated cases can be subdivided for medical purposes. However, there are some syndromes which, although relatively uncommon, are of interest.

Early infantile autism

The essential components of this syndrome, first described by Kanner in 1943, are an inability to form normal social relationships and poor development of language and of other methods of communication. The children show what Kanner called an 'obsessive desire for the maintenance of sameness'. They may reject the unfamiliar and show, e.g. in their diet, a narrow and unvarying choice. Much of their behaviour is repetitive, and their interests are specialized. In some respects their behaviour is advanced, and it has been supposed that potentially they are of normal or even superior intelligence although they perform poorly on standard tests. Their parents are often of superior intelligence and successful in their occupations or professions. The term autism has gained popular currency and is used when the intention is to emphasize the disorder in social behaviour rather than the intellectual disability.[25] The prevalence of autism, restrictively defined, is low—4.5 per 10 000 children being found in one survey.

Idiots savants

Of theoretical interest and probably related to autism are *idiots savants*, who despite poor development in most respects and failure in the ordinary subjects of tuition have acquired a store of highly specialized knowledge, or show extraordinary feats of memorizing or of arithmetical calculation, or astonishing skill in the playing of musical instruments, the making of intricate models or the drawing of detailed plans. Remarkable skill may be attained in a limited sphere of activity—a good ear for music, for instance, perhaps without any understanding of musical notation, or the recitation without understanding of nursery rhymes.

Childhood psychosis

This diagnosis tends to be made when a child shows detachment from all social relationships, regression in habits, and anomalous or inappropriate emotional responses. The clinical picture varies with the age of onset, and it has been suggested thetefore that the cases should be divided according to the age of onset, e.g. under 3 years old, from 3 to 5, and over 5. A disproportionate number of those of early onset are said to come from Social Classes I or II.

NOTES AND REFERENCES

1. Caplan, G. (1964). *Principles of preventive psychiatry.* Tavistock Publications, London.
2. Erikson, E. H. (1959). *Identity and the life cycle.* International University Press, New York.
3. Up-to-date figures for the various frequencies mentioned in this and later paragraphs of this chapter are to be found in the reports of the Office of Population Censuses and Surveys (OPCS), the occasional statistical and research reports of the Department of Health and Social Security, and in Macfarlane, A. and Mugford, M. (1983). *Birth counts: statistics of pregnancy and childbirth.* HMSO, London. Trends in the structure of families are discussed by Rapoport, R. N., Fogarty, M. P. and Rapoport, R. (eds) (1982). *Families in Britain.* Routledge & Kegan Paul, London.
4. Recent research on attachment is reviewed by Parkes, C. M. and Stevenson-Hinde, J. (eds) (1982). *The place of attachment in human behaviour.* Tavistock, London.

5. Ounsted, C., Roberts, J. C., Gordon, M. and Milligan, B. (1982). Fourth goal of perinatal medicine. *Br. med. J.* **284**, 879–82.
6. Kendell, R. E., Rennie, D., Clarke, J. A., and Dean, C. (1981). The social and obstetric correlates of psychiatric admission in the puerperium. *Psychol. Med.* **11**, 341–50.
7. Trethowan, W. H. and Conlon, M. F. (1965). The couvade syndrome. *Br. J. Psychiat.* **111**, 57–66.
8. The most comprehensive follow-up data come from Pringle, M. L. K., Butler, N. R., and Davie, R. (1966). *Eleven thousand seven-year olds; first report of the National Child Development Study (1958 cohort).* Longmans, London. The most recent report is Steadman, J. (1980). *Progress in secondary schools; findings from the National Child Development Study.* National Children's Bureau, London.
9. Bowlby, J. (1951). *Maternal care and mental health,* World Health Organisation Monograph Series, No. 2. HMSO, London.
10. Shaffer, D. and Dunn, J. (eds) (1979). *The first year of life.* John Wiley, Chichester.
11. Bowlby, J. (1969). *Attachment and loss: 1 attachment.* Hogarth Press Institute of Psychoanalysis, London.
12. Whetnall, E. and Fry, D. B. (1970). In *Learning to hear* (ed. E. B. Niven). Heinemann, London.
13. Lane, H. (1977). *The wild boy of Aveyron.* Allen & Unwin, London.
14. Shields, J. (1962). *Monozygotic twins brought up apart and brought up together.* Oxford University Press, Oxford.
15. e.g. Robinson, W. P. (ed.) (1981). *Communication in development.* Academic Press, London.
16. Rutter, M. (1981). *Maternal deprivation reassessed.* Penguin Books, Harmondsworth.
17. e.g. Liddell's experiments on goats described in CHAPTER 2, p. 16.
18. Pfaffenberger, C. J. and Scott, J. P. (1969). The relationship between delayed socialisation and trainability in guide dogs. *J. genet. Psychol.* **95**, 145–56.
19. Davis, D. R., Apley, J., Fill, G., and Grimaldi, C. (1978). Diet and retarded growth. *Br. med. J.* **1**, 539–42.
20. Stacey, M., Dearden, R., Pill, R., and Robinson, D. (1970). *Hospitals, children and their families.* Routledge & Kegan Paul, London.
21. Dunn, J. and Kendrick, C. (1982). *Siblings.* Grant McIntyre, London.
22. A useful source of information about disorders of mental development is Rutter, M. (ed.) (1980). *Scientific Foundations of developmental psychiatry.* Heinemann, London.
23. This point is taken up again in CHAPTER 7, p. 139.
24. Rutter, M. and Yule, W. (1975). The concept of specific reading retardation. *J. child Psychol. Psychiat.* **16**, 181–97.
25. That the syndrome of early infantile autism is capable of explanation in psychological and ethological terms similar to those discussed with reference to undifferentiated cases is shown by Tinbergen, N. and Tinbergen, E. A. (1983). *Autistic children: new hope for a cure.* Allen & Unwin, London.

5 Disorders of adolescence

There are several stage-points in the journey from childhood to adult responsibility: the move from primary school to secondary school at 11 years old, puberty, leaving school, embarking on a job or career, pairing, leaving home and getting married, to be followed by setting up a home and the birth of the first child. Each of these stages, spread over a decade or more, requires a new adaptation. Of particular importance are the stages involving changes in relationships with parents, peers, or potential or actual marriage partners. Breaking away from parents, pairing, marriage, and pregnancy are then the points of crisis.

At the start of the decade the child belongs to a family and relates to his peers and to other adults, amongst them being teachers. A son in an harmonious family enjoys a quiet relationship with his mother and models himself on, i.e. identifies with, his father. A daughter identifies with her mother and enjoys a quiet relationship with her father.

These relationships change gradually. A son's relationships with his parents weaken, and he renounces to a greater or lesser degree the attitudes of his father—his religious and political views, for instance. After a short period of greater warmth, his relationship with his mother weakens, and he transfers his affections from her to a girl-friend of similar age to himself. A daughter's relationships with her parents tend to weaken less, and there is still some truth in the adage: 'A son is a son until he takes a wife. A daughter is a daughter all her life.' Her father's claim on her is symbolically broken in the marriage service, but her relationship with her mother tends to continue after her marriage, so that the mother plays a part as grannie in the life of the new family.

Judging by the break of voice or the growth of pubic hair, the mean age of puberty in boys is about $13\frac{1}{2}$ years; the first seminal emission might be a better criterion, but is less readily ascertained. Judging by the first menstrual period, i.e. the menarche, the mean age in girls is about 13 years. It was over 14 years in the last century. The first seminal emission and the menarche occur relatively late in the changes of puberty and after the peak in the spurt of growth. The first sexual contact with a person of opposite sex is usually made soon after puberty, but the first sexual intercourse may not occur for several years. The mean age of marriage is about 24 years for men and 22 years for women, 1 in 10 grooms being under the age of 21 years, and 1 in 3 brides. By 40 years old, 9 out of 10 men and women have married.

Intellectual development

The use of visual imagery declines a year or two before puberty, and linguistic development makes a big advance, as does the capacity for conceptual thinking and abstract ideas. The teenager then tries to resolve along rational lines, and by theoretical discussion, the sexual, social, and occupational problems arising after puberty. Hence may emerge a devotion to academic study and an interest in psychology, philosophy, and literature especially, the student hoping to find in books an understanding of, and a rational solution for, pressing problems that he is not yet able to resolve more realistically. Creeds and theories serve in this way to relieve anxiety.

All individuals make some use of 'intellectualization' as a defence, but they differ in the degree to which it is a substitute for action. In a few it pervades all spheres of their lives. Intellectual formulations in some cases are coherent, internally consistent, and expressed in conventional terms. They are then communicated readily, and are modified or amended as a result of experience or in response to the reasoning and criticism of others. At the extreme are scientific theories, which are little distorted by personal needs, and which are continually tested against reality. In other cases intellectual formulations lack coherence and consistency, are expressed in a private language, are difficult to communicate, and persist without modification despite the criticism of others. At the extreme are poorly systematized delusions to which the individual holds firmly because they relieve otherwise intolerable anxiety.

There are other ways in which intellectual activity may serve as a defence. Some individuals accumulate knowledge for its own sake, making little distinction between the essential and the inessential and over-emphasizing detail. They tend to hold all kinds of information readily available for recall, but their learning tends to be guided by artificial standards rather than by its practical use. The choice of theory or creed during adolescence is of interest. There is usually a gradual departure from the views held by parents. In some, there is a sudden conversion to different views; in others, there is a return to parental views, i.e. 'capitulation'. Conversions tend to occur at times of crisis in relationships with parents.

Intellectualization tends to break down as a defence in the middle or late teens as the young person becomes more involved in the world outside his home and school. He then seeks experience and understanding through action. Experience leads to dissatisfaction with the world as he finds it and to a desire to reform it. Efforts to change the world, at first diffuse, gradually become more focused as he acquires more specialized knowledge and skills and hence roles. Specialization is an essential feature of healthy development during adolescence.

The establishment of identity

Social training in the family and outside it prepares the young person for the roles he is to play in adult life.[1] He has learned through experience during childhood something of what kind of a person he is. How he gets on with his peers is crucial, especially the part he plays in the gang. Learning is impeded and distorted if he stays out, or is kept out, of the gang. Preoccupation and doubts about his identity are rearoused after puberty and at each of the crises of adolescence, often in a more acute form than before. Identification with the parent of same sex or with another older person may serve for a while, or he may seek to resolve his doubts and uncertainties by emulating a public idol or finding a leader who will prescribe roles for him. He looks for someone or something to have faith in, and may espouse a religious, humanitarian or political cause, especially if this gives him a target for his anger. Or he may become a member of an adolescent 'sub-culture' and imitate the other members of it.

Gradually he develops a conception of himself which is more or less realistic. He discovers how to react to others, and how they react to him. School, apprenticeship, further education, or university give him specialized knowledge and skills, and hence roles to play in work or leisure. He learns too how to deal with social encounters. Sexual identity is of special importance. If relationships with parents have been harmonious, the young person is ready to adopt a consistent masculine or feminine role in relationships with peers. Experience in sexual relationships may confirm or weaken identity, for this is tested by intimacy. The first affair may be crucial; if it goes wrong, it increases doubts and uncertainties and adds to 'identity confusion'.[2]

Gender identity

Children learn very soon after birth to which gender, i.e. class whether male or female, they are assigned. The decision whether a new-born baby is a boy or a girl is taken immediately by parents and others in accordance with the form of the genitalia—penis or labia—and is then confirmed in innumerable ways: e.g. the choice of a name, the colour and style of clothes, the gifts of family and friends, the parents' expectations and interpretations of the baby's behaviour, and what behaviours are encouraged. Also, mothers tend to treat girls as like themselves, boys as different. What children learn during the first 2 or 3 years determines crucially their gender identity, i.e. how they see themselves in relation to the distinctions made between male and female roles in the culture in which they live.[3]

Throughout childhood and adolescence there are strong influences on them from parents, family, peers, school, and community to adopt the social and sexual roles fitting their gender. They tend to identify with, i.e. model themselves on, the parent or other adults of the same gender and to join the peer-group gang of same sex and to accept the gang's models; these are often the pop idols of the time.

There are other questions to be asked retrospectively about individuals. At what age was puberty reached? Was this early or late in relation to peers? In what degree did secondary sexual characteristics confirm their subjective awareness of gender? Was this affected by physical disability or illness? What preferences have they shown in the choice of a sexual partner? What have been the characteristics of the partners to whom they have responded? In what degree have the persons or objects arousing sexual interest had male or female attributes? For what roles in sexual intercourse, and for what coital techniques, have they shown preferences?

There has been much discussion of how far the roles assumed by men and women are determined by biological, and how far by cultural, factors. This distinction is unhelpful, however. Women, by reason of their biological constitution, are the child-bearers, and childbirth and lactation give them experiences shared only partially by men. These facts have a profound influence on the ways men and women see themselves and their expectations. On the other hand, biological factors have little or no direct influence on many of the roles men and women assume in the home and outside it. Because of the greater reliability of contraceptive methods and other things, women bear fewer children than they used to, and child-bearing and the care of children occupy fewer years. They are more free, therefore, to assume other roles. What roles they assume is determined in a complex way by the expectations others have of them and they have of themselves.

Discordant patterns

There are many departures from such simple expectations as that a child assigned at birth to the male or female gender should develop a corresponding gender identity and after puberty corresponding sexual attitudes and behaviours, with a preference for sexual intercourse with a person of the other gender. Studies of various types of discordant behaviour show how complex the processes are.[4]

Hermaphrodites

The importance of social learning in determining gender identity and patterns of sexual behaviour have been confirmed by following up children born with malformed genitalia having both male and female features. Most of the foetuses so affected are chromosomally female, but have been masculinized as a result in some cases of an ovarian or adrenal tumour, in other cases androgens or other hormones, e.g. progestin, taken in from outside during the pregnancy. Children reared as male or female as a result of decisions at birth develop, as a general rule, a corresponding gender identity, interests, and behaviour.

There is no evidence to suggest that any of the discordant patterns of sexual behaviour observed in adolescence or adult life are determined by the genetic constitution. The chromosomes of 'homosexuals', i.e. those showing a sexual interest in, or a preference for sexual intercourse with, a person of the same sex, are almost always concordant with the gender to which they have been assigned because of the form of their genitalia. However, bodily features, determined in part by the genetic constitution, play some part in determining how persons see themselves and their peers see them, but this is only one of the many factors affecting gender identity or patterns of behaviour. The physical constitution and secondary sexual characteristics of male and female homosexuals vary as widely as do those of heterosexuals. The effeminacy or butch features of the few lies mainly in the way in which they comport themselves, and little if at all in their physical constitution. Whether there are any hormonal factors is uncertain. There is little to suggest it, although it has been reported that girls affected by an excess of androgens during intra-uterine life tend to become 'tomboys' in early adolescence.

The reasons for discordant patterns are to be found in what has happened to a child from early childhood onwards. Children are subjected to many influences. A mother may encourage her child to develop interests regarded in the culture as more fitting to the other gender. Circumstances may decide that a boy plays mainly with girls and acquires their interests, or a girl mainly with boys. In the teen years a girl may join as a 'tomboy' a gang of boys, or less often a boy a gang of girls. Lacking a relationship with, or having an antipathy for, the parent of same sex, a young person may prefer the parent of opposite sex as a model. Preferences are influenced too by especially the first experience of sexual intercourse. What forms of experience are of importance may be discovered by studying such discordant patterns as transvestism, transsexual-ism, and homosexuality. The heterogeneity of the persons showing these patterns and the diversity of the behaviours so labelled should be kept in mind.

Transvestism

'Transvestists' or 'cross-dressers' wear occasionally or habitually the clothes of the other gender. They are not satisfied with 'unisex' clothing. The habit of cross-dressing may begin in early childhood, usually before 5 years old, and becomes more frequent in early adolescence. It tends to be given up at the end of the teen years, but may continue into middle age. In some cases cross-dressing reflects an abhorrence for the behaviour patterns of the same gender, but usually no more than a liking for some aspects of the behaviour of the other gender. Cross-dressers do not deny the gender to which they have been assigned or their anatomical gender. Cross-dressing may begin as a means of solace at times when a boy, for instance, feels deprived of maternal affection. Or he may put on women's clothes, commonly borrowed secretly from his mother or sister, in support of fantasies during masturbation of sexual contact with or conquest of a woman. This last, which is relatively uncommon, occurs especially when the boy has a close, identifying relationship with his mother; in a few of these cases he becomes homosexual in his orientation. Adults who cross-dress are more often male than female. The cross-dressing is often in private and becomes associated with sexual gratification. Most are exclusively heterosexual, and many are married and have children. Wives tend to tolerate the cross-dressing when they know about it, but to be unwilling to enquire into its significance. However, there are some male cross-dressers who are homosexual, and who wear female clothes as a means of attracting a sexual partner.

Transsexualism

A few transvestists, much more often male than female, believe that they have been wrongly assigned, despite the form of their genitalia, and seek surgery in order to put right what they feel has gone wrong and to be restored to what they feel to be their rightful gender. These feelings have nearly always begun in early adolescence or earlier although treatment may not be sought until the late teens or early twenties. In some cases transsexualists have shown from earlier childhood inclinations to belong to the other gender, and have modelled themselves on persons of the other gender. Transsexualist males usually accept that surgery if it is to be undertaken means reconstruction of the external genitalia. Their fantasies tend to be of sexual approaches by men while they play a female role in intercourse. Some actively seek male sexual partners. Most transsexualists show severe confusion in their identities and severe impairment in their relationships with others; in forming relationships they have been handicapped by the contradictions in their gender indentities. In many cases they have suffered severe deprivation during childhood, with a lack of any lasting relationships.

Homosexuality

Any general statement about the childhood experience of homosexuals, as of transvestists and transsexualists, should be read with caution because the samples from which it is derived are likely to be biased. The biases are obvious when samples of homosexuals are made up either of patients attending psychiatric clinics or of those who have 'come out' and announced their homosexuality, the former seeking help because they feel confined in unsatisfactory social or sexual roles, and the latter feeling that they have broken free from any fixed role and are making progress in redefining their identities.

Evidence about the relationships homosexuals have had with their parents is incomplete and inconclusive. The typical pattern in males has been said to be a combination of a close attachment to a domineering or over-protective mother, which is a source of guilt and anxiety in heterosexual relationships, and of antipathy to the father, which has handicapped the young person in developing masculine attitudes and interests. It seems likely, however, that of the greater importance is the relationship with the father, who because of his absence, ineffectiveness or cruelty has served as a poor model for his son, the closeness or quality of the attachment to the mother being of lesser importance. Whatever may have been the pattern of the relationships with parents, homosexuality is rarely the only result. Homosexuals may show other tendencies as well. In some cases the discipline in the home has been strict, and they are then notably conscientious, with a tendency to intellectualize and keep firm control over aggressive and other feelings. They may be ill at ease in their social dealings, but efficient and successful in their occupations or professions. Homosexuals of this kind are sometimes described as 'organized'; others are 'conflicted' and are predisposed to mental illness in adolescence and adult life.

In their choice of career male homosexuals have been said to shun the rougher occupations and to prefer work in the professions, offices, and personal services, but there is no clear evidence of a raised proportion of homosexuals in these occupations. On the other hand, some try to disguise or compensate for their homosexual tendencies by cultivating an excessive masculinity in the manner in which they present themselves.

That a special relationship with the mother has some importance is suggested by the finding in a sample of patients of an excess of last-born and a lack of those in the middle positions in birth order among those male homosexuals who come from large families. A curious finding is that male homosexuals tend to have more brothers than sisters. The mean parental age has been found to be raised.[5]

Other disorders in adolescence

Erectile impotence and frigidity

Normally the anxiety attached to sexual functions as a result of social learning during childhood is dissipated during courtship, the process being akin to 'desensitization' in the sense in which this term has been used by behaviour therapists. If the anxiety is not dissipated, there may be erectile impotence or frigidity at the start of a sexual partnership. These disorders reflect not only attitudes towards sexual activity but also difficulties in establishing a relationship involving more than a sexual partnership. The initiation of a sexual partnership is a crisis of 'intimacy' in which the identity of each partner is challenged. Defences are dropped, and secrets are revealed. A person unsure of himself and unable to maintain a clear sense of his own identity finds it difficult to accept the mutuality a partnership entails and feels threatened by it. The sources of the difficulties may lie in conflicts and confusions about the roles each should adopt or in persisting conflicts in relationships with parents.[6]

Sexual promiscuity in adolescent girls

Sexual desire of more than average strength is not a factor. On the contrary, promiscuous intercourse, often described as unpleasant or even repulsive, is not motivated by the desire for sexual satisfaction, but is an attempt to meet a variety of other problems. Part of the motivation may lie in the search for a sense of identity and self-worth although the result may be further confusion in identity and self-doubt. Certain factors recur in these girls' histories, such as conflicts at home, broken homes, lack of participation in organized group activities, even extrusion from peer groups, poor living conditions, and friendlessness and loneliness. In many cases the father has been absent from the home. When he lives at home, he shows no affection for, or interest in, his daughter, and may openly display his rejection of her. In many cases too, the mother has been unfaithful to her husband. Sexual activity in these cases, likewise the courting of a pregnancy, appears to be an attempt to compensate for feelings of being rejected by the father or for failure in other spheres of activity, especially in relationships. As a consequence of her promiscuity, the girl's relationships with her parents, sibs, and peers tend to deteriorate, and the promiscuous tendencies then increase.

Incest

A history of sexual intercourse with a member of the family covered by the prohibition is occasionally met with in psychiatric practice. The commonest of the incestuous partnerships is that of father and daughter, especially when the daughter is a step-child. That of brother and sister is nearly as common. That of mother and son is uncommon and occurs only when both partners are seriously disturbed already. In father/daughter cases there are usually grounds for supposing that there has been collusion on the part of the mother, tacitly even if not openly.[7]

Incestuous feelings and fantasies are part of a person's experience in the early teen years when the relationship with the parent of opposite sex is normally coloured by sexual interest. Common observation testifies to the truth of this assertion. Psychoanalytical theory supposes that every child has incestuous wishes, which are revealed in the Oedipus complex and in other ways. After puberty sexual interest is transferred from the parent to a person outside the family. This transfer may be distorted, delayed or prevented when a child has had experience of incestuous intercourse, with the result that there is fixation on, or failure to emancipate from, the parent or sibling and inability to sustain a sexual relationship with someone outside the family, this being reflected in, amongst other things, promiscuity and frigidity or impotence.

How regularly incestuous intercourse is damaging in these respects is uncertain since evidence from patients seen in psychotherapy being unrepresentative is an unsound basis for conclusions. However, it is generally accepted that parent/child intercourse is seriously damaging, brother/sister intercourse less so. But parent/child intercourse does not occur unless relationships in the family are already disturbed, which itself affects the young person's capacity to form relationships.

Anorexia nervosa

The most prominent component of the syndrome is a more or less selective refusal of food, which results in a serious loss of weight. The patient, typically a girl in her teen years, shows the pursuit of thinness and may go to extreme lengths to avoid putting on weight. The struggle to keep control over her body in this respect may be at the heart of the girl's feeling about herself. As a part of this control she regularly misuses laxatives, even cathartics, and may induce vomiting. She takes vigorous exercise in order to reduce weight. Yet she remains interested in food, and may show a particular keenness to cook or serve food for others. She may at times eat voraciously and then vomit. Amenorrhoea is an early symptom. Although starting in some cases before much weight has been lost, it is probably related to the weight loss at least partially. A high level of anxiety may be a factor too.

The refusal of food may be regarded as an instrumental avoidance response, the food being a danger signal. If she does eat, she feels uncomfortable. However, it is far from clear what the danger is that is being avoided. The habit usually begins soon after puberty, and may be a reaction to the crisis of puberty and the development of secondary sexual characteristics by a girl unprepared to assume the social and sexual roles of adult life and confused in her gender identity. The patient tends to show faulty appreciation of reality, especially with regard to her own body-image, impoverishment of emotional response and childishness, and also a denial of sexuality and a lack of interest in boys. The relationships in the families of patients tend to be strained, a common pattern being an uneasy relationship between the girl and her mother, who is domineering and insecure, and who sometimes feels threatened by the girl's close relationship with her father. A relatively high proportion of the fathers are in Social Class I and are upward mobile.

The accounts the girls give suggest that the refusal to eat is the strategy they have adopted in the struggle to achieve or preserve a degree of independence and integrity; to eat is to capitulate. They face pressures to reach the goals decreed by parents, school, and community while they are trying to discover for themselves how to live and especially how to relate to others. The struggle they feel they are engaged in is made more difficult by the mystifying contradictions in what they feel is expected of them as growing women: this is to be at the same time successful and conforming.[8]

School refusal

A distinction is made between school refusal and truancy. The school refuser stays at home with the knowledge of his mother or is kept at home, and displays intense anxiety when pressed to go to school, or complains of such symptoms as abdominal pain or headache. The truant leaves home, but does not go to school or, if he goes, does not stay. Usually he deceives his parents. Truancy is more often associated with offending, e.g. stealing, than is school refusal. The term 'school phobia' has been applied to both, although more often to school refusal. But this is related as much to leaving home and separating from a parent as arriving at school.

School refusal occurs at any age, but becomes much more frequent in the first and second year in the secondary school, i.e. amongst 11- and 12-year-olds. Boys and girls occur in equal numbers in series of cases. It is relatively common in 'only' children, and children born some years after their sibs. Separation from the mother tends to arouse anxiety at any age, and there may be difficulties on this account in getting the child to start at school. They recur when a relationship with the mother comes under strain or when the child's anxiety level rises for any other reason. The peak at 11 and 12 years old reflects in part the difficulties of settling into the more socially demanding conditions of the secondary school and in part the intensification of conflicts in the relationship with the mother at the approach of puberty. The mothers tend to be indulgent, vacillating, over-anxious and over-protective, and to communicate their own anxieties to their children. They may collude with the child because of their own need for support. The fathers tend to be weak, ineffective, and submissive. In some cases there is a crisis in the relationships in the family, due, for instance, to a deterioration in the relationship between the mother and father or psychiatric illness in the mother, in other cases, the father has recently left the home.

Addictions: smoking

The habit of smoking becomes established during adolescence. Thus 80 per cent of the men and 40 per cent of the women who are regular smokers became so before they were 20 years old. A non-smoker at 20 is unlikely to take up smoking later. On the other hand, few who have smoked more than two or three cigareetes before 20 do not become regular smokers. Many begin to smoke regularly when they leave school.

Alcohol

Most of those who in their later years misuse alcohol have begun to drink to excess in the middle or late teens. Their relationships with their peers tended to be shallow, and they experienced difficulty in forming and sustaining a heterosexual relationship. Men tended to present themselves as masculine although they entertained doubts about their sexual orientation, and to prefer the company of men. A disproportionate number lost a parent before they were 16 years old. A history of misuse of alcohol is relatively common in the families of drinkers, as is teetotalism. Drinking during adolescence serves as a means of relieving anxiety and suppressing uncomfortable memories.

The misuse of alcohol is far more common among adolescents than is the misuse of drugs, and the number misusing alcohol has been increasing steadily. The consumption of alcohol per head of population doubled between 1950 and 1980, a relatively large part of the increase being due to the increase in consumption by the young. Between one-third and one-half of 16-year-olds describe themselves as regular drinkers. Drinking is now an occasional cause of absence from school.

Heroin

The few heroin addicts before the nineteen-sixties were mostly middle-aged and had access to heroin and other drugs because of their professions. There was an epidemic increase in the number of young people addicted to heroin in the middle sixties, and a further sharp increase in the early eighties. It is not possible to say how far the increases have been due to the drugs greater availability outside the law, and how far to social conditions affecting the young, such as unemployment. Most heroin addicts have begun to misuse drugs in their middle teens. More are male than female. Most have started on heroin before they are 21. They used other drugs before turning to heroin, and continue to use other drugs indiscriminately. Few have been of stable personality. Most have resorted to heroin as a way of dealing with severe problems in their lives, and have shown depressive symptoms before they became addicted. A history of suicidal attempts is relatively common. Nearly half have suffered separation from one or both parents for a year or more before the age of 16 years. Others have come from homes in which there has been serious disharmony, and which have provided inadequate care. Many have been convicted of offences other than those involving drugs, and most have resorted to stealing in order to get money to purchase drugs. A minority have been regularly employed. About half have on-going heterosexual partnerships. Most live in a drug sub-culture and have few or no friends outside it.

Misuse of drugs

Many drugs have been misused by young people in recent years, notably cannabis, amphetamine and related compounds, barbiturates by themselves or in combination with other drugs, and hallucinogens, e.g. LSD. The work record of those misusing drugs has usually been poor. Many have been convicted of offences. Of the young persons taken into care by the local authority, about one in ten has been misusing drugs regularly; about one in four has been drinking regularly. Misuse of drugs has usually begun during the school years, and early experience of drugs has nearly always been in groups, e.g. at weekend parties. The drugs are valued because they are thought to relieve tension, give pleasurable bodily sensations, and make people more perceptive. Users of cannabis do not have any difficulty as a general rule in going without; nor do users of amphetamine, of whom only a few become dependent. Many experiment with drugs, and then stop using them. There are fashions, which rise and fall, in the chemicals chosen for their intoxicating effects when swallowed or sniffed; some have dangerous effects.

Young offenders

Young offenders are heterogeneous, but some general statements can be made about them. More boys than girls are convicted in the courts, the sex ratio being of the order of 5:1. The commonest of the boys' offences are various forms of stealing and breaking and entering. Sexual offences are the commonest for girls. Rates of conviction vary greatly from one school to another, one neighbourhood to another, and one district to another. A large proportion of offenders, when classified on the basis of their father's occupation, are in Social Classes IV or V. A large proportion come from large families. A relative lack of only, first-born, and last-born children, and an excess in middle positions, has been reported in several investigations, but the findings vary from sample to sample. The proportion of adopted children is relatively high, as is the proportion of illegitimate children.

A relatively high proportion of young offenders come from homes of abnormal composition and have suffered the loss of one or both parents because either the parents have not lived together or have divorced or one parent has died. Homes 'broken' by separation or divorce are more strongly associated with offending by the children than homes broken by the death of a parent. Loss of the father whether by death or desertion has been found to be twice as common among offending boys as loss of the mother. The loss has often been suffered during the pre-school years. When he has been present in the home, the father has tended to be indifferent or rejecting in his attitude towards the child. There has been lack of cohesion or open conflict between members of the family, and the children have also lacked support from kin and neighbours, who have tended to be hostile to the families. The offenders have had weak identifications with adults of the same sex, and have lacked supervision by their parents.

Personality disorders

Young offenders can readily be defined, with or without qualification, as those convicted in the juvenile courts. Less readily defined are 'personality disorders', which are put with 'other non-psychotic mental conditions' in the International Classification of Disease—'ICD-9', and with 'specific developmental disorders' in the American Psychiatric Association's classification 'DSM-111'. Personality disorders include 'psychopathic disorder', defined by the Mental Health Act 1983 as 'a persistent disorder or disability of mind . . . which results in abnormally aggressive or seriously irresponsible conduct on the part of the person concerned', as well as what used to be called 'psychopathic personality'.

The term 'personality disorder' is applied to those appearing to be incapable of conforming to society's code of behaviour and to be resistant to social training (the 'anti-social') and the quarrelsome, inadequate, eccentric, and excitable. The patterns of behaviour they show are regarded as maladaptive and as having become established by adolescence or earlier. A minority of young offenders suffer from a personality disorder in this sense. The term is sometimes used loosely to refer to mental disabilities resulting from brain damage, whether due to trauma or other cause or reflecting incomplete recovery from a psychotic illness. Efforts to find in dysfunction of the brain a cause in other cases of personality disorder have not produced convincing evidence.

Although they may be emotionally labile, quarrelsome or prone to violent tempers, those with personality disorders do not show sustained anxiety to any degree and are usually described as cold emotionally and callous; they may be vain or sensitive in a few respects. They show little guilt or shame, and tend to be impulsive and erratic, their behaviour being directed towards immediate gratification and being undeterred by the later consequences. Especially they are impaired in their capacity to form lasting or close relationships with others.

This may be regarded as the key feature in a varied group of disorders. Many have experienced separation from the mother in early childhood. Denied a warm, loving relationship with a parent, a child fails to identify with either parent and fails to learn, through his early relationships, appropriate attitudes and restraints. The failure of training arises out of shallow, neutral or interrupted relationships in childhood. In some cases the child becomes opposed to his parents and refractory as a result of a harsh discipline at home. The personality disorder may not be detected until several years after the psychological damage has been done—until he goes to school, for instance, where he is expected to conform to conventions, rules, and laws. Even then, although it may bring him into trouble at school frequently, the personality disorder does not have serious consequences until the late teens or early twenties when society demands more of him.

Many types of personality disorder have been described, to which various overlapping terms have been applied. The types in the list below illustrate the tendencies commonly referred to when a personality disorder is being described:

'sociopathic' or anti-social tendencies, characterized by behaviour deviating from social norms, with a disregard for social obligations;

'explosive' tendencies, by intemperance or lack of control over behaviour, with proneness to outbursts of anger or violence;

'obsessional' tendencies, by over-conscientiousness, pedantry or rigidity in behaviour in some respects, with anxiety to maintain order and control, and at the same time deep insecurity and excessive doubting and indecisiveness, with proneness to impulses, unwelcome and not acted out;

'paranoid' tendencies, by undue sensitiveness to slights or rebuffs, jealousy and suspicion of others, who are perceived as rejecting or hostile;

'hysterical' tendencies, by craving for the attention of others, dependence on them, and the histrionic display of feelings;

'introverted' tendencies, by avoidance of or withdrawal from close relationships and the disguise of feeling;

'cyclic' tendencies, by swings in mood from indolence and depression, with a fearful or gloomy pessimism, to zestful and energetic activity, elation and optimism.

SCHIZOPHRENIA

One source of knowledge about what factors are important in the disorders occurring during adolescence lies in studies made of the most severe and intractable disorders, many of which attract a diagnosis of schizophrenia. International discussions have reached broad agreement that the diagnosis of schizophrenia should depend on the presence of certain carefully defined symptoms—especially those identified by Schneider as of 'first rank'— ascertained in the course of interviewing and rating in an agreed way: the 'Present State Examination' (PSE).[9] The diagnosis depends on the description of the phenomena of the illness without reference to any theory. It is now fairly reliable in that when two or more psychiatrists undertake the PSE in samples of psychiatric patients, they tend to agree on which patients suffer from schizophrenia, and which suffer from other forms of illness. The importance given to the definition of schizophrenia arises from the assumption that it is a distinct form of disease corresponding to a specific abnormality of biological function, due perhaps to one or more pathogenic genes. However, at present the diagnosis is governed by convention, and the term 'schizophrenia' is used here as no more than a convenient rubric under to which to discuss illnesses showing certain kinds of symptoms.

Symptoms characteristic of schizophrenia

The first rank symptoms include 'primary' delusions, i.e. delusions arising as sudden intuitions, auditory hallucinations, thought echo, thought insertion, thought withdrawal, thought broadcasting, and the delusion of being under alien control.[10] There are usually also disorders of thinking and language such as incoherence, irrelevance, looseness of associations, and incongruity of verbal and non-verbal messages; and disorders in patients' feelings about themselves and reality or 'depersonalization'; and especially splitting of the self into disconnected functions such as inner and outer selves. These symptoms, which form a syndrome, typically start during adolescence and progress to serious disability and alienation in social relationships, typically in the twenties and thirties.

Certain symptoms have been found to indicate a poor prognosis: emotional flatness or blunting, insidious onset, without any precipitating event, lack of initiative, 'break-up' in the development of the personality, depersonalization, and poor psychosexual development, such as being unmarried. Follow-ups have shown that the relapse rate is high when patients discharged from hospital return to homes of high emotional response ('expressed emotion' or 'EE') as revealed in the emotion, hostility, or critical attitudes expressed at interview by the family.[11] This is so whether patients return to parents, spouse or other kin. The relapse rate is relatively low among those who return to emotionally neutral homes—of low EE.

Distortions in social development

Schizophrenic patients as a class have failed to surmount the developmental tasks normally undertaken in the teens or early twenties. Only a few of those who so fail become ill with schizophrenia, which is at the end of a chain of distortions in development. Physical or mental handicap or severe material or emotional deprivation may make it difficult for a young person to achieve independence from his parents or kin and to create an adult pattern of relationships. The lack of a job and little money restrict opportunities. Those who become ill with schizophrenia have failed for other reasons and have dealt with the resulting conflicts in a special way.

Non-integration with peer groups

Schizophrenic patients, when retrospectively investigated, appear to have remained aloof from their peers at school and in their neighbourhoods and not to have got on friendly terms with them. In some cases this has been both a cause and an effect of irregular attendance at school or school refusal. Teenagers who are the second generation of immigrants meet particular difficulties because they have to reconcile the cultural differences between their parents and their peers. For one reason or another the patients have largely missed out on the social learning that membership of a peer group or gang provides and have not acquired the social skills, forms and languages of communication, or knowledge about people that would have prepared them for their adult roles. Also they have failed to learn about—get wise to—themselves. The conception each patient has formed of himself has not been sufficiently tested and modified by continuing experience in relationships with peers.

Social drift

Schizophrenic patients have undergone a gradual deterioration in their performance at school and at work, starting usually in the middle or late teens. Academic promise has not been fulfilled, and they have not established themselves in jobs or careers in keeping with the earlier expectations of them. This 'social drift' tends to be progressive. The social class distribution of the fathers of patients as judged from their occupations, whether at the time of their birth or of their admission to hospital, is similar to that of the general population, as is the proportion of patients who had entered grammar school at 11 years old as a result of success in the examinations used in the 1950s and 1960s to select pupils. At the time of their admission to hospital, perhaps 10 years or more later, an undue proportion were in occupations which put them into Social Classes IV or V. There is thus evidence of a downward drift after puberty.[12]

In a disproportionate number of cases intelligence-test scores are found to be below average, often much lower than would be predicted from the school record or achievements before the illness began. The scores are not to be relied upon as indications of previous capacity, but they may say something about the present level of functioning. Some sub-tests, e.g. 'vocabulary' and 'information', may give evidence of a greater capacity previously.

An undue proportion of schizophrenic patients are admitted from the central and less desirable areas of cities. This effect appears to be due to a minority who are single, separated or divorced, and living alone. The residences of the majority, who have been living in a family setting, are distributed evenly over all areas. The minority living alone had previously been living elsewhere and had moved into the central areas before admission, perhaps because of their social inadequacy or their wish to isolate themselves.

Attachments outside the family

A consistent finding in the literature on schizophrenia is the small proportion of patients who have married. Perhaps four out of five male patients and two out of three female are single at the age of 30 years, by which age four out of five in the general population are married. The partners of those who have married tend to be different in age, religion, education or social class. An undue proportion of those who have married have become separated or divorced. Obviously there are several reasons for patients not marrying after they have become overtly ill. 'To the patient', it has been said, 'the imaginary mistress is more than a real one. For this reason normal intercourse is sought so little.' Even before they become ill, they have made few or no close attachments outside the family. A few have been promiscuous. A few have found atypical sexual partners. Most have stayed out of any sexual relationship and have been without friends. The first affair, if there has been one, has quickly come to an unhappy end and has added to the patient's identity confusion.

Family settings[13]

The causes of the failure to surmount the developmental tasks have been looked for in the family settings in which patients have been living, and the question has been put: in what degree are these families sociologically irregular? Even if the families are irregular, it can be countered, this might be an effect produced by the deficiencies in the personalities of the patients. However, both causes and effects are taken into account if the patterns of interaction in the families of patients are studied.

Some of the irregularities exist before the deficiencies in personalities. Certainly, there is a raised incidence of schizophrenia among the first-degree relatives. Twice as many mothers as fathers were found in the classic studies to have suffered from schizophrenia (or 'dementia precox'). Some of the relatives without schizophrenia are eccentric or suffer from more or less severe disorders of personality. There is fair agreement in the literature that more parents of schizophrenics are psychiatrically disturbed than parents of normal children, and more of the mothers are 'schizoid' in that they show some of the tendencies characteristic of schizophrenia. Whatever value these findings may have as evidence in favour of a genetic theory, they belong also to a description of the family settings.

The strength of the familial tendency in schizophrenia has been overestimated. In the early investigations, as many as 14 per cent of the sibs and 9 per cent of the parents of patients were reported to suffer from schizophrenia. However, the samples were biased, being drawn from hospital populations, and there were other deficiencies in method. Moreover, the concept of schizophrenia was very wide. If schizophrenia is restrictively defined, the proportion of parents and sibs with the diagnosis is small, too small to give much support to the hypothesis of a pathogenic gene, and too small to be given much weight in a description of the family settings. The eccentricity and strange attitudes of family members are of greater weight.

Evidence of a birth-order effect is inconclusive. An effect has been found in some, but by no means all samples. Disagreements in what has been found to be the most vulnerable position are not readily explained by reference to cultural factors. A relatively high degree of heterogamy has been found in the parents of patients. The loss during childhood of a parent whether by death, divorce or desertion has been reported to be unduly common, but a now extensive literature does not warrant a firm conclusion. That the age of both the mother and father are relatively high at the birth of the patient is generally agreed although not what the implications of these findings are. There is a relative lack of mothers under 25 years old and an excess of mothers over 30. An unexplained finding is a seasonal pattern of births, with an excess of births in the early or winter months of the year.[14]

Emancipation from parents

Schizophrenic patients have not emancipated themselves from their parents in the middle teens to become 'reasonably autonomous adults', it has been reported, and in particular have remained close to the parent of opposite sex, in whom they have shown some sexual interest. This relationship, which has often been a key feature of the family, has been ambivalent, changeable, and destructive in its effects. A son singled out for his mother's particular attention, perhaps because of his personality or for other reasons, and overprotected by her is handicapped in achieving independence outside the family; the over-protection may be both the cause and the effect of his continuing dependence. Engulfing and indulging him she creates a distance between him and his father who tends then to be excluded from the life of the family.

When disqualified in this way the father is passive and ineffectual and a poor model therefore for the son, and fails to fulfill his paternal role in this and other respects.

There is thus 'skew' in the relationships in the family, one relationship, e.g. that of son and mother, predominating while that of son and father is weak. With skew there tends to be associated some blurring of the 'generation lines', i.e. of the distinctions in roles between parental and child generations. The lines are also blurred when the normal age differences are departed from, as happens, for instance, when the mother has step-children of a similar age to herself, or a child has nephews and nieces of his own age, or the father is a generation older than the mother. Blurring of the generations contributes to the patient's confusion about his roles in the family.[15]

Interaction between the parents

Often a striking point about the family of a patient with schizophrenia is that the mother and father have never been normally attached to one another. The nuclear family has not been formed normally because one or both parents has remained attached to one of their parents or sibs. The heterogamy of the parents, which reflects their choice of a partner, may be the indirect result of conflicts in the family. In some cases there has been open rivalry between the parents for the affection of the patient when a child, or between the patient and one parent for the affection of the other. In some cases there has been open discord about other matters, and in other cases the relationship between the parents has been a quiet one, lacking real interest and lacking reciprocity and complementarity in roles. The marriages have shown 'schism', and the coalition between the parents in bringing up the child has been defective. In nearly every case the parents' sexual life together has been unsatisfactory from the beginning of the marriage, and has deteriorated in the years before the onset of the illness. Estrangement in this sense cannot be regarded as the result of the illness, as has sometimes been suggested. The high rates for separation and divorce, on the other hand, might be attributable in part to the illness.

Patterns of communication

The literature gives some support to the claim that communication in the families of schizophrenic patients tends to be blurred, poorly understood, inconsistent, wandering, disruptive, and illogical. The parents have adopted styles of communication that impair the child's capacity to communicate with others outside the family. One of the themes of recent research lies in studies of the responses made by patients and their parents to the Rorschach ink-blots in order to discover what goes wrong between them. Parents and patients show similar disorders. They do not share a focus of attention. They fail to convey a sense of closure. The meanings of their responses are left tentative, indefinite, incomplete, inconsistent or contradictory.[16] These disorders are similar in many respects to the lack of integration, preoccupation with small detail, and hypotheses of poor quality that have been shown to affect the responses made in tests of visual perception.

'Double binding'

One of the earliest and most often quoted descriptions of patterns of communication in the families of schizophrenic patients refers to the disorganization of the patient's behaviour produced by the double-bind quality of the messages they receive from their parents or other members of their families. Double-bind messages offer alternatives both of which are liable to be met with disapproval, have unpleasant connotations, or present unresolvable paradoxes. Two conditions are necessary for the double bind to produce disorganization. There must be an obligation to respond, and comment on the messages must be forbidden. Repeated experience of double binds teaches patients to make responses that are ambiguous or paradoxical and disguise true feelings.

The essential disabilities

Unconventional communication habits

Unconventional communication habits have been said to be the cardinal symptoms of schizophrenia. They are in a sense appropriate to, or even necessary in, the *Alice in Wonderland* world created for patients by their parents although they handicap them in social relationships outside the family. In this world family myths are maintained that give false pictures and mask or deny realities. Defences tend to be 'transpersonal'. By insisting on the denial of sexual interests, for instance, parents regulate the young person's inner life in order to reduce their own anxieties. The untrustworthiness of the cryptic and idiosyncratic messages in the family creates 'mystification'. Patients do not acquire habits of assessing through reality testing the objectivity of what they perceive. The unreliability of their distinctions between fantasy and fact originates in the inconsistency with which their parents validate their experiences as real. They learn to avoid issues giving rise to anxiety in themselves or their parents by evasive or irrelevant responses or by blocking. The incongruity of their verbal and non-verbal messages serves to confuse the issues.

Confusion over social roles

As they emancipate themselves teenagers normally become reticent with their parents about their doings outside the home and opt out of their parents' conflicts with one another. This separation between the generations frees teenagers to work out their relationships with peers and to form special attachments. In the histories of schizophrenic patients failure to separate is revealed in the parents' undue interest in the patient's developing sexuality, undue frankness about their own marital difficulties and the blurring of distinctions in roles. Patients are pulled by one or other parent into playing adult roles in the family, but these roles are left ill-defined. The roles played by the parents tend to be changeable and ambiguous and to show some reversal of the normal gender roles. Also, family members collude in creating the illusion of perceiving and meeting each other's needs while true reciprocity and mutuality are lacking; this has been called 'pseudomutuality'.[17]

In normal families parents form a coalition but tolerate initiatives by the children. In the families of schizophrenic patients, social interaction is dominated by one parent, more often by the mother. The domination is subtle—sufficient to deny the child outlets for aggressive impulses, but not provoking open rebellion. The resulting confusion together with a general lack of confidence engendered by the parents, who tend to regard the world as threatening, and with a lack of social skills makes it difficult for them to establish roles outside the home. Not being able to resolve social, sexual, and occupational problems in practical ways, the young person turns to theoretical studies in for instance psychology or philosophy in the search for understanding.

Patients' conceptions of themselves

The conditions in their families have not been conducive to the formation of a sense of identity. The failure of the parents to provide models for identification, the confusion of the roles in the family, and the lack of successful experience in relationships outside the family all contribute to confusion of identity. This is further confused by failure to disidentify with the parents during adolescence. Gender identity especially tends to be confused. This is shown in uncertainties about sexual orientation which after the illness has begun are often expressed in delusional ideas. The patient may express doubt whether the gender to which he has been assigned is correct; he is less certain of its incorrectness than is the transsexual.

In order to compensate for weakness of identity and feelings of inferiority and unworthiness, patients tend to develop unrealistic conceptions of themselves. These are supported by fantasies of goodness, cleverness, and power, and are later to be expressed as grandiose delusions. They may be revealed in boasting, and their peers then regard them as conceited and strange. They live more and more in a pseudo-community in which they are as their fantasies dictate, and their thoughts are increasingly expressed in a private or autistic language with an excessive use of metaphors which are not labelled as such. Paranoid ideas serve to rationalize their sense of being unfairly treated and the discrepancies between fantasy and reality.

Various stratagems preserve a distorted conception of self. A person may continue to suppose that he is uniquely gifted if he evades every situation in which this conception is put to the test. In this way he loses any opportunity for real achievement, and goes on denying the reality. The gap between potentiality and achievement tends to widen. He may try to make the world more receptive to him by becoming a reformer, fanatic or criminal or through wish-fulfilling fantasies. Achieving little or nothing, he may suppose that circumstances have been unfavourable to him, with delusions that others have been hostile to him. Grandiose and paranoid delusions serve to preserve his conception of himself.

Schizoid defences

Uncertainty about what and who he is makes a person feel unreal and precariously differentiated from the rest of the world; this is one aspect of depersonalization. Patients shun relationships in order to preserve their fantasy conceptions and autonomy. Otherwise they feel they would be engulfed. An extreme manifestation of the struggle to preserve identity in this way is the muteness and immobility of the catatonic state. However, the most characteristic of the schizoid defences is 'splitting'. Under threat from outside a person preserves a sense of identity by splitting his inner, first or real self from his outer, second or false self. The outer self observable by others is felt to be only precariously under the control of the inner self. Splitting like this is self-defeating. Avoiding experience because it appears threatening, the inner self feels increasingly empty. The inner self can only be real in relation to real people or as it has been put: 'The sense of identity requires the existence of another by whom one is known.'

The overt illness

Schizoid defences are fragile, and breakdown may be triggered off by a small change in circumstances to which the patient is unable to adapt by reason of the weakness of his identity. An example is the 'crisis of intimacy' when the patient is pressed into a close relationship with either a parent or sexual partner. Intimacy is tolerable when there is firm self-delineation. Sexual intercourse is especially threatening because the sense of fusion with the partner is felt as identity loss. An extreme example is the honeymoon psychosis described by Bleuler.[18]

Defences break down in other circumstances.[19] The relationships between the parents and the patient tend to be passing through a critical phase, and the conflicts may then be revealed in a clear form. The mother's ambivalence towards the patient, her confusion about the roles she should play in his life, and the discords between the parents are exposed. One or other parent may become ill too. Each reacts to the patient's illness with guilt and anxiety, and may make efforts to restore the relationship with him, or take energetic steps to have him removed from the home.

The circumstances in which the acute illness begins appear to fall into three groups: (i) events making the parent of opposite sex and the patient more dependent on one another, e.g. when the other parent becomes ill, leaves the home or dies, or another person on whom the parent has been dependent, such as grandparent, uncle or aunt or sibling, goes away or dies; (ii) the appearance of a rival, e.g. when the parent takes a lover or remarries, the other parent returns to the home after a period of absence, the parents are reconciled after a period of discord, or another child is born; and (iii) other events which revive conflicts, e.g. the death of a sib, engagement or marriage of the patient, the patient's pregnancy or his wife's pregnancy, or a parent's illness or death.

In the face of events such as these there are various paths open to the patient which offer some prospect of relief from intense anxiety. He may take flight and leave home; the flight may take the form of a fugue in which he loses any awareness of his identity. He may attempt suicide or more rarely homicide, perhaps parricide; suicide is sometimes an attempt to destroy unacceptable aspects of the self. He may stay at home and deal with the new realities in a psychotic way, e.g. through denial and dissociation with cessation of reality testing and compensatory fantasies. There may be a terrifying loss of identity as well as uncertainty about the boundaries between self and non-self, and 'first-rank' symptoms may appear: his private and inner thoughts are being read by bugging, his autonomy is being destroyed by alien powers, and so on. Any attempt to form a therapeutic relationship with the patient is then fraught with difficulty because either his interest is not aroused or he does not reliably distinguish between his own thoughts and feelings and those emanating from the therapist, whom he may then regard as intrusive and threatening.

Course and prognosis

About one-quarter of those admitted to hospital for the first time in whose cases a diagnosis of schizophrenia is made on the strict criteria of first-rank symptoms as ascertained by the PSE make a full recovery and do not suffer a further attack. Many, perhaps most, of the others become more or less severely disabled, in social relationships especially. Some leave home. Others become a burden to their families. A few stay in hospital, and a few are re-admitted after shorter or longer periods in the community.

In some cases symptoms such as delusions and hallucinations, incoherence in language and eccentric and unpredictable behaviour persist to a disabling degree although they are less in evidence than during the acute illness. In some cases these symptoms fade, but the patient lacks drive and initiative, appears apathetic, and shows poverty in emotional expression; what little he conveys verbally or non-verbally is vague. Social withdrawal, poverty of speech and other classic symptoms tend to become more marked if the patient becomes 'institutionalized' in a ward with a restrictive regime.[20]

The symptoms persisting or recurring have usually been attributed to 'intrinsic' impairments which have their origin in dysfunction of the brain. Alternatively they may be explained as reflecting reorganization in a disintegrating system of relationships after a crisis and a period of instability, which amounted to illness. Patients actively withdraw from relationships which have caused them anxiety, isolate themselves, and abandon activities in which they have experienced pain. A few kill themselves.

Many of those with persistent symptoms become unemployed and unemployable because of their indifference or slovenliness. Some are able to continue in their jobs if these do not require any close contact with people and may be valued because of their special skills or meticulousness. Some of those who stay at home settle into a routine in which they show little initiative and do little. Some embark on strange hobbies or become collectors. Some become dependent to a childish degree on a parent or other relative; a 'symbiotic' relationship between a mother and a son with chronic schizophrenia may occasionally be observed. Those who leave home tend to adopt a mode of life which keeps them out of any close relationships. They may shut themselves away in their own homes or live in lodging houses where they can avoid anything other than shallow and transient relationships.

Themes in the psychopathology of schizophrenia

Several themes recur. (1) The distortion in the patient's social development and his failure to form a sense of identity, because of the confusion of the roles in his family and the inconsistent and conflicting attitudes. (2) The unconventional habits of communication he acquires during childhood: these hamper him in communicating with others outside the family. (3) His failure to emancipate himself during adolescence, to achieve independence and to develop a new, more adult pattern of relationships with relatives, peers, colleagues, and a sexual partner. (4) Confusion about his social roles and his gender identity prevents mutuality in relationships. (5) The behaviours characteristic of schizophrenia are to be seen as stratagems adopted in order to relieve interpersonal conflicts. This relief tends to be achieved by attenuating or reducing social contacts. In this way he achieves a degree of stability. (6) If pressed into a relationship, his behaviour tends to disorganize rapidly, because he lacks the skills a sound identity would have given him.

The disorder in interpersonal processes makes worse, and is made worse by, the disorder in intrapsychic processes. (7) The gap between the patient's fantasies, which make up his conception of himself, and the realities of his situation tends to widen. (8) His conception of himself is preserved by reducing or suspending the testing of reality, or is reconciled with reality by holding to delusions. (9) The gap is reflected in the split between the inner and the outer self. The outer self, which is in touch with reality, tends to be disowned by the inner self. (10) The auditory hallucinations characteristic of schizophrenia represent the comment, or a running commentary, addressed to the inner self by the outer self. (11) The inner self regards the outer self as an agent who intrudes, and interprets hallucinations in terms not of psychological processes but of paranormal powers.

There are several themes in the psychotherapy of schizophrenia. (12)

Admission to hospital gives the patient protection while he is a danger to himself or others, and a moratorium away from the setting in which he has broken down. (13) The appropriate medication, claimed by some to have a specific effect on the underlying disease process, reduces distress and the impact of reality at a critical time. (14) Patients are encouraged in the community of the ward and the occupational therapy department to engage in activities involving co-operation and communication with others, and to acquire the skills which equip them for a more independent life outside hospital.

In one-to-one psychotherapy the therapist keeps a certain distance so that he is not felt to be intrusive. He fosters the patient's sense of identity and otherwise builds up his confidence and self-esteem. He encourages him to 'meta-communicate', i.e. talk, about his experiences, his delusional ideas especially, and their meaning for him. The relationships in his family are discussed, and he is encouraged in initiatives to change the way in which he relates to family members and to become more independent.

Plans are made for discharge from hospital. Discussion with his relatives, usually in his presence, modifies their attitudes towards him and changes their expectations and demands. They are encouraged to change their style and to become less critical of, and less involved in, what he does. Reducing the face-to-face social contact of the patient with a relative of 'high expressed emotion' is of great importance. Social intervention along these lines has been shown to reduce greatly the risk of relapse. The relapse rate is at its lowest when psychotherapy related to the everyday life of the patient and his family is combined with drug therapy,[21] 'family management' being more efficacious than individual therapy. At best all three forms of treatment are provided.

NOTES AND REFERENCES

1. Coleman, J. C. (ed.) (1979). *The school years: current issues in the socialisation of young people*. Methuen, London.
2. Erikson, E. H. (1968). *Identity: youth and crisis*. Faber & Faber, London.
3. Rutter, M. (1970). Normal psychosexual development. *J. Child. Psychol. Psychiat.* **11,** 259–83.
4. Bancroft, J. (1974). *Deviant sexual behaviour: modification and assessment*. Clarendon Press, Oxford. See also Pincus, L. and Dare, C. (1978). *Secrets in the family*. Faber & Faber, London.
5. Refer to CHAPTER 1, p. 7.
6. Masters, W. H. and Johnson, V. E. (1970). *Human sexual inadequacy*. Churchill, London.
7. Renvoize, J. (1982). *Incest: a family pattern*. Routledge & Kegan Paul, London.
8. Macleod, S. (1981). *The art of starvation*. Virago, London.
9. Wing, J. K., Cooper, J. E. and Sartorius, N. (1974). *The description and classification of psychiatric symptoms: an instruction manual for the PSE and Catego system*. Cambridge University Press, Cambridge. See also Wing, J. K. *Reasoning about madness*. (1978). Oxford University Press, Oxford.

10. The description of first-rank symptoms is derived from Schneider, K. (1959). ·
    Clinical psychopathology (5th edn). Grune & Stratton, New York.
11. Brown, G. W., Birley, J. L. T. and Wing, J. K. (1972). Influence of family life on the
    course of schizophrenic disorders: a replication. *Br. J. Psychiat.* **121**, 241–58.
12. Goldberg, E. M. and Morrison, S. L. (1963). Schizophrenia and social class. *Br. J.
    Psychiat.* **109**, 785–802.
13. Much of the account given in this section is derived from Lidz, T. (1973). *The
    origins and treatment of schizophrenic disorders.* Hutchinson, London. Bateson, G.
    (1973). *Steps to an ecology of mind.* Granada, St. Albans, Herts. Laing, R. D.
    (1971). *The politics of the family and other essays.* Tavistock Publications, London.
14. A recent paper is Shur, E. and Hare, E. H. (1983). Age-prevalance and the season
    of birth effect in schizophrenia: a response to Lewis and Griffin. *Psychol. Bull.* **93**,
    373–7.
15. Fleck, S. (1960). Family dynamics and origin of schizophrenia. *Psychosom. Med.*
    22, 333–44.
16. Refer to CHAPTER 3, p. 47. See also Hirsch, S. R. and Leff, J. P. (1975).
    Abnormalities in the parents of schizophrenics (Maudsley Monograph No. 22).
    Oxford University Press, London; Reiss, D. (1976). The family and schizophrenia.
    Am. J. Psychiat. **133**, 181–5.
17. Wynne, L. C., Ryckoff, I., Day, J. and Hirsch, J. (1958). Pseudomutuality in the
    family relations of schizophrenics. *Psychiatry* **21**, 205–20.
18. Bleuler, E. (1950). *Dementia precox or the group of schizophrenias.* International
    University Press, New York.
19. Brown, G. W. and Birley, J. L. T. (1968). Crises and life changes and the onset of
    schizophrenia. *J. Health soc. Behav.* **9**, 203–14.
20. Wing, J. K. and Brown, G. W. (1970). *Institutionalisation and schizophrenia.*
    Cambridge University Press, Cambridge.
21. Themes in the treatment of schizophrenia are discussed by Goldstein, M. J.,
    Rodnick, E. H., Evans, J. R., *et al.* (1978). Drug and family therapy in the after-
    care of acute schizophrenia. *Archs gen. Psychiat.* **35**, 1169–77. Leff, J., Kuipers, L.,
    Berkowitz, R., Eberlein-Vries, R. and Sturgeon, D. (1982). A controlled trial of
    social intervention in the families of schizophrenic patients. *Br. J. Psychiat.* **141**,
    121–34; and Falloon, I. R., Boyd, J. L., McGill, C. W., Razani, J., Moss, M. B. and
    Gilderman, A. M. (1982). Family management in the prevention of exacerbation
    of schizophrenia. *New Engl. J. Med.* **306**, 1437–40.

6 Disorders in adult life

CLASSIFICATION OF MENTAL DISORDER

The system now in use in Britain is the ninth revision, in 1978, of the International Classification of Diseases—ICD–9.[1] It divides mental disorders into three classes: psychoses; neurotic disorders, personality disorders, and other non-psychotic mental conditions; and mental retardation. The psychoses are subdivided into: organic psychotic conditions, which include various types of dementia and brain syndromes; other psychoses, which include schizophrenic psychoses, affective psychoses, and paranoid states; and psychoses with origins specific to childhood. The neurotic disorders, in the second of the classes, include anxiety states, hysteria, phobic state, and obsessive-compulsive disorders. Also in this class are several types of personality disorder, sexual deviations, alcohol and drug dependence, non-psychotic disorders specific to childhood and adolescence, and a variety of other syndromes. Mental retardation, in the third of the classes, is subdivided according to its degree.

A more advanced system is that elaborated by the American Psychiatric Association and published in the *Diagnostic and Statistical Manual of Mental Disorders*—DSM–III.[2] Described as 'atheoretical with regard to aetiology', it starts from a definition of mental disorder in which the key phrases are: 'a clinically significant behavioural or psychological syndrome or pattern', 'in an individual' and 'not only in the relationship between the individual and society', which is 'associated with either a painful symptom (distress) or impairment in one or more important areas of functioning (disability)'. DMS–III evaluates each case on five axes, the first three of which, I clinical syndromes, II personality disorders and specific developmental disorders, and III physical disorders and conditions, constitute the diagnostic assessment. This is supplemented by ratings on axes IV and V each on a seven-point scale of 'severity of psychosocial stressors' and 'highest level of adaptive functioning past year'. The classification on axes I, II and III is broadly similar to that of ICD–9 although the criteria are more stringently defined.

An agreed classification of mental disorders and the nomenclature that goes with it are essential for some purposes in a scientific psychiatry. Amongst other things, they provide the common language in which professional colleagues can inform each other about individual patients, and they enable investigators in different centres to collate their research findings. Without them epidemiological studies would hardly be possible. Nor would it be possible to repeat a trial of a treatment in order to confirm, or refute, the results of a trial elsewhere, or to make comparisons. Also, any classification draws attention to the respects in which patients differ from one another, and which should be included therefore when describing a particular patient.

Yet the applicability of a classification, however atheoretical it is claimed to be, is limited to the purposes for which it was devised. The classification ensures similarity in certain respects in the cases classed together, but because it does so it raises the risk of circularity in arguments. The class of the disorder may be an important item in the description of a patient although it may be argued that more important and less arbitrary items are age, sex, occupation, the manner in which the patient presented, the presenting symptom, and the level of disability. It is of little or no importance when the questions being asked are about the processes involved in a symptom. Also, it is often a less important consideration when deciding whether to admit a patient to a psychiatric hospital than is the quality of the support network available to the patient in the community or the degree of his disengagement or extrusion from the network.

Mental Health Act 1983

Special legislation is necessary to define the circumstances in which compulsory powers may be used to override the normal personal rights of individuals and to provide safeguards against the abuse of the powers. These are required when patients incapable of protecting themselves or their interests are at risk of being neglected or exploited: when, not realizing that they are ill, they can only be treated against their wishes at the time; or when they have to be detained and treated for the protection of other persons.

Three conditions have to be satisfied before a person is liable to be detained under the Act: he suffers from mental disorder of a nature or degree which warrants detention in a hospital; detention is necessary in the interests of the patient's health or safety; or for the protection of other persons; and other methods of care or treatment are either not available or not appropriate.

In the Mental Health Act 1983, mental disorder means mental illness, severe mental impairment, mental impairment, psychopathic disorder, and any other disorder or disability of mind. A person is not to be treated as suffering from mental disorder by reason only of promiscuity or other immoral conduct, sexual deviancy or dependence on alcohol or drugs. For some of the purposes of the Act, the class of mental disorder has to be specified. About 95 per cent of those detained under the Act are said to suffer from mental illness.

Mental illness is not defined in the Act. By 'severe mental impairment', which with some change in emphasis replaces 'severe subnormality' in the 1959 Act, is meant 'a state of arrested or incomplete development of mind which includes severe impairment of intelligence and social functioning and is associated with abnormally agressive or seriously irresponsible conduct on the part of the person concerned'. In cases of 'mental impairment', which replaces subnormality, the impairment of intelligence and social functioning is 'significant'. The definition of 'psychopathic disorder' has been given in Chapter 5 (p. 102). 'Mental deficiency' was the term in general use until the 1959 Act replaced it by severe subnormality and subnormality, but these terms were used very little except when the Act demanded it. 'Mental handicap' gained currency as an alternative to them, and is now widely used in the National Health Service, without being precisely defined.

These terms have had or have a certain usefulness in an administrative context when special arrangements for care or medical treatment are under discussion, but are liable to be misleading if used otherwise. Although they say something about the severity of a person's disability, and serve to justify the use of compulsion, they say nothing about its nature or causes or the person's needs otherwise.

It is perhaps surprising that mental disorder and, especially mental illness have been so little defined in the legislation. It tends to be argued that they are incapable of a legal definition except in a very broad sense because of the variety of the forms they take. The question whether a person is of unsound mind or mentally ill has been left therefore to the judgement of doctors. One reason for this lies in the social history of psychiatry.[3] The price paid in the seventeenth century, in the 'age of reason', for the preservation of the virtues of order, reason, and work was the 'sequestration' of those beyond the pale. These whose behaviour was seen as a threat to reason and order were kept under control in the houses of correction in Germany, the hôpitaux généraux in France and, less restrictively, the workhouses in Britain. The development of psychiatry at the beginning of the nineteenth century brought with it the identification of the 10 per cent or so of those so brought under control who could be regarded as insane and within the province of medicine. They were the curable although they might require firm therapeutic restraint for a time.

Nowadays the doctor supports his judgement that a person suffers from mental disorder by stating in the terms in current use in medicine what form of disorder it is. There is a tendency to accept more readily as mental disorder those cases in which the symptoms conform to one of the recognized classes. In support of the opinion that admission to hospital should be compelled under the Act, he presents evidence to show in which important areas of functioning the person is impaired, or in what respects he is unable to cope with the demands of ordinary living, his appraisal of the world around him and his position in it is out of accord with reality as perceived in the culture, or he is a danger to himself or others.

A note on the history

A classification of mental disorders was first proposed at about the time medicine assumed the care of a proportion of the sequestrated. Thus Pinel in 1798 divided them into four groups, mania, melancholia, dementia, and idiocy, while remarking that medical science was not sufficiently advanced to warrant a more detailed classification. In the second half of the nineteenth century a distinction was made between acute, primary, and curable dementia, on the one hand, and chronic, secondary, and incurable dementia, on the other. Secondary dementia, which was regarded as hereditary and progressive, included neurosyphilis, which was often diagnosed, as well as what later became known as dementia precox. After lumbar puncture had been introduced as a technique in 1890, and the Wasserman complement-fixation test in 1906, it became clear that in only about one in three cases diagnosed as neurosyphilis was the diagnosis correct. Some of those misdiagnosed were cases of dementia precox (or schizophrenia).

Emil Kraepelin, after studying thousands of case histories, proposed a comprehensive system of classification, much of which has been carried over into contemporary classifications. He distinguished between the endogenous disorders, caused by inherent constitutional factors, and the exogenous, caused by external factors. The pattern of a disorder, he noted, depends also on the age at which it starts. He made in 1896 the crucial distinction between dementia precox, starting in adolescence or early adult life, which is endogenous and progressive, and manic-depressive psychosis, now called affective psychosis, the course of which is cyclic, with intervals of normality between attacks.

Supposing the disorders to arise from metabolic or other defects, Kraepelin described the manifestations of the disorders as if they were neurological signs, and certainly not as reflecting continually changing processes of adaptation. This bias still influences the criteria applied in contemporary systems. It was corrected in some degree by Bleuler[4] when in 1911 he gave to dementia precox the new name 'schizophrenia'. This he described in terms giving more prominence to the psychological processes. Impressed by the variety of the cases, he spoke of the group of schizophrenias, and pointed out that the course was not inevitably progressive.

Support for Kraepelin's view that the functional psychoses fall into two classes, in his terms, dementia precox and manic-depressive psychosis, has been found in the raised incidence of schizophrenia, but not of manic-depressive psychosis, in the families of patients suffering from schizophrenia, and the raised incidence of manic-depressive psychosis, but not of schizophrenia, in the families of patients suffering from manic-depressive psychosis. Occasionally a child of a manic-depressive parent is found to suffer from schizophrenia, while the reverse is said to be exceptional. These 'pedigree' studies give support to the view that there are two distinct classes of pathogenic genes, and also of metabolic defects, corresponding to the two classes of functional psychosis.

Not all the evidence justifies this distinction. The pattern of many psychoses is atypical, some of the symptoms being schizophrenic and some affective. In the families of patient suffering from atypical psychoses, schizophrenic, affective, and atypical illnesses occur. The results of statistical analysis of the distribution of symptoms in series of patients have in general failed to confirm the distinction.[5] However, it continues to be widely accepted as fundamental in the classification of the functional psychoses.

Forms of illness

Although the pattern of the mental disorder conforms in some cases to one of the classes as defined in a recognized system, in other cases it does not and is mixed or atypical. However, disorder in social relationships occurs in nearly all mental illnesses in adult life. While he is ill, the patient is alienated, i.e. estranged in greater or lesser degree from family, peers or friends. He feels he is on his own, and does not belong to any community. He is egocentric and does not associate himself with others or espouse any cause. He breaks off transactions with others and ceases to communicate or co-operate with them. Sometimes he feels that he is under attack, more often that he is unworthy or bad. Depressive attitudes like these form part of most of the illnesses for which an adult patient seeks help. He goes to a doctor or other helper because he feels doubt about the outcome and that the fault lies in him rather than the circumstances. He chooses a doctor if he supposes the fault to be medical rather than moral or legal.

Many who are ill in a broad sense do not go to a hospital or seek help from a doctor. Some go for help to a clergyman or solicitor or faith healer, for instance. Some shut themselves away in their own homes. Some become vagrant or travel abroad in order to get away from family and friends. Some adopt a mode of life which keeps them out of close relationships. Some seek casual or promiscuous relationships in an attempt to find acceptance and affection, but to be broken off if they become too serious. Some turn to drinking or drugs in order to get relief from anxiety. Some find solace in bars and clubs on the outskirts of society. Some, denied the satisfactions of human relationships, seek vicarious satisfactions in the accumulation of wealth or knowledge or in political power. Others who feel rejected by the community and out of sympathy with it do not feel constrained by its laws, customs and conventions, and offend against them, feeling justified in doing so because of a sense of grievance at unfair treatment. All these forms of illness, although seen only occasionally in hospital practice, have to be taken into account in any discussion of mental disorders in adult life.

Sex ratios

Among in-patients in psychiatric hospitals in England there are more women than men in the ratio of about 3:2. There is only a small preponderance of women in the younger age-groups, but the ratio for those over 55 is 2:1. There are no official figures from which to derive sex ratios for those attending out-patient departments or day hospitals or centres, but there are probably many more women than men in both cases. The ratio for agoraphobia, the onset of which is typically in the mid-twenties, is 3 women to 1 man. There are more women than men among those who take psychotropic drugs regularly.

The reasons why there are more women than men are uncertain and complex. For those over 55 years old the proportion of women in the population is rising because of their greater longevity. In the age-group 60–64, for instance, 6 per cent of men and more than 20 per cent of women are widowed; for 65–74, 14 per cent of men and 40 per cent of women. Three times as many wives lose husbands as husbands lose wives. A widowed man is much more likely to remarry than a widowed woman.

The effects on women of disturbances in the family appear to be more often of a kind for which psychiatric treatment is sought by the patient or the relatives. When there are open conflicts between husband and wife, it is more often the wife who seeks help from a doctor or marriage guidance counsellor. On the other hand, several of the forms of disorder not often seen in hospital practice are commoner in men. In prisons men outnumber women by 5 to 1. There are more men in common lodging houses. Alcoholism is commoner in men. In most classes of offenders there are many more men than women, but the proportion of women has been rising.

Other reasons lie in the social roles of men and women and the support they are given. The roles expected of women, other than housekeeping and childcaring, are less clear-cut. A man is expected to go out to work, for instance. Whether a woman should do so is seen to depend more on circumstances. He has the support of workmates; she is more dependent on the support of family and neighbours. The present high rates of unemployment among both men and women may prove to have an effect on the sex ratio.

A preponderance of women in psychiatric hospitals is not found in every country. There tends to be a preponderance of men when mental-health services are poorly developed and there are few in-patient facilities. In Eire, on the other hand, there are more men than women although the admission rates are higher than in Britain.

CRISES IN ADULT LIFE

The birth of a child as a crisis for each of the parents has been discussed in the previous chapter. Amongst other developmental crises in adult life are marriage, the death of a parent, the emancipation of children and their departure from home, for women the loss of their maternal role, and in both men and women retirement from work.

Among accidental crises are the breakdown of marriage, desertion of the spouse and divorce, the premature death of the spouse, the physical illness of the person himself or accident, illness or death of others, promotion at work, failure to gain promotion, loss of a job through redundancy or other cause, and the untimely pregnancy of a daughter. Among less severe crises are the infidelity of a spouse, house-moving, burglary or fire in the home, and a quarrel or lawsuit.

All these are examples of the untoward events sometimes called 'life events'—reported in the histories of patients as being related to the onset of a mental illness more or less directly.[6] Each event brings about, or threatens to bring about, a change in the patient's relationships with family or others, the challenge to the system not being compensated by the homeostatic restoration of the relationships. The essence of the change lies in loss, separation, disappointment or change in role.

Marriage

About 80 per cent of husbands are older than their wives, the mean difference in age being 2.5 years when the husband's age at marriage is between 25 and 35 years, and 1 year when it is less than 25. Husbands and wives tend to be similar in ethnic origin, religion, social class, education, and intelligence, i.e. to show homogamy, to a degree capable of expression in statistical terms. They tend to have lived close, but not very close, to one another.

Getting married usually means also the weakening of ties with parents, perhaps removal to a home in a new district, and brings changes in the lives of each, e.g. in financial matters, leisure habits, and friendships. Husband and wife form a partnership, of which they expect, in the words of the Church of England marriage service, 'mutual society, help and comfort . . . both in prosperity and adversity'. Marriage prepares for the procreation and socialization of children.

There are three stages in the transition from the single to the married state:[7] the period of courtship or engagement, the honeymoon, and early marriage. Various problems arise: intra-psychic conflicts in each of the partners, difficulties in settling the roles each is to play and the rules to be followed, overt influence or interference by others, such as a parent or other family member, and hidden difficulties arising from attitudes to significant outsiders, such as a previous boy-friend or girl-friend. Failure to complete the tasks of adjustment set by the marriage may result in the sometimes acute illness of one of the partners during the courtship period or honeymoon. A mounting distress or dissatisfaction may bring one or both partners to seek professional help, typically several months after the marriage was formalized.

Several questions may then be asked about the marriage, as about any other partnership, such as that between those cohabiting. What is its extent? Is it more or less comprehensive, or narrow, as in a liaison? Is interaction continual, frequent, intermittent or occasional? What is the degree of the commitment? Is the partnership seen as lasting, transitory or *ad hoc*? Do the partners do the same things, and have joint roles in which they co-operate and reciprocate? Are they competitive? Are their roles segregated and complementary? How closely do they regulate one another, and how sensitively? Is one controlling, and the other dependent? How intimate is the relationship? Do they confide in one another, and reveal their troubles? In what degree do they test against reality their perceptions of one another? Do their perceptions of their relationship and of the part each plays in it agree? And are there any significant outsiders?

Divorce

The number of divorces increased steeply after the change in the law in 1971, but the annual increases are now small. Of those married in 1968, 11 per cent had divorced within 10 years. About one in four of those married in the mid-1960s are expected to have divorced after 25 years. If current trends continue, about 30 per cent of the marriages now being contracted will end in divorce. Divorce rates reach a peak after 4 years of marriage and remain high until after 11 years. They decline when the partners are in their late thirties, and decline further when they are in their forties and fifties. They are relatively high for all durations of marriage when the wife's age at marriage was under 20 years, and also when the marriage is childless or there is only one child. They do not vary much with occupation, social class or religious affiliation. They are higher for remarriages than marriages. In 70 per cent of cases the petition for the divorce is made by the wife.

A large number of children are affected by the divorce of their parents, 60 per cent of the couples divorcing having children under 16 years old. In 1975 some 202 000 children in England, of whom 145 000 were under 16, were affected by the divorce of 120 000 couples.[8]

As in all crises there is a period of instability, usually preceding by months or years the completion of the divorce in law, during which husband, wife, and children work through their loss and the grief, anger, and protest going with it. The resentments of husband and wife may be acted out in struggles over the arrangements to be made for the children. These struggles serve to perpetuate the relationship and to postpone the need to face the bereavement. Each finds a degree of stability eventually in a new, reorganized system of relationships. The children are of course affected in many ways by the restructuring of their lives. Sometimes their grandparents are brought in to play a bigger part in their care. Whether the experience of the divorce of parents has a long-term effect on the children is open to question. It may be expected to affect the partnerships they form subsequently.

Many of the divorced remarry, about one-third doing so in any one year. About 15 per cent of marriages are now remarriages. Some cohabit, i.e. live as husband and wife without a civil or religious ceremony having taken place, but cohabitation is typically a prelude, not an alternative to remarriage. Some form other partnerships. Others live on their own or with a child or children, then often in poor circumstances, being dependent on supplementary benefits.

More than a half of the parents caring for a child or children on their own do so as a result of separation or divorce.

Marital status

The single, widowed, and divorced are over-represented among those admitted to psychiatric hospitals, the rates for the single and the divorced being much higher than for the widowed. In the single and the divorced the incidences of schizophrenia and of psychoses associated with alcoholism especially are high; that of manic-depressive psychosis is about the same as in the married.

How is marital status related to the causes of mental illness? The best way of looking at it is to suppose that the personality traits associated with single status or predisposing to marriage breakdown predispose also to mental illness. but the breakdown of marriage and bereavement are also crises out of which mental illness may arise.

In samples of patients admitted to a psychiatric hospital, a recent bereavement of a parent, spouse, sib or child is reported several times more often than would be expected if there were no association with the illness. There is a preponderance of women over 40 years among those so bereaved and admitted. If referrals to all agencies providing psychiatric care are considered, widows are over-represented by comparison with the married, especially those in the age-groups 25–39. The time relations between widowhood and referral suggest that the illness arises during the transition into widowhood.

Realignment crises

Mental illness, especially depressive illness, in those in the forties and fifties is often the result of a combination of crises: the death of parents, the drifting apart of brothers and sisters after their parents' death, the departure from home of sons and daughters, and changes in the relationship with the spouse at the end of the child-bearing period. Women retire from their parental role when their children become emancipated and leave home. The generations separate at least for a while. Reunion occurs in some cases after a period of years.

The point may be made in striking terms. Consider 50-year-old women living in Britain. Fifty is the commonest age for the menopause, although the average is a year or two younger. The average age of their mothers, if they have survived, is 78 years, and this is the commonest age of death in once-married women. In fact, about half the women of 50 have a mother alive; about one-quarter, a father. Fathers, dying on average at 72, and three years older than mothers, are typically lost in the early forties. The average age of daughters is 23, which is near the average age for marriage. Many women thus meet within a few years crises in the relationships of greatest importance to them.

The menopause

As a cause of psychiatric symptoms special importance has been attached to the menopause—the 'change'—which is taken to mean much more than the final cessation of the menses. 'Hot flushes', although not uncommon at other times of life, are often regarded as the cardinal symptom. Attitudes towards the menopause are an extension of those formerly held towards the menstrual flow, which is regarded by some women as cleansing, by others as debilitating. For the latter the menopause comes as a relief. Surgical removal of the uterus, in relief of more or less serious gynaecological symptoms, tends to be accepted readily by women in their forties. Psychiatric symptoms in the forties and fifties tend to be attributed to the changes in endocrine functions associated with the menopause. Whatever part these changes may play, the menopause is also of significance because women feel that they are changed by it. It marks for them the end of the capacity to bear children. More importantly it brings with it a sense of loss of femininity and value as a sexual partner, which in some cases is welcomed, in others regretted. In itself a developmental crisis, it tends to be accompanied by other crises of greater importance although less often recognized to be so.

A mother who has been dependent on a daughter for company and emotional support tends to become anxious and depressed when the daughter's growing independence threatens to deprive her, and she may become definitely ill when the daughter is about to leave home or has just left home, especially if the circumstances are unhappy. Illness in reaction to a son's emancipation is less common, but may occur in a skewed or schismatic family. The mother may recover quickly when the daughter returns, as she commonly does, to settle down near her parents. She is then likely to find a new role as grannie to sustain her. If the timing is favourable, the gap between her retirement as parent and her re-employment as grannie is filled by taking responsibility as a daughter for the care of infirm parents. This last role may well provide opportunities for the revival of relationships with her sibs.

Some men meet difficulties when a decline in their capacity for athletic pursuits in their forties or in their sexual capacity in the fifties obliges them to revise their conception of themselves. Especially at risk are those who set store by their physical prowess, and who become disabled as a result of an accident or disease. Physical ill-health may contribute to the decline, and a man may also have to accept that many of the hopes and ambitions of his twenties and thirties will not now be fulfilled, and in particular that there are limits to his career prospects.

Redundancy and unemployment, as accidental crises, may not be met without entering into a period of serious instability for a while, because they challenge not only the conception a person has of himself, but also the assumptions and expectations of others about the roles he plays in his family. Men may become depressed when a daughter becomes engaged, married, becomes pregnant or leaves home, if these events have not been prepared for. The support and comfort he gives to his wife is reduced if he becomes depressed as a consequence of these or other crises in his life.

Whether a married couple stay well in their fifties and sixties may depend on how successful they are in reorganizing their relationship with one another. For 25 years more or less, husband and wife have been preoccupied with separate activities, he typically in pursuing his career, and she in bringing up children. For this reason there has been a degree of estrangement between them. After the children leave home, and the nest is empty, they become more dependent on one another. Her demands on him tend to be greater than his on her while he is active outside the home, but the position may be reversed when he retires from work. Some married pairs cease for one reason or another to have regular sexual intercourse after the wife's menopause, and this may be associated with some weakening of their attachment to each other. She may give him a lower priority than her grandchildren in her daily arrangements.

Single persons in their fifties tend to turn to siblings for company and support, and adopt a parental role towards nephews and nieces or godchildren, and a grandparental role towards grandnephews and grandnieces. A single person without a family may make a kind of family with a colleague or friend, who is also single, widowed or divorced, or find a 'quasisibling' as a companion. Many of these relationships are more stable and supportive than are marriages, but crises in them may be followed by illness in the same way.

DEPRESSION

If in adolescence and early adult life the most characteristic form of illness is schizophrenia, that in the thirties, the middle years of life and subsequently is depression. This belongs to the affective psychoses in the ICD–9. Usually two out of three in samples of patients being treated for depression are women. Depression is common. Thus 15 per cent of a sample representative of women living in Camberwell, a predominantly working-class area in London, were found by Brown and Harris[9] to have suffered from a definite psychiatric illness within the 3 months prior to the interview, practically all of them having been depressed. Another 18 per cent had definite psychiatric symptoms although not severe enough to rate as clinical depression. The prevalence of depression is relatively high in the working class.

The disturbance of mood, which is reflected in gloom, sadness, wretchedness or misery, is seen as the cardinal feature of clinical depression. The self seems worthless, the outer world meaningless, and the future hopeless, it has been said. Two types of depression have been distinguished: 'endogenous' and 'reactive', the former appearing to have arisen spontaneously, and the latter to have been provoked by an external event. 'Psychotic' and 'neurotic' are better terms for these two types since they are descriptive and do not imply what the causes are.

Hallucinations and delusions occur in psychotic, but not in neurotic, depression. In psychotic depression there has usually been loss of weight. Sleep has been disturbed, with early morning waking especially. The patient tends to feel at his worst in the early morning. The mood is one of misery, the hopelessness being more general and more profound than in neurotic depression. In this there is increased emotionality, with indecisiveness and helplessness. The patient feels at his worst in the evening, and has difficulty in getting to sleep. Those with psychotic depression tend to be older, those with neurotic depression younger.

Whether the two types are distinct has been much discussed. Against the distinction is the finding that the scores on rating scales in series of depressed patients are distributed normally without any evidence of bimodality.[10] On the other hand, the factor analysis of symptoms has shown two constellations of symptoms, i.e. syndromes, corresponding to the two types. But the investigation in which this method was used depended on dividing patients into two classes on variables such as age, which have a continuous distribution, i.e. as older or younger, and on variables such as sleep disorder, which do not readily submit to being dichotomized, i.e. as early-morning waking or difficulting in getting to sleep.[11] The two constellations can be regarded, therefore, as artefacts of the method.

The distinction would probably have been abandoned, had it not recently been discovered by Brown and Harris that in cases of psychotic depression the 'past loss' of a parent or other significant person, i.e. loss occurring 2 years or more before the illness started, tends to have been due to death, and in cases of neurotic depression, due to separation. This discovery suggests that there is between the two types a qualitative difference independent of age.

Hypomania

Much less common than depression is hypomania or mania, which is linked with depression in accordance with the theory that there is a disease-entity 'manic-depressive psychosis' attributable to a cyclic process in the body. The difference between hypomania and mania is one of degree, the patient's restless activity being open to influence by others in hypomania, but not in mania. The hypomanic patient is elated and excited, with a pressure of activity and flight of ideas. The association of one idea with another is comprehensible, often witty, in hypomania, but not in schizophrenia.

Only a few per cent of the depressed give a history of hypomanic symptoms. The illness of these few is described as 'bipolar', that of the many as 'unipolar'. Another way of looking at the relation between depression and hypomania is to suppose that depression is typically preceded by a phase in which the patient tries to remove what he sees as threats to his well-being by intense activity. The flight of ideas then reflects the high level of anxiety. When the intense activity fails, depression supervenes as a result of the repeated stimulation without reinforcement. Depressed patients commonly speak of their discouragement after making great efforts to cope. Also, the hypomanic patient often gives the impression that he is restlessly active in order not to give way to his grief, distress or tearfulness.

Provoking agents

Most of the Camberwell women who developed depression during the year of Brown and Harris's study had been affected by a 'provoking agent', i.e. a serious life-event or major difficulty. In about one-quarter of the cases of depression, a provoking agent was apparently absent. These patients seemed to have been unduly susceptible by reason of being older, over 40 years, or of having had a 'past loss' or a previous episode of depression. But only one-fifth of those affected by a provoking agent had developed depression. This finding raises the related questions: What creates the vulnerability of the minority? What protects the majority?

A confiding relationship

Brown and Harris found that an important factor in creating vulnerability, but not by itself a cause of depression, is the lack of an intimate, confiding relationship with husband, or boy-friend or with a close friend, mother or sister. Among those affected by a provoking agent, 4 out of every 10 women who lacked a confiding relationship had developed depression, compared with only 1 in every 10 of those who enjoyed a confiding relationship with someone seen at least weekly.

Whether a person becomes depressed when affected by a provoking agent seems to depend therefore on the support given by kin and the social network. The pattern of the support changes at different stages of life, the level of the support tending to be reduced when parents die, ties with sibs weaken and children leave home and after retirement from work. These things can account for the rise in the prevalence of depression with age.

Differences in the quality of the support account partly for Brown and Harris's finding that a higher proportion of working-class women, 1 in 3, than of middle-class women, 1 in 12, became depressed when affected by a provoking agent. There are other reasons for the higher prevalence of depression among working-class women. They meet greater difficulties, e.g. in health, finance, housing and living conditions. Serious events affect them more often, and the events tend to be more serious. Middle-class women, on the other hand, have a wider range of choice in all these matters, and are given greater protection through the social network to which they belong. Also, they are more likely to enjoy a confiding relationship with a husband. Moreover, their self-esteem is higher.[12]

Brown and Harris found three other groups of women to be especially vulnerable; those with three or more children under 14 at home, those not going out to work, and those who had lost their mothers before they were 11 years old. The reasons for the vulnerability of the first two groups are to be found in the degree and quality of the support they receive. How losing mother before 11 creates vulnerability is less certain.

Parental loss

Nearly half the Camberwell women who had lost their mothers before 11 developed depression when there was a provoking agent, compared with only 1 in 6 of the other women. Loss of mother after 11 was not associated in any way with depression, nor was loss of father at any age, nor loss of a sibling. Brown and Harris's evidence on the part played by loss of the mother before 11 stands out from the confused findings of the many researches into the contribution made by parental loss during childhood to vulnerability to psychiatric illness in adult life.[13] It has been widely believed over many years that parental loss is of importance because it affects the development during adolescence of a sense of social and sexual identity. However, there have been difficulties in finding the incidence of loss, however defined, in the populations from which research samples of patients have been drawn. Control samples collected from other hospital departments are hardly acceptable as representative. General-practice samples are satisfactory if care is taken to ensure representativeness, although the allowances that should be made for any differences in social class or year of birth are difficult to determine.

The probable reason why Brown and Harris's finding stands out is that their sample of depressed women is more widely representative of depressed women than are the depressed women referred to psychiatrists. It is known that women with young children at home have relatively little contact with their general practitioners, and are less likely to be referred to psychiatrists when they are depressed. Early loss of mother and three or more children at home were found to be correlated in the Camberwell sample.

DELIBERATE SELF-HARM

Suicide

The pioneer in research into suicide was Durkheim.[14] His methods were systematic and, although his statistical procedures were unrefined, his evidence still deserves consideration. His main findings have not been questioned, and his work provides a model of the way in which social data can be used to suggest hypotheses about the causes of a disorder, in terms of its social context rather than of processes in families. He denied that 'extra-social' factors, e.g. either 'organic-psychic' or physical factors like climate or temperature, play a significant part in causing suicide, and argued that its occurrence can be explained by reference to social structure and its ramifying functions. He collected data to show how suicide rates vary in relation to a large number of variables: age, sex, marital status, education, religious affiliation, urban or rural residence, civilian or military occupation, nationality and race, economic and political factors, and time of day or year. This list has been added to in more recent investigations.[15]

He concluded that the strength of the suicidal tendency varies inversely with the degree to which a person is integrated into a social group. He recognized three types. Egoistic suicides are the result of excessive individualism when the person lives for himself instead of performing his duties to society. Altruistic suicides are the acts of persons living in a closely-knit group with a strict code of honour, who sacrifice themselves because they feel an obligation to do so, e.g. the captain of a ship who allows himself to drown when his ship sinks, the officer who shoots himself when his unit is defeated in battle, or the sick who kill themselves when they do not want to be a burden on their relatives. Anomic suicides occur when regulation by society is upset by a crisis in the social situation.

The death rates from suicide are compiled from the verdicts reached at coroners' inquests. Conclusions from them have to be cautious, therefore, whether a death is attributed to suicide or accident or other cause not being wholly reliable. Rates for the population as a whole are affected by the demographic structure, the proportion of the elderly especially. The rate for England and Wales in recent years has been of the order of 8 per 100 000 population over 15 years old. Suicide under the age of 15 years is uncommon. The sex ratio is about 1.5. In men the rate rises steeply in the fifties and sixties, reaching a peak at about 85 years old. In women the peak is in the decade 55–64.

The rate is higher in the single than the married, and the married without children than the married with children. It is higher in the widowed than the single, and higher still in the divorced. Very high rates are recorded for elderly men recently widowed, living alone and out of contact with their families.

The rate tends to be higher in Protestants than Catholics, probably not because of any difference in doctrine, but because the former are brought into a community in lesser degree. It tends to be higher in towns than in the country, and higher still in large towns. These differences are probably due in part to the greater number of elderly in large towns and in part to the greater isolation to which those living in them are liable. The effects of social class are complex; in general, the highest rate is in Social Class V. Poverty by itself does not seem to have any influence on the rate. This is affected more by the cohesion of the social network.

Durkheim found that rates tend to increase from January to July in countries north of the equator, and to decline in the second half of the year. The peak has been earlier in recent decades, being in April in 1951–60. There is a lesser peak in October. These and other seasonal variations have yet to be explained.

There was a peak in the rates in males during the years 1931–4 when there was an economic depression, rising unemployment, and social disorganization. The rates fell during the two world wars. There was a dramatic fall in the nineteen-sixties at about the time domestic gas became much safer, and a further fall during the nineteen-seventies, the trough being in 1977 when the standardized mortality rate (SMR), 100 in 1968, was 82 for men and 80 for women. It has now risen in 1980 to over 90 for men and nearly 90 for women, the upturn being more marked in men in the younger age-group.

Up to 1962 the commonest method of suicide was the inhalation of domestic gas, but the incidence of death from this cause fell sharply in 1963 and subsequently. Drug overdose has become the most common method for both men and women. This is the cause of death in one in three suicides in men, and two in three in women. Hanging and strangling are common in men, less common in women. Drowning is relatively common where there is ready access to deep water.

Non-fatal deliberate self-harm

This has been defined as a deliberate, non-fatal act, whether physical, drug overdosage or poisoning, done in the knowledge that it is potentially harmful, and in the case of drug overdosage, that the amount taken is excessive. For every fatal act of self-harm there are 20–30 non-fatal acts, as judged by admissions to hospitals. Of these, over 90 per cent are drug overdosages, of which there has been an epidemic over the last two decades, perhaps now tailing off.

The rates rise after 12 years old. In the early teen years those for girls are five times those for boys. The peak age is in the twenties, when there are two to three times as many women as men. The rates fall sharply as age increases, levelling out in the sixties and seventies, when the rates for men and women are more nearly equal. In more than half the cases, the drug taken is one used in psychiatric treatment. Overdose of barbiturates was very common at one time, but now accounts for less than 1 in 10 cases; the proportion among the older patients is rather higher. Benzodiazepines are now the most frequent of the drugs misused. Young people take aspirin or paracetamol relatively often.

The rates have been shown to be high among those living in the areas in cities which are the most overcrowded and have the poorest amenities. The reasons why this is so are complex. Amongst other things, such areas tend to contain a relatively high proportion of socially mobile young people who are living away from their relatives, and who have little stability in their lives.

Self-harm has been regarded as a form of appeal to others for help in meeting an intolerable situation, i.e. as a way of drawing attention to distress. In support of this view it is argued that the harm often falls far short of what would be expected to cause death, that the act is done in circumstances in which intervention by others is probable or even certain, and that the act often has the effect of getting help for the person. On the other side it can be argued that some of those who harm themselves express a strong wish to die, that few admit the intention to get help, and that a certain proportion, possibly about 10 per cent, do die from deliberate self-harm sooner or later.

Certain signs in a patient who has recently harmed himself are taken to indicate a high risk of a further act proving fatal. The recent act was potentially dangerous, especially if there have been other acts, each more serious than the previous one. The patient is clinically depressed. He suffers from insomnia. He does not avail himself of offers of help. The therapist fails to form an easy relationship with him. The older the patient, the greater is the risk of a fatal outcome. The recent death of a close relative or friend is a warning sign, as is a recent quarrel or break up of a relationship. Awareness of a serious or life-threatening illness adds to the risk. A further question is: how readily available is an effective method of producing a fatal result?

Particularly at risk are young people living away from home, women with young children at home who lack a confiding relationship and elderly men who are recently bereaved, isolated, and in poor health.

Some of those who survive an act of self-harm did have some intention to die, but their plans, which could have proved fatal, went awry, in some cases because they were inefficient, indecisive or vacillating. These characteristics are shown in some degree by all behaviour at times of high anxiety. The most ruthless acts are carried out by those who are depersonalized or psychotic. Some who survive have underestimated the difficulties of bringing an end to their lives. Some were playing with the idea of death. Some were seeking not death but relief from intolerable distress. Some were expressing anger and protest, and chose a method which pointed a finger at those they wished to accuse. A very few were trying not to destroy themselves, but to mutilate or deform in accordance with psychotic ideas.

The setting in which acts of self-harm are made is nearly always one of crisis and disorganization in the patient's family. Some have suffered a recent bereavement. Some have quarrelled with a key person in their lives. Several investigations have been carried out in order to decide whether an undue number have suffered the loss of a parent during childhood, and, despite their technical faults, it does appear likely that loss of a parent during childhood is a predisposing factor. It appears likely too that a recent crisis is followed by an act of self-harm when it revives unresolved conflicts in earlier relationships.

The view that in some cases at least acts of self-harm represent appeals for help has drawn attention to what other alternatives are available to those in distress or despair. What else can they do? How can support and help be made more accessible? One result has been the development of services, notably that provided by the Samaritans, which offer help under circumstances acceptable to those at risk. Women, it seems, those in their twenties especially, are less able than men to find other ways of getting relief from distress. Men are more prone than women to act out their anger and distress in violent behaviour and to seek relief from alcohol; drinking as a method of self-harm is more likely to be monitored by others. A relationship with a therapist may help the patient to develop a more constructive approach to the problems in his life.

Another way of reducing the number of fatal acts is to identify more often those most at risk and then to provide help and support or even, exceptionally, to use the powers conferred by the Mental Health Act to compel admission to hospital, where the patient can be given some protection. At least as important are the measures taken to reduce the availability of potentially fatal methods of self-harm, e.g. by inducing more care and restraint on the part of doctors in the prescribing of drugs and exercising greater control over poisons and guns. A notable example is the reduction of the carbon monoxide content of domestic gas before the less dangerous North-sea gas replaced that derived from coal. Another example is the policy of limiting the access of the public without supervision to high places from which a person can fall to his death. There is now a greater awareness of the need to remove or reduce the dangers of self-harm, in the same way as other health hazards, as soon as they are recognized. This gives importance to studies in the epidemiology of deliberate self-harm.

Unemployment

It would seem reasonable to suppose that unemployment, the lot now of one in seven of the working population, would affect the incidence of deliberate self-harm. It reduces a person's participation in society, reduces his social contacts, removes the structure of his daily life and lowers his sense of status and self-esteem. National statistics are said to show that death rates have risen as unemployment rates have risen. Also the follow-up of samples of the unemployed have shown higher death rates than comparable samples of the employed for all causes, but especially from accident and suicide. The longer the unemployment, the more ill-health a person tends to suffer. Yet how far unemployment is causal is uncertain. Sometimes it is caused by ill health, such as chronic bronchitis or alcoholism. There are many methodological pitfalls, and a firm conclusion cannot yet be reached.

NOTES AND REFERENCES

1. World Health Organisation (1978). *Mental disorders: glossary and guide to their classification in accordance with the ninth revision of the International Classification of Diseases.* World Health Organisation, Geneva. See also Cooper, J. E., Kendell, R. E., Gurland, *et al.* (1972). *Psychiatric Diagnosis in New York and London.* Oxford University Press, London.
2. Task Force on Nomenclature and Statistics of the American Psychiatric Association (1980). *Diagnostic and statistical manual of mental disorders.* American Psychiatric Association, Washington D.C.
3. Doerner, K. (1981). *Madmen and the bourgeoisie: a social history of insanity and psychiatry.* Blackwell, Oxford.

4. Bleuler, E. (1950). *Dementia precox or the group of schizophrenias*. International University Press, New York.
5. Kendell, R. E. and Gourlay, J. (1970). The clinical distinction between the affective psychoses and schizophrenia. *Br. J. Psychiat.* **117**, 261–6.
6. Dohrenwend, B. S. and Dohrenwend, B. P. (1981). *Stressful life events and their contexts*. Prodist, New York.
7. Rapoport, R. (1967). The study of marriage as a critical transition for personality and family development. In *The predicament of the family* (ed. P. Lomas). Hogarth Press, London.
8. Wallerstein, J. S. and Kelly, J. B. (1980). *Surviving the break-up: how children and parents cope with divorce*. Grant McIntrye, London.
9. Brown, G. and Harris, T. (1978). *Social origins of depression*. Tavistock Publications, London.
10. Kendell, R. E. (1976). The classification of depressions: a review of contemporary confusion. *Br. J. Psychiat.* **129**, 15–28.
11. Kiloh, L. G. and Garside, R. F. (1963). The independence of neurotic depression and endogenous depression. *Br. J. Psychiat.* **109**, 451–63.
12. The complex relations between depression and marriage difficulties are reviewed by Hinchliffe, M. K., Hooper, D. and Roberts, F. J. (1978). *The melancholy marriage*. John Wiley, Chichester.
13. Birtchnell, J. (1970). Early parent death and mental illness. *Br. J. Psychiat.* **116**, 281–8; Recent parent death and mental illness, ibid., pp. 289–97. Depression in relation to early and recent parent death. ibid., pp. 299–306; The relationship between attempted suicide and parent death. ibid., pp. 307–14.
14. Emil Durkheim's monograph on *Suicide*, now translated into English, was published in 1897.
15. Morgan, H. G. (1979). *Death wishes?—the understanding and management of deliberate self-harm*. John Wiley, Chichester.

7 Disorders of the elderly

Of the population of England and Wales 11 per cent are from 65 to 74 years of age; this proportion is falling. About 4 per cent are from 75 to 84, and 1 per cent, 85 or over. The number in the last two age-groups will be about 10 per cent higher in 1990. There are twice as many women as men over 75. Two-thirds of the women and one-third of the men of this age are widowed.

Of those aged 65 years or more, 94 per cent live in private accommodation, 2 per cent in residential accommodation, 3 per cent in hospital, and 1 per cent in a hotel. Of those in private accommodation one-third live on their own; two-fifths live with a spouse or other member of a family. Seven out of ten live in a household in which there is no one under the age of 65. Many of the elderly live in substandard accommodation with poor amenities. Half live close to the subsistence level.

Patterns of social interaction

Most old people fight hard to preserve their status, sense of identity, and independence, and are sensitive to any suggestion that they are unable to look after themselves, but confidence is precarious, especially nowadays in their capacity to remain solvent financially, and they take care in the spending of money, sometimes to the point of miserliness. They prefer their own front door and 'intimacy at a distance', but try to retain effective contact with their children even when they are not living near. They see their daughters more often than their sons, and turn for help more often to their daughters.

Disengagement

A cardinal tendency in the elderly is disengagement, with a weakening or severance of relationships with other members of society. It is gradual, difficult to resist and usually accepted, although reluctantly. Already in the twenties and thirties there is increasing specialization and hence narrowing in job and leisure interests. As the children grow up, time may be found again to re-engage in social activities outside the home, but in the fifties the network of kin loosens, with the death of parents and often then also the weakening of ties with sibs. Children leave home and move away. This means retirement for the mother from her maternal role. For the father retirement from work comes a decade or so later. Relatives and friends move away or die, and are not replaced.

The elderly disengage more in modern industrial societies, when there is a fixed retirement age, than they used to do in rural communities. Retirement under 65 years old is becoming more usual. Older men and women tend to be pushed out, especially from leadership roles, as a result of social pressures. Society's expectations and the restrictions on the roles open to the elderly mean that they lose the status and identity they were previously given by their membership of a working community. Men, having depended more on their friendships at work, have weaker ties with their children, sibs, and neighbours than their wives have, and are more vulnerable when they retire from work and also when they are widowed. Women are sustained in their sixties by their closer ties with their children, their daughters especially, and may retain their position as the functional and emotional centre of the family. Their ties with sibs, especially sisters, tend to be preserved. On the other hand, they lose their husbands by death three times as often as men lose their wives.

The 'life satisfaction' of the elderly has been found to be related positively to their level of social interaction.[1] Many have no intention to disengage and maintain former relationships and activities or enjoy new ones. Mothers become active again as grandmothers or even as great-grandmothers. Men find new things to do which give them a position in the community. People marry again even in their eighties and find satisfaction from doing so.

The changes in the circumstances of their lives mean, as a general rule, that husbands and wives become more dependent on one another. The soundness of the marriage is tested when the terms of the partnership have to be revised to take account of the new circumstances. This is especially so when one of the partners has become more dependent on the other by reason of ill health.

Those most at risk

The indifference shown by some of the elderly towards social interaction has been attributed to their acceptance of disengagement, but may be due not so much to 'isolation', i.e. lack of opportunities for social interaction, as to 'desolation', i.e. turning away from social interaction because it has become painful as a result of bereavement.[2] A widow may disengage because she has not acquired during her marriage the social skills which would enable her to re-engage as a single person. Or she may feel an obligation to her dead husband not to replace him. On the other hand, she may join up in a companionship with another women, who may be a relative, a former colleague or acquaintance.

Especially at risk because disengagement is likely to progress to a serious degree are the single, the divorced, the widowed and the only child, those who have moved away from their families, those whose family ties have always been loose, as is relatively common in Social Classes IV and V, and those who have shown low levels of social interaction over many years.[3] In the last group are those who suffered serious mental illness in their teens or twenties, failed to establish an adult pattern of relationships and become alienated after the death of their parents.

In many of those who become ill mentally in their sixties and seventies[4] there is evidence of social withdrawal over many years, often as a result of failure to adapt to the realignment crises in the fifties. Also at risk are those whose level of social interaction has been reduced by ill health, especially deafness or reduced mobility due to arthritis, giddiness or visual impairment and those who have failed to adjust to a colostomy or facial deformity after a stroke or operation or losing teeth. A person who has dropped out as a result of illness may find it difficult to re-engage. A degree of dementia may reduce social interaction and be a cause of estrangement.

Mental illness may begin when social contacts hitherto just sufficient to give the person some reassurance and to define for him his identity are reduced further. This may happen because of the loss of a relative or friend, or even a dog or a cat, or because an intercurrent physical illness prevents continuation of membership of a social network.

Some old people feel that there is nothing more they need or want to do and await death with composure. Let it come when it comes. Some want it to come soon because existence without a loved one or in pain, physical or psychological has become meaningless. Others are distressed by the prospects of becoming dependent on others.

The suicide rate in women reaches a peak in the decade 55–64 years. The suicide rate in men, after rising steeply in the fifties and sixties, continues to rise even in the eighties. The risk of suicide is at its highest among elderly men, recently bereaved and living on their own, who are out of touch with relatives; the risk is increased further if a man also suffers from a life-threatening illness.

A few deny mortality and push any thought of death out of mind, and a few are fearful. Most talk readily of their expectations, which are more or less realistic, of the length of time remaining to themselves, spouse or friends. They review their life experience, and may become preoccupied by the unresolved conflicts—the unfinished business.

Disengagement creates conditions which favour recall of their past, about which the elderly tend to talk freely. By doing so they remind themselves and others of the esteem in which they were then held, and thus achieve some reinstatement in fantasy. They reveal to children and friends things previously held secret, and try to put right what has gone wrong in their relationships. They seek reconciliation with those from whom they have been estranged, or take steps to make amends or come to recognize that to make amends is no longer possible. Grievances may be recalled and become troublesome. Some are tormented by guilt; some project on to others the shortcomings in their lives. All the defence mechanisms operating at other ages, denial, wish fulfillment in fantasy, projection, displacement, etc. operate also in the elderly. Depression is relatively common, and has been said to affect about 10 per cent of those over 64.

Mental functioning

The intellectual capacity of many elderly shows no decrement even in the eighties. However, there is some evidence in the scores on intelligence tests of a decrement in those who have been living in institutions, perhaps because they have been dependent and lacked intellectual stimulation. In general, the elderly show a change in style in their performance on tests as age increases towards greater hesitation and caution; they tend to respond more slowly. There may be some loss of mental capacity even if it does not show up in scores on tests, but any loss in an individual as age advances tends to be small relative to the differences between individuals. Knowledge and grasp of a specialized field may be preserved into an advanced age.

Dementia

A small proportion of the elderly suffer from 'dementia'. By this is meant a clinical syndrome, the crucial feature of which is a more or less general impairment of intelligence, memory, personality, and skills, without impairment of consciousness.[5] Typically it is progressive. The proportion has been said to be 2 per cent in those aged from 65–69 years, and 10 per cent in those over 80. These figures are not reliable because there is no way in which the degree of dementia can be reliably estimated, and no precise answer to the question: at what point does the loss of mental capacity with ageing become dementia?

The causes of dementia lie in various kinds of diseases of the brain, the commonest of which is cerebral atrophy as a result of the degeneration of brain tissue. Cerebral atrophy is now sometimes called 'Alzheimer's disease' although this term used to be applied only to a particular form of atrophy. Next most common is cerebro-vascular disease or 'multi-infarct' dementia. Other causes are trauma, inflammation (e.g. encephalitis), toxic (e.g. carbon-monoxide poisoning), hypoxia (e.g. as a result of an anaesthetic mishap), and metabolic. The physician has to remain alert to the possibility of disease outside the brain, e.g. myxoedema, congestive heart disease or intracranial tumour.

In cases in which a diagnosis of dementia is reasonably certain, there tends to be some impairment in abstract thinking, visuo-spatial orientation, and memory for recent events. The patient may show difficulty when he has to cope with more than one thing at a time and divide his attention efficiently between them, and when he has to change his 'set' in an object-sorting test, i.e. the principle on which he sorts. Judgement is impaired, and he lacks insight in that he seems to be unaware of the deficiencies in his behaviour or, especially, his memory. Typically, the dementing patient is forgetful without being distressed by being so, whereas the depressed patient overestimates his difficulties in remembering, his complaints being out of proportion to any observable impairment. Failure to recall names especially tends to trouble the depressed, but not the dementing. The mood of the dementing tends to be one of indifference or mild elation. In some cases there is emotional lability; tearfulness, laughing or a flare up of irritation or anger then occurs suddenly without sufficient cause.

The clinical picture varies not only with the amount of neuronal loss but also with the site. The infarcts due to cerebro-vascular disease tend to be localized. When an infarct is in the vicinity of the speech area in the dominant hemisphere, dysphasia is a prominent symptom, which is usually associated with loss of motor function on the other side of the body. In a right-handed person the speech area is in the left cerebral hemisphere, so with dysphasia is associated some paralysis of the right face, arm, and leg. In a left-handed person, the speech area may be in either the right or left hemisphere, so with dysphasia is associated paralysis sometimes on the right, sometimes on the left. Infarcts in 'silent' areas of the brain may cause significant neuronal loss without there being any detectable neurological signs. When there are multiple infarcts, the course is a 'step-wise' loss of mental functions, with a degree of recovery after each episode.

In cases of cerebral atrophy the course is a gradual, at first insidious, progressive decline in performance, with some impairment of memory for recent events and loss of intellectual capacity. Blunting of sensibility and coarsening and disinhibition of behaviour are late effects. The degree of the dementia is probably in proportion to the amount—the 'mass'—of the cortex affected, in accordance with the 'mass-action' theory of cortical function, and is largely independent of the site. 'Computed tomographic scans' of the brain suggest that there can be substantial loss of cortex before unequivocal signs of dementia appear. Impariment of memory disproportionate to the loss of cortex occurs when the floor of the third ventricle is affected, as it may be when there is a tumour near it or in some cases of amnesic syndrome due to alcohol.

Covering up

While the dementia is not severe, a person may learn to cover up the deficiencies in his performance. The devices he uses are similar to those used by patients with a residual defect after incomplete recovery from diffuse brain damage. Difficulty in finding his way about may be dealt with by restricting walks to familiar territory, studying maps or getting written instructions. *Aides-mémoires* compensate for forgetfulness of recent events. Keeping to a routine or an excessive orderliness reduces the chance of being caught out. A name forgotten is covered over by a circumlocution or replaced by a wrong name. A sister's name may replace that of a daughter, the address of an earlier home that of a later.

The diagnosis of dementia is strengthened if the mistakes are not corrected, or if in formal tests wrong responses persevere, and if self-critique is lacking. Dementia is more likely if the events talked of are not given a context in time or place, or are transposed to an earlier occasion. 'Undated memories' are said to be characteristic of the dementing, but they occur also when a person anxiously recalls painful events.

The diagnosis of dementia is unreliable because many of the tendencies held to be characteristic of dementia are also shown by the elderly who are not dementing. Aware of the limits of their physical powers, the elderly become cautious about what they take on. The degree of control they want to impose on their circumstances may be unrealistic. Generally, they adopt a mode of life which takes account of their disabilities, but these are revealed when they are obliged to move out of their routines. They readily become panicky when they fear they cannot cope, their behaviour then disorganizes, and they become agitated and angry, sometimes very angry, sometimes violent. A 'catastrophic reaction' of this kind may suggest dementia but is an unreliable indication of it. An elderly person is vulnerable when, like King Lear, his expectations are unrealistic and are not met, or when he is unduly sensitive to any slight. However, his control over his situation may be threatened both because of the circumstances and because of impairment in his mental functions. In either case paranoid ideas may colour behaviour or be openly expressed.

When the disability is more severe, the question may be put: is it due to depression or dementia? But this question may be misleading since they may co-exist. Brain disease makes a person less able to adapt when a crisis arises in the system of relationships of which he is part, because of a loss or quarrel or change in role made necessary by a change in dependency needs. Not adapting he becomes depressed. Or his depression reflects his awareness of the decline in his mental or physical powers. Some of the causes of the decline can be removed, e.g. those due to inappropriate medication (a common cause), chronic infection, dietary deficiency, deafness, and loss of mobility due to foot conditions. A relatively common mistake when a diagnosis of dementia is being proposed is failure to recognize the part played in the impairment of mental function by depression.[6]

The patterns of behaviour adopted by the elderly represent attempts to compensate for any decline in their powers. The decompensation which occurs when a pattern is not suited to the circumstances may be rapid and produce confusion, which is usually reversible. At the same time the dementia is uncovered. But there may be a degree of recovery after a period of instability as a result of reorganization in the system of relationships and the development of a new pattern.

Dying

Difficulties arise when members of the family and doctors, in order to defend themselves against their own anxieties, deny that a person is dying. Yet they often do so. Those who have had experience of talking with the dying testify to the frequency with which they consider death to be a possible or probable outcome of their illnesses and welcome opportunities to talk about their feelings. Evasions and untruths prevent them, not only from taking ordinary practical measures to put their affairs in order, but also from working out their relationships with those near and dear. To open up communication may be of great help, and make possible reconciliation with those from whom there has been estrangement. Family members, too, are helped, and their reactions to bereavement when it comes are less distressing and follow a shorter and easier course.

The dying suffer from fears of several kinds. They fear pain. They fear losing control over their feelings and behaviour and, especially, over bowel and bladder. They fear becoming dependent and being abandoned. They fear, too, the loss of status they suffer when they have to give up their roles in the family, and the weakening of identity when they have to give up the activities which distinguished them. Sometimes they are angry that they have become ill, and that their illness has not been dealt with. They regret the unfinished business, such as helping their children to become independent or making provision for spouse or other dependents. In consequence, they may feel that they are unworthy or have failed. On the other hand, they may get some relief from distress through fantasies in dreams or daydreams of reunion with dead members of the family or dead friends. They may turn back to a belief in religious ideas. They may achieve a sense of surviving through identification with the living to whom they are able to give.

The disturbed feelings arising out of the recall and re-evaluation of the painful experiences of earlier phases of their lives may be transferred into their relationships with those caring for them, such as spouse, nurse or doctor. The past may become more preoccupying as they regress and become more dependant. The carers, if they can accept the disturbed feelings, then have the opportunity to help them to come to terms with the past. Progress may be very rapid as death approaches.

NOTES AND REFERENCES

1. Crawford, M. P. (1971). Retirement and disengagement. *Hum. Relat.* **24,** 255–78.
2. This tendency was shown by some of the widows included in a survey of the structure of families in Bethnal Green, London: Townsend, P. (1957). *The family life of old people.* Routledge & Kegan Paul, London. A more recent survey is Bowling, A. and Cartwright, A. (1982). *Life after death: a study of the elderly widowed.* Tavistock Publications, London.
3. Kay, D. W. K., Beamish, P. and Roth, M. (1964). Old-age mental disorders in Newcastle upon Tyne: a study of possible social and medical causes. *Br. J. Psychiat.* **110,** 668–82.
4. A convenient review of the illnesses of the elderly is Levy, R. and Post, F. (eds), (1982). *The psychiatry of late life.* Blackwell, Oxford.
5. Lishman, W. A. (1978). *Organic psychiatry.* Blackwell, Oxford.
6. For an example of the use of mental tests in the differential diagnosis of the normal, depressed, and dementing elderly see Kendrick, D. C., Gibson, A. J., and Moyes, I. C. A. (1979). The revised Kendrick battery: clinical studies. *Br. J. soc. clin. Psychol* **18,** 329–40.

8 Methods of psychotherapy

Psychiatry is sometimes regarded by patient and public as the means by which displeasing or disturbing behaviour is brought under control, and as being successful when symptoms are reduced or suppressed. The use of drugs is successful in this sense if it reduces the amount of disturbed behaviour even if it does nothing to modify the underlying tendencies. However, the aim of psychotherapy is more ambitious. It is to enable behaviour tendencies and attitudes to be modified by experience and thus to relieve suffering. Much of disordered behaviour has shown itself to be resistant to modification by ordinary experience. The problem is therefore to create the special conditions in which learning will be resumed or, as Frank put it, to bring about the arousal and display of attitudes under conditions in which they can be influenced, i.e. in which new learning can take place.[1]

The term psychotherapy is restricted to procedures carried out within a relationship between patient, or client, and therapist which is professional in two senses. Firstly, the therapist uses his knowledge and skill for the benefit of the patient and having regard to the objectives agreed between them. He recognizes an ethical code, and does not exploit for his own ends the patient's dependence on him. The patient is free to terminate the relationship whenever he pleases. Secondly, the therapist is guided by a scientific theory giving him some understanding of the processes concerned in psychotherapy. Also, he has had supervised experience in the methods he uses, and these methods have been evaluated.

The term 'patient', which in its derivation implies suffering, is usually preferred in the health service, 'client', which implies listening, in the social services. In its modern use, 'client' means one who uses the services of a professional. Counselling, which may be regarded as a special form of psychotherapy, depends on conveying information and giving advice or guidance, or even conciliating or arbitrating, on matters more immediate and practical than are usually the issues in psychotherapy. It gives less importance to the expression of feelings or the discovery of their origins in past experience.

How can behaviour tendencies and attitudes be modified by psychotherapy? What are the essential processes? Here are some of the answers that have been given.

Supernatural powers

In ancient Greece, in Aeschylus's play *The Oresteia*, for instance, Orestes' madness is depicted as the guilt and suffering resulting from the pursuit of the Furies, who as agents of the divinely appointed order inflict madness as a form of vengeance, chiefly on those who have murdered their kindred. They confront him as soon as he has killed his mother. In modern terms, they are projections, as hallucinations, of ideas about the anger of the dead mother. He recovers when the pursuit is called off as a result of Athena's mediation and his trial by jury at the Council of Aeropagus. The Furies are transformed into gracious spirits, and he is declared by Apollo to be cleansed of pollution. The court of justice, by regulating impulsive violence, restores law and order and upholds the civic state. For Orestes the sequence is confession, expiation, and reconciliation.

Until the Renaissance in the fifteenth and sixteenth centuries it was usual to attribute misfortunes or disorder and unnatural acts to supernatural powers, like those manifest in witchcraft. There has been a popular belief at all times in history, as even today, that there are humans who, having made a pact with the devil, as Dr Faustus did in Marlowe's play, assume supernatural powers. Conflicts between people are then seen as fights between God and Satan, good and evil.

Those suspect of heresy or responsibility for unnatural or subversive acts are accused of witchcraft and devil worship. So to accuse serves the purposes of the accusers and justifes the actions they take. These may be extreme when there is no social institution to regulate them. When there is such an institution, interpersonal conflicts can be acknowledged and reviewed, the legitimacy of the interests in conflict being recognized. It is then possible to seek accommodation and reconciliation through negotiation and compromise. In modern practice, the negotiation takes place formally or informally in a variety of settings, sometimes in a consulting room or clinic, only exceptionally in a court. Anger, shame, and remorse are expressed. The issues are clarified, and attitudes modified. Goodwill is restored. The exercise of power is regulated.

Yet already by the start of the seventeenth century it was being said that supernatural explanation whether of witchcraft or demonic possession is unnecessary. External agents such as evil spirits were replaced in explanations by humoral processes, and the seat of diseases such as hysteria was moved from the uterus to the brain.

Any explanation in terms of supernatural powers is to be regarded as a metaphor to be translated so far as it may be possible to do so into the terms of natural science. Not translated it makes a moral judgement over a social or interpersonal issue which tends to be destructive of one side or another and of human values in general. It makes no analysis of the issue, and embarrasses attempts at reconciliation. Moreover it tends to be accepted as soon as it chimes in with an emotional need. But a medical explanation in the terms of internal, humoral processes, although now widely accepted in other contexts, does not provide an alternative, nor the terms into which to translate ideas about evil spirits. Instead, the spirits who are thought to possess the patient are to be regarded in psychological terms as representations of his 'other self', partly or wholly split off. The conflict between good and evil is then intra-psychic, or interpersonal in so far as the other self represents another person.

Exorcism

There are still some who believe that disordered thoughts, feelings or behaviour or bodily discomforts are due to possession by evil spirits, and some patients too talk occasionally of being possessed, or claim that malignant influences are putting voices or thoughts into their heads. 'The voice was given me, but I was not the master of it; I was but the instrument' is how Perceval put it in his narrative of his schizophrenic illness.[2] Patients or relatives may ask for exorcism, a method of healing depending on the use of spiritual power, e.g. through appeal or adjuration, to expel the spirits. Some patients value and wish to retain them. In some cultures possession confers prestige, and permits a person to assume roles not otherwise open to him, especially a sick role, which exempts him from normal social responsibilities.[3]

Exorcism, although it carries the danger that it makes the patient more disturbed, has been found to be effective in some cases at least. To what processes its effects are due is uncertain. It may be that seeking exorcism a person acknowledges his guilt indirectly and transfers to those undertaking the exorcism some of the responsibility for the control of unacceptable impulses. Also, he gains some support through interacting with the healer and witnesses, who become involved in his affliction.

In the nineteenth century discussions centred on two themes: the integration into society of the mentally ill through 'moral management', with the cultivation of self-control over disruptive tendencies, and the relations between suggestibility, hypnosis and hysterical symptoms, and the use of suggestion and hypnotism in treatment.

Psychoanalysis

The end of the nineteenth century saw the development of psychoanalysis, which provided a more comprehensive explanation of the effects of psychotherapy than had previously been attempted. Psychoanalysis was remarkable in two main respects. It recognized, firstly, that the symptoms of mental illness, which might otherwise be regarded as accidental or capricious products of the breakdown of the functions of the brain, have meaning in that they express ideas and feelings derived from experience or, especially, from the 'unconscious'; and, secondly, that even the strangest manifestations of insanity, as well as of lesser disorders, and slips of the tongue, errors, wit, dreams, and artistic productions can be explained in terms of psychological processes. These were regarded in the early days as intra-psychic, later as interpersonal as well as intra-psychic. The next step was to discover through what processes symptoms were relieved.

Abreaction and catharsis

In the early days of psychoanalysis Breuer and Freud showed that the recall of a traumatic experience could lead to the relief of anxiety and other symptoms, and supposed that this was due to the release or 'abreaction' of the emotion pent up with the experience when it was 'repressed'. Abreaction has thus a purifying effect, which can be described as 'cathartic'; one of Breuer's patients called it 'chimney sweeping'. The term 'catharsis' may also be used in the more general sense of purging emotions through vicarious expression, e.g. by hearing, reading or seeing representations on the stage of the exploits of others. In purgatory the soul is cleansed by suffering and expiation.

Early psychoanalytical theory referred to excitation in the central nervous system being discharged, when a traumatic experience is recalled, in accordance with the homeostatic 'tendency to keep intracerebral excitation constant'. The degree of benefit has been held to depend on the intensity of the emotional expression. Ideas of this kind linger on, but have not been seriously entertained since the Second World War when methods intended to produce 'excitatory abreaction' had a vogue, e.g. the intravenous injection of methedrine or inhalation of ether, the patient being encouraged to cry, shout, and struggle while reliving the experience. The outcome was said to be better when anger rather than terror was expressed, full recall of the experience being unnecessary. Similar displays of emotion are encouraged at times by some religious sects.

An alternative explanation of the relief of symptoms after feelings have been expressed is that exchanges are initiated with another person. A child refused a toy screams and kicks. What matters is not the discharge of emotion but the consequent interaction with the mother and its outcome. The benefit the bereaved derive from expressing their feelings to others and talking about their loss is due to the effect that doing so has on their relationships with them.

Blocking and distortion of emotional expression are characteristic of many forms of mental illness. Many depressed patients, for instance, are unable to communicate their feelings, perhaps especially their anger. The therapist tries to create the conditions in which they can do so, e.g. by responding himself in a way which encourages expression. While expressing their feelings, patients start to re-formulate the issues.

The undoing of repression

Freud soon gave up the idea of catharsis and then argued that painful memories, being 'excluded from association' by repression, achieve 'psychic autonomy'. Although not then at the disposal of the patient in the way his more commonplace memories are, they may recur in dreaming or other 'dissociated' states with 'the undiminished vividness of recent events' and 'an astonishing integrity and intensity of feeling'. The therapeutic process lies in the undoing of repression, i.e. making conscious the unconcscious, so that the circumstances in which the symptom first appeared can be recalled. The memory then 'becomes merged in the great complex of associations, and is ranged alongside of other experiences which perhaps contradict it; thus it undergoes correction by means of other ideas'.[4]

Hypnotism

Freud, following Breuer, used hypnotism for a while as a method for the uncovering of traumatic experiences. Hypnotism induces a state of heightened suggestibility ('hypnosis') with the aid of various artifices. However, he gave up the method, which is still controversial, in favour of free association and interpretation, which became the essential features of the psychoanalytical method. His reasons for doing so were that its effects on symptoms were capricious, short-lived, and unreliable. It has the serious disadvantages that it increases the patient's passivity and dependency and strengthens belief in the magic of the therapist's powers.

Narcoanalysis

Another method of bringing about the recall of memories is the giving of a drug either by mouth or into a vein. The drugs used most often while the method was in vogue during the nineteen-forties and fifties were narcotics, such as barbiturates, given into a vein—hence the term 'narcoanalysis'. Recall and discussion are facilitated because the drug, like alcohol, loosens the tongue by, it is said, removing inhibitions. What is recalled under the influence of alcohol is not wholly or even largely truthful, despite the tag '*in vino veritas*'; the popular term 'truth drug' is a misnomer.

Free association and interpretation

Freud took an important step forward when he developed free association as a method of circumventing the resistances to the recall of traumatic experiences. When protected from distractions and encouraged to relax and allow their thoughts full rein and expression, patients reveal through free association a wide range of experiences not otherwise recalled. This recall from the recent and remote past is piecemeal, gradual, and progressive. Anxiety is kept to a minimum because the patient sets his own pace. The therapist interprets the gaps, hesitations, and digressions in what is recalled. That is, he explains what they mean, and he puts what is recalled into a context of other ideas. Interpretation, as well as being explanatory, is thus also 'transformative' in that it is intended to affect the patient's attitudes. Nevertheless, the free-association method is very lengthy.

Transference

The recall of repressed memories is also facilitated, Freud soon discovered, by the 'transference' of attitudes previously held towards parents or other significant persons into the patient's relationship with the therapist. The transference is 'positive' when the patient is compliant, 'negative' when he is defiant. A positive relationship may by itself relieve symptoms, but this is no more than a 'transference cure'. A strong, persistent transference, with dependence on the therapist, amounts to a 'transference neurosis'. 'Counter-transference' means the transfer of the therapist's feelings into the relationship with the patient; these have to be recognized and overcome.

It was the habit at one time for the psychoanalyst to sit unseen behind the patient who lay on a couch. This encouraged the development of fantasy about him, and he became a blank screen on to which the patient projected his feelings. However, the emphasis gradually moved from the analysis of what was recalled during the sessions or in dreaming to the analysis of the transference relationship. This became the main therapeutic tool of psycho-analysis and its hallmark in the years between the wars. The transference relationship is an inevitable necessity, Freud argued. Psychoanalysis does not create it. It brings it to light so that it can be combatted at the appropriate time. It has to be dissolved before treatment ends so that the patient can re-assert his independence and resume an adult role; dissolution proves difficult in some cases.

Confession

The recall and reporting of past experience may bring with it acknowledge-ment, i.e. self-accusation made before someone in authority, of fault or offence. It may then be called 'confession'. The patient when confessing is contrite and remorseful, and reaffirms the rules and expectations of the social group of which he is a member. He is then in a better position to try to restore his relationships with others, and symptoms may be relieved as a result. But in confessing he may disown his offences as the work of the devil.

Psychotherapy has been regarded as a secular form of confession which is more suited to the attitudes now prevailing among the middle classes. But there are important distinctions. The psychotherapist tries to create the conditions in which the patient can re-evaluate his own experience for himself. He refrains from judgements about right and wrong, and removes, so far as he can, pressures on the patient to conform. The positive transference, by giving him status as an authority, encourages a patient to be contrite but his aim is to free the patient so that he can decide for himself what rules he wishes to follow in his relationships. He encourages the patient to accept that what he has done are facts about himself, which he may wish to repent.

Overcoming the resistances to recall

Repression, i.e. active forgetting, of an experience is a 'defence mechanism' in that it protects the person from the anxiety associated with the experience. It may be regarded as an instrumental avoidance response that serves to remove the person from a danger situation. One of the ways in which repression is maintained is engagement in other activities. When recall is imminent, the person starts doing something else. Restless activity, it should be noted, is a common feature of mental illness, and there are many patients who become anxious if they do not busy themselves continuously. Obsessional habits and rituals may also play a part in maintaining repression, and in mania, or hypomania, the incessant activity and flight of ideas serve a similar purpose. Another way of maintaining repression is transformation of the experience into a fixed, stereotyped memory, expressed usually in verbal terms, occasionally in visual images. This memory is recalled readily, although capriciously and without emotion. It is an impoverished and inaccurate representation of the original events, no more than a token, although it may give an impression of vividness.

The defence may partly fail when the person is tired, in the hynogogic state before going to sleep, while dreaming, under hypnosis or under the influence of drugs. In all these conditions there is a degree of disengagement. What is then recalled is a selective, fragmentary version of the original events, filled out with fantasies of recent origin.

To recall the experience is to re-enter in thought the danger situation. Psychoanalysis makes this possible by requiring the patient to disengage from business in hand and to withdraw attention from other things. The re-entry is in easy stages, the patient setting his own pace and being allowed to avoid the painful areas up to a point. Interpretation of the gaps in what is recalled puts some pressure on him, so that his tentative explorations range further and further into the painful areas.

The part played in the relief of symptoms by the recall of traumatic experiences has gradually been re-evaluated as a result of the shift in emphasis that gives more importance to the analysis of the transference. Freud supposed that what was recalled during psychoanalysis had been stored in memory more or less intact because repression had prevented it from being incorporated into 'schemata'. This supposition has been abandoned as the recognition has grown that what purport to be memories are versions of past events which have been reconstructed in the light of contemporary attitudes. What is recalled throws more light on the present than the past, and is seen rather as an indicator of recovery than a cause of it. What has not been recalled has been withheld rather than repressed. His developing relationship with the therapist gives the patient the confidence to reveal his preoccupation with versions of his past experience. The aim of treatment came thus to be redefined, not as lifting amnesia for traumata of the past, but as opening up communication within the transference relationship.

Interpersonal processes

Psychoanalysis was at first dominated by 'instinct' theory, which supposed that symptoms reflect the vicarious discharge of energy derived from instincts which because of frustration has not been discharged normally. Symptoms thus arise out of intra-psychic processes. The positive transference was valued because it provided the conditions for the expression of the 'tension' resulting from the frustration of instincts as well as for the recall of traumatic experiences.

Recall was facilitated because the transference supplied the contexts and orientations of childhood. The patient adopted the role of child and imposed on the therapist the role of parent, and wanted to be told what to do, thus shifting the responsibility for taking decisions to the therapist. This display of the attitudes held towards parents and the growing recognition of the difficulties produced by positive transference gave support to views that illnesses arise because the attitudes acquired through unhappy experiences in childhood permeate all the patient's relationships, especially those with his spouse, children, and other members of his family as well as with peers and colleagues.

These attitudes reappear in his relationship with the therapist. If in his relationships with others he tends to crave affection or reassurance or to be passive, dependent, domineering, shy, distant, sensitive, suspicious, hostile, negativistic or mendacious, he is likely to show similar tendencies in his relationship with the therapist. This transference provides opportunities therefore for modifying them. The aim of therapy is then to work out a satisfactory relationship with the therapist.

In 'transactional analysis', a specialized approach to psychotherapy, attention is paid to the position a person adopts in a transaction with another, whether as 'adult', 'parent' or 'child', and to what he does to manipulate the relationship in order to achieve a position more favourable to his purposes; this is the 'game' he plays. If he becomes a 'child', for instance, and the other a 'parent', he is relieved of the responsibility for taking decisions, and he may try to establish this kind of relationship with the therapist. Because patients tend to attribute power and authority to him, the therapist may have to take care not to assume the position of 'parent' and insist that the responsibility for decisions lies with the patient.

Interpersonal processes have assumed a greater importance in modern psychotherapy than intra-psychic processes, and the emphasis has also shifted from an instinct to a social theory, from biological to social factors, from history-taking to analysis of the here-and-now, from reasons for the genesis of symptoms to reasons for their persistence, and from acute symptoms to faulty habits and attitudes. These changes began in the nineteen-thirties, the lead being taken by the 'Neo-Freudians' who had moved to USA from Europe. In the special conditions of the war years, group therapy first developed as the means by which psychotherapy could be made widely available.

MEDIATION

There was a further shift in emphasis in the nineteen-sixties and seventies. The re-enactment of the conflicts of the past within the relationship with the therapist came to be regarded as less important than the changes brought about in the patient's relationships with members of his family, colleagues, etc, outside the therapeutic sessions. These relationships 'can change as a result of experience, supervised by the therapist, in a group, i.e. in 'group therapy', or in the family, i.e. 'family therapy'.[5]

The therapist is then a mediator, an outsider who intervenes in order to bring about a change in relationships, and especially to reconcile. In work with a couple, he serves as a go-between or third party. He may serve as a broker who helps patient and spouse, or patient and other person, to negotiate the terms on which they are to relate to one another. He is then a catalyst of change. Occasionally he gives advice or arbitrates. Mostly he promotes conversation between the parties. His relationship with the patient is temporary and to be broken off as soon as it has served its purpose.

Other changes took place in what the therapist does. Psychoanalysts used to restrict themselves to work with the patient and seldom had any contact with any other member of his family. If the spouse was ill too, it was usual for him or her to be treated by a colleague. If the patient was a child, the mother was normally seen by a psychiatric social worker. That is, members of families were treated separately.

When illness is regarded as arising out of processes in the family, the therapist may interview other members of the family either separately or together with the person who has come forward as the patient. Or he may share the work with a second therapist, each 'co-therapist' seeing one of a couple. They may then come together as a foursome. To see the couple, or several members of the family, together is informative because the co-therapists can observe directly the interactions in the family.

There are some advantages to be gained if one co-therapist is male, and the other female. Working as a co-therapist provides opportunities for improving techniques, as a result either of observing the other or of discussing afterwards with the other what happened during the session, perhaps in the presence of a supervisor.

Referral as a crisis

People seek the help of a psychotherapist when they are ready to question the terms on which their relationships are based, or when the system of relationships to which they belong has begun to decompensate, and a crisis is imminent. Matters may have already reached a crisis as a result of a significant event which challenges the system. Sometimes the event is of no more significance than the straw which breaks the camel's back. Sometimes the seeking of professional help is seen as a way of warding off the crisis and preserving the system as it has been. More often the patient is anxious about the effects of the decompensation and wants help and support while he copes with them. Sometimes the system is stable, but the roles it imposes are felt to be unsatisfactory by the patient or another of its members.

A three-act scenario

The psychotherapist may be helped to plan his strategy if he sees what he does in the context of the three-act scenario of a well-made play.

In Act I—*challenge*—something happens which challenges the assumptions two or more people make about each other and brings the system of their relationships to a crisis. Homeostasis fails, and the system decompensates.

In Act II—*exploration*—the crisis is followed by a period of instability or 'disequilibrium' while the implications and consequences of the crisis are explored. Attempts are made to work out terms on which to restore the relationships.

In Act III—*reorganization*—there is no return to the status quo. In some cases there is a gradual 'working through' to a new, perhaps more mature pattern of relationships, with some redistribution of the offices and roles and the responsibilities which go with them. Those concerned are satisfied with the new pattern, which is flexible and modifiable. In some cases the relationships stabilize on terms more restrictive than before and more disabling to one or other or both partners. In some cases there is a progressive estrangement and then separation. Sometimes events move towards tragedy: a disastrous, perhaps fatal conclusion.

Crises in a system are broadly of three kinds: 'structural'—a member of the system drops out or threatens to do so; 'conceptual'—something happens which causes perceptions, assumptions or expectations to be re-evaluated; and 'developmental'—the roles which a person accepts or which are expected of him change because of a developmental change, perhaps a biological change such as puberty, or physical disability.

Let us return to the example given in CHAPTER 1 of a lovers' quarrel. The terms of their partnership are challenged, let us suppose, by the discovery by one of the infidelity of the other. This brings the system to a 'conceptual' crisis. During the ensuing period of instability they try to resolve the difficulties in their relationship constructively, but so far in vain. At this point one or both may seek help from psychotherapy or counselling. The one seeking help has usually accepted that at least part of the fault lies in him, and the seeking of help reflects partly some loss of hope of finding without help a way out of the difficulties and partly some revival of hope that a way may yet be found. He may still be actively reviewing what has happened and looking for a solution. If so, he tends to show more or less intense anxiety. Or he may have become dejected and discouraged, i.e. depressed, as a result of his continued failure to find a solution. Or he may show some denial of the difficulties or other defences, with which is associated some relief of anxiety.

In these cases the psychotherapist adopts a strategy intended to encourage further exploration and then reorganization to form a new pattern of relationship. The crisis being recent, he tries to stop defences from being established, to arrest 'contractile processes', to keep the options open and to prevent stabilization of the system in a way likely to reduce the flexibility and modifiability of the relationships in it.

The strategy is different when there has already been reorganization and stabilization of the relationships, but on more or less unsatisfactory terms for one or more of those concerned. After a crisis in a marriage the relationship may be restored, but with a shift in positions, one of the couple taking a position more of parent, and the other more that of child. Alternatively, one accepts, and the other projects, the blame for the difficulties, which are not resolved, the former, who is more often the wife, losing self-esteem and becoming liable to depression. One or both may accept a new belief system which offers security and confirms identity, but which is more restrictive.

In such cases the objective of psychotherapeutic intervention may be to destabilize in order to release the couple or the members of a family from a deadlock in the games they are playing with one another. This is to restore flexibility and modifiability and to enable learning to be resumed.

Recent crisis

A person who has recently suffered a painful experience, such as a quarrel, loss or failure, may show during the period of instability a tendency to withdraw and may be encouraged to do so by his relatives. He may go away on holiday, for instance, or be admitted to hospital for a rest, or be removed in some other way from the situation in which he has broken down. Temporary withdrawal is beneficial when it breaks a vicious circle of increasing anxiety and decreasing efficiency, or when it allows the person to reassess the situation and plan his return to it. Also, it gives time for the situation itself to change, perhaps to his advantage. But powers of adaptation do not always recover with the rest. On the contrary, rest may favour the establishment of neurotic defences; it may strengthen avoidance tendencies. The psychotherapist has to decide therefore when to encourage the patient to return. To do so too early runs the risk that he will not cope and will suffer further pain or failure. To do so too late runs the risk that defences become firmly established.

Immediate return

The popular belief is that the sooner the rider who has taken a toss gets back into the saddle, the more readily he will do so. There is probably some truth in it although there is no systematic evidence on which to decide. Similarly, the driver, the pilot or the workman who has sustained an accident regains his confidence more easily if he resumes soon. Again, those who break down during active fighting in war are said to be more likely to make a return to active duty if they are not evacuated to base hospitals, but are treated near the fighting so that they make an early return to it. The student who has fled from the examination room can more readily be got back into it the same or next day than if his return is held up. An immediate return to school is recommended when a child is showing a tendency to refuse to go. The spouse who has left the home after a quareel is persuaded to return immediately on the supposition that the longer the delay, the greater the difficulties.

Forced solutions

Suggestion, persuasion, cajolement, coercion, offering bribes, etc, directed at getting a person to return, are occasionally successful before defences become established. Often they fail, but are continued because they nearly prove effective. They tend to fail at the brink because, in accordance with the principles of learning theory, the closer the danger, the stronger the avoidance tendency. Phobic patients do not overcome their fears even when great pressure is put on them to do so. In cases of anorexia nervosa, starvation is not sufficient to overcome aversion from food. The punishment of avoidance tendencies does not work. If it does eliminate a particular avoidance response, a new method of avoidance, i.e. a new symptom, appears.

The patient may be forced to return, on the analogy of the forcing of rats in Masserman's experiments to return to the food-box. The forced solution is the traditional sink-or-swim method. The consequences are not always advantageous. The child sometimes does sink. Psychiatric casualties in wartime when forced back into combat through the coercion of custom, duty, authority, and the threat of disciplinary action wander off in a fugue sometimes or throw their lives away. The pilot returning to duty immediately after an accident may be clumsy and inefficient. The student forced back into the examination room may become disorganized or depressed. The young man with sexual difficulties, flinching from marriage, but forced into it by pressure from his family, may become seriously disturbed.

Forced solutions are seldom practicable, for sufficient pressures cannot be brought to bear on the patient, who can usually find a way of escape—a more sympathetic doctor, for instance. Yet they are often resorted to with an optimism not justified by the results. Anyone who has attempted a forced solution in a case of anorexia nervosa knows of the lengths to which the patient goes to evade the pressures on her, and of the variety of the devices to which she resorts. A special example is the removal in narcoanalysis of the defences preventing the recall of a traumatic experience. This is often effective although sometimes the patient falls asleep.

Learning in easy stages

A different method is to give back to the patient as much control over his situation as possible and, in particular, to remove all coercions. He will then re-engage with the other or others and make tentative explorations of the issues. He does so without becoming anxious if he is free to withdraw at any time. This method, which resembles the 'desensitization' method of 'behaviour therapy', depends upon learning in easy stages, gradualness being an essential feature. The psychotherapist plans the patient's experience no more than is necessary to ensure that the patient does not meet a situation he cannot master. Confidence is built up through success, and the explorations are then extended in extent and duration. The patient prepares for the difficult by learning first to master the simple.

Consider a case of 'neurotic' amnesia of recent onset. Direct questioning is rarely if ever effective in removing the amnesia. The psychotherapist proceeds by opening up communication with the patient on trivial matters, which the patient can deal with easily and without embarrassment, the range of the conversation being gradually extended, and the patient being allowed to retreat from any topic which raises anxiety. Gradually he will gain the confidence to talk about matters of importance. This method is better than using drugs to remove defences, as in narcoanalysis, for it helps to establish a good relationship and does not make loss of memory appear mysterious and beyond the patient's control.

A similar method can be used in the treatment of other losses of function. These are regarded as instrumental avoidance responses, which are abandoned when the person acquires new ways of coping through learning in easy stages. The learning takes place if he is given control over the situation, which he can then explore. It is facilitated by social imitation where others are seen to be coping more or less successfully. This both shows how and gives confidence. Discussion with others similarly affected, in the course of group therapy, may have similar effects.

Confirming reality

The instability after a crisis is severe in some cases. There may then be disorganization of behaviour, loss of sense of identity, and uncertainties about what is self or non-self, or what is internal experience or external event. If reality testing is suspended, and these uncertainties are not relieved, the illness may be regarded as a psychosis.

In other cases the patient expresses his thoughts and feelings in idiosyncratic messages, which convey information in a disguised form. The messages may be difficult to understand when they are expressed in metaphors, or when the verbal messages are not sufficiently amplified or qualified by non-verbal messages through, for instance, posture, gesture or facial expression. The non-verbal messages may appear to contradict the verbal. Examples of unclear messages given during a quarrel are to swallow 20 tablets of aspirin or to smash a favourite vase. They are imprecise in important respects although their meaning may be guessed at. What is it that the person dares not express more precisely?

The psychotherapist confirms the patient's identity through the relationship he forms with him. He helps to define reality for the patient and to corroborate his perceptions. He interprets unclear messages and encourages their translation into less opaque terms. By doing so he helps the patient to define the issues in more specific, less general, terms. He counteracts the loss of self-esteem or any rate makes the loss less general. When the crisis arose out of a quarrel, he mediates between those involved.

Treating depression of recent onset

Most patients described as depressed positively avoid certain things. To others they intend to return although for the present they are inactive and discouraged from doing so. There are thus both avoidance responses and unresponsiveness due to habituation, the former reinforced when they relieve the anticipation of danger and the latter, tending to recover. The effects of both are similar in that they keep the patient out of the situation in which he experienced pain or failed to cope. While he stays out, there is a deadlock. Not regaining control he continues to avoid the situation and to be depressed in relation to it. The avoidance is not uncomfortable. With the depression is associated a more or less general hopelessness and loss of self-esteem, which are to be reduced as a result of treatment.

The method is similar to that of learning in easy stages. The first step is to reduce the demands made on the patient. In the easier circumstances of the hospital ward, for instance, he may achieve small successes, the effect of which is to restore responsiveness and to build confidence. He is put to do simple things at first, for his efficiency is likely to be greatly impaired, and then allowed to extend gradually the range of his activities. He may make visits to his home, brief to start with and to be cut short if he feels threatened or distressed. At the same time he is encouraged to explore through recall the painful experiences related to the crisis which he has hitherto avoided, whether they involved a quarrel, loss or disappointment. This is akin to the procedure of 'guided mourning'.[6] Confidence is restored slowly but progressively. To recover fully, he has to redeem his position in his family, although perhaps on new terms, to bring about a reconciliation with those from whom he has been estranged, and to engage in new relationships.

Electroplexy (ECT) is sometimes administered as a means of breaking the deadlock, although much less often than it used to be when little was known of the psychological processes. It is not known how ECT brings about its remarkable effects in cases of depression. However, it restores responsiveness temporarily, and enables the patient to make a start on putting right what has gone wrong in his relationships. How much he benefits seems to depend upon what he does during the period of relaxation immediately following the treatment. This is an opportunity for the ward staff to develop their relationships with him.

The timing of the administration of ECT or other treatment intended to counteract depression, such as 'anti-depressant' medication, is a matter of judgement. Depression protects from the effects of excessive stimulation, and is helpful until the time is ripe for the patient to re-engage. After a disaster or severe bereavement, sudden, unprepared for or in distressing circumstances, the patient needs time. The right speed is one at which the patient can regain confidence and self-esteem through coping successfully, however limited the gains may be at first. Even then other defences are likely to appear and last for a while during the second phase of recovery. The risk of suicide is incurred when the patient beginning to recover is encouraged with misguided optimism to re-engage with his problems too soon and suffers a set-back. With depression is always associated anger at others and especially at one's self.

PROMOTING CHANGE

Psychotherapeutic help is sought, less often during the period of instability, more often after relationships have been stabilized, but on terms unsatisfactory or disabling to one or more of these concerned, who feel themselves to be in an impasse. A couple may feel, for instance, that they are trapped in a relationship which involves them in destructive behaviour towards one another. Much of what they do is self-defeating and repetitive, but they do not learn from it. The aim of psychotherapy is to destabilize the relationship and promote change.

The psychotherapist has been called 'an outside agitator', but this supposes that he is partisan, for instance, in the struggle of a young person to break free from the oppression and mystification of his family.[7] His aim is to liberate, but he is at pains to be impartial and not to take sides either for or against any of those involved. There are several things he can do.

History taking

There is a tradition in medicine that before treatment comes diagnosis, but this is a poor model for psychotherapy. Treatment starts as soon as, or even before, patient and therapist meet. What happens between them initiates changes in the way the patient sees himself and others, and impetus is lost if the therapist attends to the mere gathering of information. This is of no value for research, unless specifically planned for this purpose, and there is no point in collecting data for some ill-defined research in the future. Gaps in knowledge about the patient and his relatives can be filled in due course.

History taking should be educative for the patient and the others involved with him. It is more important for the patient than the therapist to see 'meaningful connections' between current attitudes and both remote as well as recent experiences. That the therapist asks about his relationships with parents, sibs, peers, and previous partners, and what has happened to them, rather than about, say, physical symptoms, directs his attention towards aspects of his past life to which hitherto he has given little importance. Doing this may by itself start him off on a review of his attitudes.

Intruders

In the course of the history taking one or more persons are usually identified with whom the patient has quarrelled and not been reconciled, or whose loss he has failed to mourn. These persons are likely to intrude, like the ghost of Hamlet's father or the stranger in Ibsen's *Lady from the Sea*, at some stage in the psychotherapy. The intruder in psychotherapy with a couple is often a parent or a former lover of one of them. It may even be useful to have a fourth chair in the consulting room as a symbol, i.e. a reminder that there are others not present who have to be considered.

Who participates?

Decisions have to be taken at an early stage on how to proceed. Should the person presenting as patient be treated on his own on a one-to-one basis? Should a couple be treated conjointly, i.e. talking together with one or two therapists? Should each be treated independently or collaboratively, i.e. each with a co-therapist and with occasional discussions as a foursome? Should several couples be treated in a group by one or more therapists? Should each join an independent group? Should other family members be brought in and be treated as a family group? Which members? Or the whole family? Different institutes show different preferences. The collaborative method especially has found favour, but there is not yet sufficient evidence to answer questions about the indications for or against each method.[8]

What the therapist does

The therapist's aim is to create the conditions in which attitudes are elicited and reviewed, in which issues are defined, and in which in due course the patient and those relating to him can take, after due consideration, decisions for themselves. He gives full support to the responsibility of each of the participants to decide and act on his own behalf. He may indicate what things should be put on to the scales, but he is 'non-directive' in that he leaves it to the patient and others to decide how much weight should be given to each of them.

Much that he does is intended to restore the confidence and self-esteem of each, but not of one at the expense of the other. He tries to ensure that any confusion a person may feel about his identity is relieved as he reviews in the course of the history taking and subsequently what kind of person he has been and has become.

He provides security so that each participant feels that he can take risks in exposing feelings, opinions, and ideas. Like a referee he ensures that confrontations or disagreements do not get out of control, and that the rules required by courtesy and respect for others are not broken. He tries to sustain an optimum level of anxiety while ideas and feelings are being worked through, at times dampening down and at times stirring up.

In conjoint or family therapy he may break the pattern of interaction in order to expose attitudes to review. When the pattern is one in which one of a couple holds forth and the other says little, for instance, he invites the latter to comment on or answer the points the former has made. He may briefly take one side or the other and alternate. Or he may put the question 'across', asking the one how the other had mourned the loss of a parent or child. By doing so, he may bring to light sharp discrepancies between the evaluations of the two about what has happened.

He poses apt questions, as Socrates did, which throw doubt on the formulation of a problem and show that neither of a couple nor the therapist understand it. They can then agree to co-operate in efforts to arrive at an understanding. He makes interrogatory suggestions, which are tentative interpretations or 'meta-communications' about what has been said. He thus encourages comment on what symptoms express. Comment reveals the meaning of a symptom when it supplies the missing part of its context.[9]

The art of psychotherapy lies in getting right the timing, explicitness, and firmness of interpretations. Put by interpretations into a different frame and a broader context, symptoms, as well as what has happened or been said, cease to be puzzling or disturbing. Adding a further piece to the jigsaw, as opportunities to do so arise, may make the picture clearer, but there is a danger that it is too easy to get the picture wrong if the therapist relaxes his sceptical and hence empirical attitude. This may happen when therapist and patient are convinced that their understanding of the patient's predicament is correct because it is based on their 'consensual validation' of the evidence they have jointly uncovered. It has been argued by some that truth can be discovered in dialogue, and that consensual validation is an essential process in benefitting the patient. Yet this may mean sharing delusions and suspending the testing of the evidence against reality.

Psychotherapy conducted along the lines indicated above, since it deals with interpersonal processes, uses verbs and adverbs rather than nouns and adjectives, and does not reify. Thus it speaks of failing to recall rather than a memory defect or of being depressed rather than depression. It thus avoids what Whitehead called 'the fallacy of misplaced concreteness'. Illnesses not being assigned to a diagnostic category, such as anxiety state or depression, patients are not labelled. Symptoms are not reduced to an underlying process, but are put into a context of experiences in relationships. This approach does not preclude other non-psychotherapeutic approaches to the symptoms.

SCHOOLS OF PSYCHOTHERAPY

The many schools of psychotherapy differ in, amongst other things, the theory which guides the treatment, how the aims of treatment are formulated, and what techniques are used.[10] Here are some examples of schools, with a brief indication of what distinguishes them.

Psychoanalysis

The theory formulated by Freud is a comprehensive psychopathology, importance being given especially to the unconscious and mental mechanisms such as repression.[11] Symptoms are devious, substitute expressions of the libido when expression in more adaptive ways has been frustrated. The libido is mainly derived from infancy onwards from sexuality. The theory is 'dynamic' in that it emphasizes movement and process. The objective of treatment is to make conscious the unconscious and thus reconstruct the past and give insight, i.e. understanding; it is an 'insight-oriented' therapy. Its main technique is interpretation of what is recalled during free association, in dreaming, and in symptomatic slips, and of the resistance to recall. It elucidates the transference relationship. It is typically a one-to-one therapy.

Analytical psychology

C. G. Jung, when he seceded from psychoanalysis in 1913, shifted the emphasis so that the libido was held to be made up of aggressive and other urges as well as sexual ones. He introduced the concepts, amongst others, of 'complexes', i.e. clusters of ideas underlying disorder, which delay responding in word-association tests, and the 'collective unconscious' made up of primordial ideas or 'archetypes'. The aims of psychotherapy are to integrate the dissociated parts of the personality and restore wholeness, and to foster individuation, by which the person becomes aware of his wholeness and completeness and discovers his creative potential. The analysis centres on the present and the weakness of the patient's attack on it. Dreams are explored as creative imagination which has significance for the future.[12]

Individual psychology

Alfred Adler, who seceded from psychoanalysis in 1910, emphasized the role played in the genesis of symptoms by the 'will-to-power', which is reflected in striving for success and in self-assertion and in its obverse, a sense of inferiority. A person adopts a style of life intended to compensate for a sense of inferiority, the roots of which lie in physical, psychological, and social handicaps. More important than the causes of neurosis is its purpose and especially what 'secondary gain' it achieves through influencing others. The goals of treatment, which are made more or less explicit in discussions between patient and therapist, lie in modification of the life-style after this has been examined, in order to achieve 'self-realization'. Therapy is seen as educative. The therapist fosters a relationship with the patient in which he acts as a concerned, helping friend.

Analytical psychology and individual psychology both anticipated trends in the development of the schools derived from psychoanalysis. More weight came to be given to the social rather than the biological factors in mental illness, especially by the 'Neo-Freudians', to the weakness of the Ego rather than the strengths of the forces of the Id, and to distortion in the conception of self, and less weight to the recall of traumatic experiences and hence to a regressive transference relationship. With these trends there has been associated some diversification in techniques, with less dependence on free association, and a preference for a more mutual adult relationship between therapist and patient, which is seen as a basis for creating the conditions in which the Ego can gain strength and distortions in the conception of the self can be corrected.

Existential psychiatry

This last objective reappears as the characteristic feature of 'existential psychiatry', which is the relief of the falsification of the self. Therapy is intended to support and re-establish a sense of self and personal authenticity, and to restore freedom to take decisions. Therapist and client engage in 'an obstinate attempt of two people to recover the wholeness of being through the relationship between them'. In order to assist the search for meaning and 'self-actualization', therapy promotes an expanded and realistic appraisal of the world. 'Mind-expanding' drugs, such as the hallucinogens used to be claimed to be, could be taken in furtherance of this objective. The significance of objects in the external world, which is the subject matter of the branch of psychology known as 'phenomenology', lies not in their material properties, location or identification, but in their qualities and meaning as perceived. This distinction refers to the contrast—a key concept of 'existentialism'—between the existence of natural objects and the existence of man endowed with will and consciousness.

In 'European existentialism', which developed mainly in France under the shadow of the death camps and the struggle against Nazism, the key concepts have been dread, anguish, despair, and nausea. Anxiety is the dread of being alone or being nothing; its essence is the feeling that the self is threatened. Existentialist meaninglessness is given a meaning within a relationship. Therapist and patient stand on the level of their common reality ('Dasein'). 'Being with' one another is the essence of the therapeutic relationship.

Client-centred therapy

This popular school, which derives some of its ideas from existential psychiatry, was founded in the nineteen-forties by Carl Rogers as a 'growth therapy'. Its aims are to see the client as he sees himself and to discover how he construes reality. Its central tenet is that 'the growthful potential of any individual will tend to be released in a relationship in which the helping person is experiencing and communicating realness, caring and a deeply non-judgemental understanding'. Much depends therefore on the qualities of the therapist who to be effective has to display 'non-possessive warmth, genuineness and accurate empathic understanding'.[13]

One of the special techniques of the school is 'encounter'—'a method of human relating based on openness and honesty, self-awareness, self-responsibility, awareness of the body, attention to feelings, and emphasis on the here-and-now'. Encounter groups provide conditions for self-discovery to emerge through interaction in a supportive, permissive, non-authoritarian, theory-free, and threat-free group setting, in which participants can become sensitive to their own reactions.

Similar in some respects to encounter groups are 'sensitivity groups' (a technique developed by Esalen's 'Human Potential Movement') which aim at producing change by promoting 'self and interpersonal awareness'. 'T-groups' (T stands for training), which are conducted by 'facilitators', are workshops in which the focus is on authority and leadership issues, communication processes and the dynamics of group change; participants discover how others see them.

The criticism to be made of client-centered therapy, and in lesser degree of existential psychiatry, is that it lacks any consistent set of ideas about the nature and causes of the difficulties it is intended to relieve, other than broad references to the oppression of late-bourgeois society. It is not grounded in a psychopathology, and tends to denigrate specialized knowledge as authoritarian. 'Therapy based on learning theory is ineffective', Rogers asserts, 'because the therapist then permits as little of his own personality to intrude as possible', and more extremely, 'No approach which relies upon knowledge, upon training, upon the accepting of something that is taught, is of any use'. These views reflect the school's rejection of the medical model. This model 'I am the doctor, and I have the knowledge and ability to cure you, and you are the patient who is sick, and who requires my help' is 'usually quite debilitating'.

At best, therapeutic sessions are educational exercises in the 'honest' and 'direct' communication of feelings, in which masks are dropped. But the setting in which self-disclosure takes place is one of regressive dependence on the group, in which the participants are expected to conform to the group's expectations. The bonhomie is suspect. Defences are abandoned under conditions which do not favour re-integration. Feelings are not focused as they are in 'psychodrama' when they are given a context.

Ideas about self-fulfillment, self-actualization and wholeness, especially when they are related, as they often are, to notable achievement, are subjective and naïve. They may be attractive when first considered because they fit well into popular ideas about what healthy functioning means in a competitive culture.

Behaviour therapy

An active movement in the treatment of neuroses by methods based on theories of learning developed during the nineteen-sixties.[14] 'Behaviour therapy', as it was called, was highly controversial to start with, partly because of the trenchant criticisms its advocates made of psychotherapy, especially the lack of evidence that it is efficacious, and partly because of the grandiose claims they made for the scientific status of behaviour therapy and for the results it achieves in treatment. Yet the design of the trials on which this last claim was based was slovenly. The claims have now been modified. The earlier dependence on outmoded theories of learning, like Pavlov's, has been corrected, Pavlov's theory being replaced by Skinner's theory of operant conditioning, which is not very different in its essentials from Freud's 'pleasure principle'.

As the theory and methods of behaviour therapy have been elaborated, the distinctions between it and other forms of psychotherapy have become blurred. There have been trends recently for behaviour therapists to take on more complex problems, e.g. 'guided mourning' and to pay more attention to attitudes, thoughts, and feelings. As a result of the development of 'cognitive therapy',[15] the aims of behaviour therapy have been widened to include the correction of faulty conceptions of the self and the world.

There are still some distinctive features. Behaviour therapists tend to present themselves to patients as experts and assume a greater degree of control over the treatment situation than is usual for psychotherapists or counsellors of other schools. They impose the conditions of the treatment in ways similar to those that are traditional in medicine, and their patients are correspondingly passive. However, they are now less inclined to be didactic than they used to be, and more inclined to encourage initiative and co-operation on the part of the patient. They tend to select those patients whose disorders are circumscribed, e.g. tics, stammering, bedwetting, refusal of food as in anorexia nervosa, overeating, indecent exposure, and transvestism. They have taken a special interest in phobias. Also, they define the goals of treatment in more specific terms than other therapists tend to do, and they relate to the goals the procedures to be followed. They give more importance to an explicit 'contract' between patient and therapist about what is to be done and what is to be the responsibility of each.

Desensitization

One of the most widely used methods of behaviour therapy is desensitization. In the desensitization of a phobia, the feeblest item of a list of anxiety-evoking stimuli is repeatedly presented to the imagination of the deeply relaxed patient until no more anxiety is evoked. The next item in the list is then repeatedly presented, and so on, until eventually the patient responds without anxiety and in a new way to stimuli previously strongly evocative. Teaching the patient 'deep muscle relaxation' is said to be necessary to the success of the method, although the general lowering of the level of anxiety and the repetition of images may be more important.

Desensitization is said to depend on what Sherrington called 'reciprocal inhibition'. The patient has learnt to respond to a danger signal by making an avoidance response, which is associated with anxiety. If the danger signal is so attenuated that the response is not evoked, he acquires a new mode of response, such as relaxation, which inhibits anxiety. Each occasion of anxiety weakens the avoidance response, and this is replaced.[16]

One of the early trials of desensitization showed it to be more efficacious than 'insight-oriented' psychotherapy in the treatment of university students disabled by anxiety in relation to public speaking.[17] A sample of students so treated showed a greater reduction in anxiety immediately after the treatment and 2 years later than a sample treated by insight-oriented psychotherapy. The latter sample did no better than a sample allowed a non-specific relationship with a therapist. Both these two samples did better than a sample given no treatment. The results of other trials suggest that desensitization is efficacious in the treatment of many phobias.

Flooding

Another method of behaviour therapy, of more theoretical than practical importance, is 'flooding' ('implosive therapy'). A person is exposed continuously to a danger signal; he is free to make a previously learned instrumental avoidance response, but this is made ineffective. The aim is to extinguish the anxiety response through massed practice, the response being repeatedly evoked without being reinforced. He is then the more able to learn a new more adaptive response.

Aversion

The painful effects of a neurotic response do not reduce the tendency to make it because they occur after it, usually long after. Ordinary punishment is usually ineffective for the same reason. To be effective, it has to be administered in close association with the stimulus evoking the response. The method of aversion depends on giving the punishment immediately after the stimulus and before the response. The treatment of alcoholism provides an example. An injection of apomorphine is given, which after a predictable interval makes the patient vomit. He is given an alcoholic drink immediately before the vomiting is due to begin. Drinking alcohol and vomiting come to be associated with each other when the procedure has been repeated several times. For one reason or another—probably because the psychological processes are more complicated than the theory allows for—the results fall short of what might be expected, and aversion methods of treating alcoholism have largely been abandoned. An aversion method using faradic stimulation has been applied with perhaps some success in the treatment of such aberrant sexual behaviour as fetishism and transvestism.

The 'bell' method of treating bedwetting has been regarded as an aversion method. The first drops of urine wet a pad in the child's bed. Conductance in the circuit being increased, the bell rings, in theory immediately before the flow of urine begins. The big claims once made for this method have not been sustained, but the method is probably efficacious and continues to be used. It works in some cases although the theory is probably wrong. Providing the equipment has effects on the child other than aversion. Proper trials have proved difficult to mount because so many children become 'dry' at night soon after their first attendance at a clinic.

Other methods

The weight given by behaviour therapy to the effects on learning of reward, or reinforcement, has influenced practice in several areas of psychiatry, notably the rehabilitation of patients who have been in hospital for a long time or the training of the mentally handicapped. The reward offered may be an object the patient wants, e.g. money, cigarettes or a sweet or more often approval or show of affection by a member of staff. 'Token economy' schemes have been widely applied, the patient being given, if he performs an agreed task correctly, in caring for himself or participating in ward activities, a token which he can exchange for something else he wants or a privilege. Part at least of the success of such schemes is due to the greater interest, motivation, and involvement of the staff, and part to the direct reward of the required response. In training the mentally handicapped, the reward has to be immediately related to the required response.

Social-skills training

Behaviour therapy has also influenced what is done to help persons experiencing difficulties in their social relationships because of their lack of skills, which they have either not acquired through lack of opportunity or not practised. Particular forms of assertive behaviour or of 'dating', i.e. making an appropriate approach to another person in order to invite a partnership, are modelled, rehearsed, coached, and discussed, usually in a group of others similarly handicapped. Similar in its methods although developed from a different tradition is 'milieu therapy'. Its aim is to offer the patient, in a structured and protected environment, a graded series of problems so that he can acquire through learning from suitably planned experience the skills and confidence to be able to participate more fully in social activities. The essence of a 'therapeutic community', a concept derived from psychotherapy, lies in the collaboration of staff and patients in creating conditions in which opinions and feelings can be freely expressed.

Two other behaviour-therapy techniques are widely used, more often in combination with such other techniques as desensitization than by them-selves. 'Relaxation exercises' where the patient is instructed how to achieve the progressive relaxation of voluntary muscles. This instruction, strongly supported by suggestion, is often recorded on tape so that the patient can play it back at suitable times, e.g. for the patient experiencing difficulty in getting to sleep, before going to bed. 'Biofeedback' is a relatively simple device which gives the patient information about his physiological state, with reference to the bodily concomitants of anxiety, e.g. pulse and respiration rate. Skin conductance is the easiest to monitor in this way. The information serves as reward to the patient's efforts to relax. Both techniques help to relieve some of the symptoms of those liable to become anxious in relation to particular situations.

THE EFFICACY OF PSYCHOTHERAPY

The criticism has justifiably been made that there is a striking paucity of evidence that any of the techniques of psychotherapy is efficacious, i.e. does what it is supposed to do. Claims have often been made for a technique when symptoms have been relieved, or recovery has occurred, without showing the relief or recovery to be attributable to the technique. Two-thirds of those treated by psychotherapy, it has been asserted, improve to a marked extent within 2 years of the onset of their illnesses, however they are treated. The literature contains numerous accounts of the difficulties that prevent a proper trial from being undertaken, but there is a growing recognition that despite the difficulties each technique should be subjected to a systematic trial, and there is a growing number of instances of the successful completion of a trial.[18]

Randomized controlled trials

The best and only satisfactory form of trial is the randomized controlled trial.[19] The patients selected as likely to benefit from the technique are divided into two samples by 'random allocation', in the sense that each patient has an equal chance of being allocated to each sample. This is usually done by giving each patient a number and allocating him in accordance with a table of random numbers. Random allocation allows it to be assumed that the two samples are similar in respect not only of those characteristics known to be important, but also those which although not known to be important might affect the result. If they are too few to ensure equal allocation, the patients available can first be 'stratified' so as to ensure that equal numbers of patients with known prognostic indicators are allocated at random to each sample.

Those in the 'experimental' sample are treated by the technique under trial; those in the 'control' sample either receive no treatment or are treated by another technique. To deny a possibly efficacious technique to some patients is ethically justifiable while it is being evaluated or is in short supply. A common practice is to regard the patients in the control sample as being on the waiting list for the technique if the trial shows it to be efficacious. Before the trial a decision is made on what number of patients should be regarded as sufficient. The trial lies in the comparison of the outcomes in the two samples, the conventional statistical tests of significance being applied.

The patients eligible for the trial, i.e. those for whom the technique is suitable, and who have agreed to participate, are selected, before being allocated, on criteria defined in such a way as to make it possible for others to replicate the trial. These criteria are likely to include age, presenting symptoms, and class of illness as well as ability to co-operate in the technique. Every patient selected and allocated must be included in the comparison of outcomes. To include only those in whose case the technique has been successfully applied is to beg the question of efficacy. The trial is only of value if the technique itself and the procedure for applying it are clearly described so that it can be replicated.

Trials of drugs use the 'double-blind' method in which neither the patient nor the therapist knows to which sample the patient has been allocated, but this method is not feasible in the trial of a psychotherapeutic technique. For this reason the assessment of all the selected patients on which the comparison of outcomes is based are made as a general rule by researchers independent of those applying the technique. It is usual for the researchers to make similar assessments at the start of the trial. The assessments afterwards are made at a time agreed beforehand. This is usually as soon as the application of the technique has been completed. They may be repeated at follow-ups after intervals of, say, 6 months or a year.

The assessments should use the best methods available; these are likely to include standardized rating scales of symptoms and of attitudes. They should be broadly based and take into account not only the severity of symptoms, but also aspects of well-being and of the quality of life and the level of functioning at work and in social and sexual relationships. They should look for unwanted or untoward effects. Enquiries should be extended so that account can be taken of the observations of the patient's spouse or those living with, or caring for, him.

Comparison of the outcomes in the two samples should show in what respects the outcomes differ. It may also show what are the characteristics of those who benefit from the technique and of those who do not. If so, the criteria on which patients are selected can be revised and more tightly defined.

There are many other questions to be asked when a psychotherapeutic technique is being evaluated. Is it efficient, i.e. economical, in the use of staff and other resources? What are its costs in financial terms? What is the incidence (or prevalence) of the conditions in which it is efficacious? Are there sufficient staff or other resources to make it generally available? If not, to what conditions should priority be given?

NOTES AND REFERENCES

Those who want to read more about some of the points made in this Chapter might start with one of the recently published introductions to psychotherapy.

Brown, D. and Pedder, J. (1979). *Introduction to psychotherapy: an outline of psychodynamic principles and practice.* Tavistock Publications, London.

Bloch, S. (ed.) (1979). *An introduction to the psychotherapies.* Oxford University Press, Oxford.

Bloch, S. (1982). *What is psychotherapy?* Oxford University Press, Oxford.

Storr, A. (1979). *The art of psychotherapy*. Heinemann, London.
1. Frank, J. D. (1973). *Persuasion and healing: a comparative study of psychotherapy* (2nd edn). Johns Hopkins Press, Baltimore.
2. Bateson, G. (ed.) (1974). *Perceval's narrative: a patient's account of his psychosis 1830–1832*. William Morrow, New York.
3. Lewis, I. M. (1975). *Ecstatic religion: an anthropological study of spirit possession and shamanism*. Penguin Books, Harmondsworth.
4. One of many critiques of psychoanalysis is Wyss, D. (1966). *Depth psychology: a critical history, development, problems, crises* (trans. G. Oun). Allen & Unwin, London. Freud's ideas on the fate of memories of traumatic experiences are reconciled with Bartlett's theory of remembering in Davis, D. R. (1951). The wonderful freshness of memories in hysteria. *Br. J. med. Psychol.* **24**, 64–8.
5. One of the many accounts of family therapy is Walrond-Skinner, S. (ed.) (1979). *Family and marital psychotherapy*. Routledge & Kegan Paul, London.
6. Mawson, D., Marks, I. M., Ramm, I., and Stern, R. S. (1981). Guided mourning for morbid grief: a controlled study. *Br. J. Psychiat.* **138**, 185–93. See also Pedder, J. R. (1982). Failure to mourn, and melancholia. *Br. J. Psychiat.* **141**, 329–37.
7. A critique of Laing's concept of the therapist as an outside agitator is Collier, A. (1977). *R. D. Laing: the philosophy and politics of psychotherapy*. Harvester Press, Hassocks.
8. For a discussion of the procedure in conjoint therapy see Hinchliffe, M., Hooper, D., and Roberts, F. J. (1978). *The melancholy marriage: depression in marriage and psychosocial approaches to therapy*. John Wiley, Chichester.
9. For a discussion of the basic techniques in talking with patients see Bandler, R. and Grinder, J. (1975, 1977). *The structure of magic:* Vol. 1 (1975) *A book about language and therapy* and Vol. 2 (1977) *A book about communication and change*. Science and Behaviour Books, Palo Alto, California.
10. The reader's scepticism will be kept alive if he has read Szasz, T. (1979). *The myth of psychotherapy*. Oxford University Press, Oxford.
11. Farrell, B. A. (1981). *The standing of psychoanalysis*. Oxford University Press, Oxford.
12. Storr, A. (1972). *Jung*. Fontana, London.
13. Rogers, C. R. (1976). *On becoming a person: a therapist's view of psychotherapy*. Constable, London. Rogers, C. R. (1973). *On encounter groups*. Penguin Books, Harmondsworth.
14. An up-to-date account is Marks, I. M. (1981). *The cure and care of neuroses: theory and practice of behavioural psychotherapy*. John Wiley, Chichester.
15. Beck, A. T., Rush, A. J., Shaw, B. F., and Emery, G. (1979). *Cognitive therapy of depression*. Guildford Press, New York.
16. Wolpe, J. (1959). *Psychotherapy by reciprocal inhibition*. Stanford University press, Stanford, California.
17. Paul, G. L. (1966). *Insight versus desensitization in psychotherapy*. Stanford University Press, Stanford, California.
18. An early attempt to assess a psychotherapeutic technique objectively is Malan, D. H. (1981). *A study of brief psychotherapy*. Plenum, New York. A recent review of the results of assessing psychotherapeutic techniques is Epstein, N. B. and Vlok, L. A. (1981) Research on the results of psychotherapy: a summary of evidence. *Am. J. Psychiat.* **138**, 1027–35.
19. Cochrane, A. L. (1972). *Effectiveness and efficiency*. Nuffield Provincial Hospitals Trust, London.

Index